REPOSITIONINGS

REPOSITIONINGS

Readings of Contemporary
Poetry, Photography, and Performance Art

Frederick Garber

The Pennsylvania State University Press
University Park, Pennsylvania

Permissions to reprint photographs have been granted by the following: Mary Boone Gallery for Barbara Kruger; Sophie Calle for Sophie Calle; John Coplans for John Coplans; Terry Dennett for the estate of Jo Spence; Allan Kaprow for Allan Kaprow; Metro Pictures for Cindy Sherman; Duane Michals for Duane Michals; Real Comet Press for Jo Spence; Royal Photographic Society for O. G. Rejlander; Carolee Schneemann for Carolee Schneemann; and Mira Schor and Segue Foundation for Mira Schor.

Permission to reprint my previously published essays has been granted as follows: *American Poetry Review* for "Pockets of Secrecy, Places of Occasion: On Gerald Stern"; *Hartford Studies in Literature* for "Re Positioning: The Syntaxes of Barbara Kruger"; *North Dakota Quarterly* for "The Talk Poems of David Antin," first published in 1987; *Open Letter* for "Presence and Its Discontents: Carolee Schneemann and Steve McCaffery"; *Poetry East* for "No One Can Live in Place of Us"; University of Oklahoma Press for "Generating the Subject: The Images of Cindy Sherman," from *Postmodern Genres*, edited by Marjorie Perloff, Copyright © 1988 by The University of Oklahoma Press.

Library of Congress Cataloging-in-Publication Data

Garber, Frederick.
    Repositionings : readings of contemporary poetry, photography, and performance art / Frederick Garber.
        p.   cm.
    Includes bibliographical references and index.
    ISBN 0-271-01408-3 (cloth)
    ISBN 0-271-01409-1 (paper)
    1. Subjectivity in literature.   2. Subjectivity in art.
    3. Poetry, Modern—History and criticism.   I. Title.
PN56.S46G37   1995
809.1'9353—dc20   94-12433
                                             CIP

It is the policy of The Pennsylvania State University Press to use acid-free paper for the first printing of all clothbound books. Publications on uncoated stock satisfy the minimum requirements of American National Standard for Information Sciences—Permanence of Paper for Printed Library Materials, ANSI Z39.48–1984.

For Nicholas James Paulson

Contents

Introduction 1

1 Places of Lyric Occasion: On Gerald Stern 17

2 The Histories and Poetics of Jerome Rothenberg 43

3 David Antin: The Boundaries of Talking 61

4 Presence and Its Discontents, 1: Carolee Schneemann and Steve McCaffery 86

5 Presence and Its Discontents, 2: Performing Photographs 118

6 The Photographic Self-Portrait: Fissures and Ideologies 160

7 Generating the Subject: The Images of Cindy Sherman 190

8 The Syntaxes of Barbara Kruger 212

Index 237

Introduction

Walter Benjamin's suggestion that the first third of our century was the age of the end of aura seems, in retrospect, to time the event half a century too early. That initiating period is more precisely drawn as the age which understood that aura would have to go, the age that took the invention of the photograph, still and eventually moving, as a signal to the undoing that would ensue. Yet even to state these points is to begin to qualify them. This was also, after all, the age when jazz emerged from the encounter of tribal polyrhythms, field songs, and European harmonies to become, along with film, one of the two major new arts in the first third of the century. No art has more of an interest in the immediacy and upfrontness, the dazzling sense of presence that characterizes aura, than this music that privileges the creation of a solo developed in and for the contemporary moment. Such dialectics suggest that aura did not die with the invention of the photograph, still and eventually moving, at least not so quickly as Benjamin had argued. Such dialectics also suggest that it would take an aggressive postmodernism to make that undoing fully, ultimately, happen. Such dialectics argue that aura's doing and undoing occur at the same time, perhaps even in the same event, that this simultaneity makes modernism ambiguous, radically ambivalent, innately self-contradictory. What do we do with modernist photographs that celebrate aura? What, that is, do we do with Eugène Atget and Edward Weston, who seem to have sought by design to counter the radical nature of their medium, its infinite reproducibility, with images *about* uniqueness and presence, what Weston, in his notebooks, repeatedly called essence? Accusations of nostalgia cannot contain or control achievements like Atget's and Weston's or, for that matter, like Rilke's, whose images of essential centrality share a platform with some of the major modernist instances of precisely the breakup of aura that the centering denies. What to do with the Rilke of the *Neue Gedichte* in terms of the Rilke of *Malte Laurids Brigge*, the latter text being one, like Pound's *Cantos*, that works over (not out; no modernist text worked them out completely) those internecine issues? Similar concatenations persist into Charles Olson's *Maximus*, suggesting the power of the probing the issues received in early modernism.

What the *Neue Gedichte* show—consider the Buddha poems as well as the poem on the panther—is that aura has to do not only with the center of art and the center of the making of art but with an obscure, enigmatic depth into which the world disappears, a mysteriously present place, a place of mysterious presence. That place is unavailable to those who stare at the panther from the other side of the bars but it is there all the same, taut, central and certain, there as surely as it is in Rilke's poems on Buddha. Images of the world enter the panther through his eyes, moving into the tensed stillness of his limbs ("der Glieder angespannte Stille"), ending in the site that centers the panther's being (the last word of the poem is "sein"). It is precisely such essentialism that Weston praises and explores, not only in the familiar peppers and artichokes (allegories of sexuality, sexuality itself a metonym of radical desire), but in cacti and Mexican commodes, a corpse and women's bodies. Much of Atget's feat was to deliberately stake out places that had no human presence in order to show auratic centrality in that which the human walks through and has, for the moment, abandoned.

Atget and Weston worked in an art that, Benjamin suggested, categorically denies any centralization of presence. Rilke, on the other hand, worked into the *Neue Gedichte* a profound understanding of what the lyric had come to say on the nature of personality. He affirmed, especially, the grounding of the lyric in a centralized self that is, at once, the site and source of the lyric's making. That has been the notion of the lyric since the middle of the eighteenth century, and however much it is now under the severest of attacks, it remains widely professed and upheld. An argument for the wholeness and coherence of self, its fullness of presence in the immediate moment, has for long grounded our understanding of the lyric, so that a particular conception of the nature of the self and a particular conception of a certain mode of poetry have implied each other (implicated each other) since at least Edward Young and his 1759 *Conjectures on Original Composition*. If that sense of self inherits the humanist understanding of what sits at our centers, it has come to frame that center within a mode of poetry that, surely because of Poe, has come to be identified with poetry itself. Yet even Poe had doubts about the qualities of selfhood: he argued for its grounding in a sense of active centrality that goes back to Descartes, then wondered whether its wholeness was no more than an illusion. That is why his sense of the link between self and lyric poetry meets and is *sometimes* mastered by an equally potent sense that this link will snap precisely when that sense of self comes seriously into question.

It was so questioned in Dada, which grounds much of the art that followed its brief turn in the limelight, grounds specifically much of the poetry and art we shall be looking at in this study. A look at the photographs of Man Ray after an immersion in Weston puts all the ironies of Dada on sardonic display. That is especially so in his Rayograms, in which he, by putting objects directly onto light-sensitive paper, turned out spectral images that undo the essence Weston had argued for, following as he did a Blakean/Emersonian tradition that was the ultimate target of Man Ray's maneuverings. Much the same effect occurs in Man Ray's films, which suggest a Nature nothing like that which Emerson and Weston knew. Yet Dada too tensely compacts the complexities of the undoing of essence to find any such play in one art alone. Still, in the *Lautgedicht*, Dada did what some essentialists had dreamed of but had not dared to do: remove meaning for the sake of pure sound. This seemed to do away with any maker not only of meaning but of the site where meaning sat. Dada privileged sound beyond what any had done before; it privileged the essence of sound that emerges in purely immediate and up-front radical being. Lexical signifiers give way and give in to sound so immediate that it signifies only itself, its unequivocal presence.

That same conglomeration of sound and presence appeared in the Zurich cabarets where Dada did itself nightly. In that sardonic self-doing it added questions of performance to those questions of subject and genre basic to modernism. When Hugo Ball dressed up in a suit that startlingly recalled the Tin Man in *The Wizard of Oz* (the suit parodied more than Cubist readings of self; only Dada would have fused L. Frank Baum and Picasso), he was not only suggesting the breakup of humanist readings of self as whole and awesome and infrangible to its core; he was moving these issues into the immediacy of *act*, taking the issues, that is, out of the static, unshakable core for which humanism had argued and putting them into history. Dada created for those issues an oxymoronic condition that held intense immediacy *and* the undoing of immediacy, a paradox that its successors were to pursue through arts that, whatever their medium, seemed grounded in performance. (We shall see that simultaneous doing and undoing in a poem by Mark Strand that knows its Emerson *and* its Duchamp). One of Dada's prime contributions was to bring performance to the forefront of these issues, filtered through Duchamp into every postmodernism. That pervasiveness of performance, its fundamental role in determining postmodern practice, has yet to be deeply explored, yet to be faced in all its implications. It appears not only in current poems but in the photographs that define many of the claims of postmodern art. It is not that the lyric has been supplanted by photography and performance but—a much more difficult question—that the poem and the photograph have absorbed the performative, as Dada suggested they should. To shift the metaphor slightly: the performative has been inscribed into current poetry and photography. It appears in poems that have been called post-lyric, in Susan Howe, for example, though initial suggestions appear in David Antin's talk-poems. It also appears in photographs that explore the possibilities of combining performance (the modernist version of performance stresses immediacy) with the act of making photographs (which has, from its beginning, incessantly stressed absence).

What follows explores a number of implications of these unlikely relationships, testing out their arguments in the light of this history by establishing a framework that looks much like the one we have just been inspecting, a framework that begins with an elaborate sense of self as compact and central. In Chapter 1, which is on Gerald Stern, that act of establishing a framework comes through in the reading of self as a town-meeting. Chapter 1 gathers together facets and phrases, old histories and new, relatives and those whom Stern has glimpsed only once but with whom he remembers the profoundest of relations. Stern is one of our purest examples of a classically modernist-humanist self, secure in its location whatever the battering it takes, whatever the fractures and failures it endures (here, as Eliot says in a comparable context, the ghost of Coleridge beckons from the wings). The sense of a pummeled but centralized self as the ultimate source of making, and the relation of that self to the nature of the lyric, establishes a theme for the subsequent chapters, a touchstone of radical self-locating from which the rest of the book departs (in several senses). This book could then be read as a narrative of an exile that grows clearer as it develops. The chapter on Stern can thus be taken as an ironic *Genesis*, the remainder of the book as the rest of a Pentateuch.

Putting the point another way: Stern stands at the origin of this text as Rilke stood in the history we have sketched, though Stern shows nothing of Rilke's fundamental ambivalence, Rilke's radical dialectic that knows no resolution. Putting Stern next to Rilke puts Jerome Rothenberg and David Antin next to the Dada that succeeded Rilke and the earliest modernism, a place that makes manifold sense for a number of reasons. Not only do Rothenberg and Antin (frequently paired though their differences are considerable) stem directly from Dada but they do as Dada did, bring into these questions of lyric centrality a sense of the movement of history that *has* to disestablish certain early modernist claims for the positioning of self and its "natural" home in the lyric, the claims continued in Stern. Rothenberg's sense of history is exceedingly complex. Aware of the assertions, demands, desires of early modernist positionings (Rothenberg thinks of some of them as mainstream modernist claims), he also acknowledges and seeks to work with history. Antin's awareness of those issues emerges in the private history of any of his talk-poems, their shift from nearly spontaneous performance through various later stages until they end up on a page that (like Rothenberg's in another way) probes the question of margins and their relation to temporality. That both Rothenberg and Antin also figure among our major performance poets establishes the interplay of self-positioning, old questions of the lyric and new questions of performance, as basic to our times; basic also, therefore, to the chapters that follow. This introduction and Chapters 1 and 2 establish, through a reading of poetry, a framework for the rest. They position the text for explorations into other media, performance and photography and performance photography (which includes not just the photography of performance but the far more difficult question of photography *as* performance).

Indeed, Chapters 4 and 5, "Presence and Its Discontents" argue not only the importance of performance for exploring these issues but the importance of how performance and its attendant complexities infuse, invade, and invest the positionings of other arts. It does all this while affirming how genre and subjectivity speak of, speak *as*, each other in incessant dialogue. Such mutual speaking comes ominously to mean that if either self or genre fractures through the pressure of present dubiety, the other will unravel at precisely the same time, for precisely the same reasons. That performance may be a way of handling the resultant fragmentation ("handling" need not mean putting Humpty together again) is one of the major suggestions that emerge from this book. Consider the modes of performance of Carolee Schneemann and Steve McCaffery. Modernist performance routinely speaks of the bodily as a perceptible essence of presence (Dada's stress on the materiality of language promotes a verbal counterpart). Sexuality is an ancient metonym for the bodily (recall the Venus of Willendorf), that figuring emergent in late modernist implications in the performances of Carolee Schneemann. It emerges boldly, brassily (compare the work of Carol Finley) but with a sometimes concomitant sense that the truth claims of presence can foster uneasiness. Schneemann's confidence in presence, confirmed and supported by her intense eroticism, seems at times to foster precisely its opposite, suggesting through the use of film within performance that presence can be queried, that the secondary can speak through all those primaries. This is the Rilkean quandary again, played out in no nostalgia but in intelligent recognition that whatever one's loyalties, there are subtexts at play even in what seems the staunchest recall of modernism. Similar contraries phrased in very different tonalities run through the work of Steve McCaffery, staunch in its rejection of any modernist recall. The cover photograph of his *North of Intention* picks up precisely those issues, playing with language and/as mask to urge the undoing of late modernist confidence. Such assurance about the relations of presence and physicality turns eloquently sardonic in his openly clumsy performance as a Chinese ventriloquist speaking out of a tape recorder, suggesting the omnipresence of the absolute secondary.

Such speaking comes through again in a poem by McCaffery that initiates a reading of performance photography, an impossible fusing of media that does as much as any such move to undo confident claims for the fixity of genre. Chapbooks by Allan Kaprow probe the ironies in work that mixes text as the script of performance with how-to photographs that picture a previous enactment of that which is proposed. Text, image, and performance work from several temporalities in Kaprow's chapbooks, not always quite the ones we expect from each. That working undoes not only generic expectations but certainty about the place of the subject within them, or to be more precise, the place and time of the subject within them. Though Kaprow's narratives are immersed in temporality, they do not put the time of the subject into any coherent telling. Photographic narratives by Sophie Calle and Duane Michals probe these issues in terms of the photographer as performer, a role in which the actor occupies no single place, a role that is, in fact, a bundle of positionings whose coherence is put to the test by the actor's peregrinations. The actor is fractured by a scene in which the artist, traditionally invisible, partakes and takes pictures, no single role sufficing, no group definitive. (With one ironic exception the photographer is always invisible in Calle, part of her toying with expectations). Calle's narrative representations show all these gestures happening, show a making exceeded in prominence by the passion that overlays all other facets of the scene. What seemed in Rilke to be definable if not harmonious now slips from definition. Performance photography, hinted at in Dada and later developments, suggested even in Schneemann, whatever her sympathies, emerges in our time as more than a slick conglomerate. It dramatically explores the repositionings of self, those shiftings made possible through a play of text, image, and act that undoes the boundaries each has claimed for itself. Calle's narrated pursuit of a man she met only once takes the blunt sexuality of Schneemann's self-enactments, the mysteries of the chase in Vito Acconci, into a major postmodern reading that puts behind itself old and comforting frameworks, rejects them under the pressures of an unforgiving eroticism that acknowledges only itself.

What Calle suggests in her pursuit, what Michals suggests by building a pyramid out of loose stones with the "real" pyramids of Egypt as a backdrop, is that in such actions one is always performing oneself. These images are therefore photographic self-portraits. Such portraits in such a medium elaborate every facet of the problems of fixity that haunt all photographs. (Technical terms like "focus" and "fixing" take on, in photographs, decentralizing ironies). Such portraits question the fixity of that which does the making as well as that which it makes, as though photographs were enjoined to attack the sort of positioning claimed in, for example, older readings of the lyric. Of course such aggressiveness links as well as divides: the lyric, too, argues that in every mode of making there is always a sense, a facet, in which one is making oneself. One tailors oneself to the lyric moment (the time of the lyric is always the time of the moment) as well as tailoring the moment to one's more fix-ed self.

From Calle's frank hiding of self we move through mandatory ironies to that which is more openly a photographic self-portrait, to images like those of John Coplans and Jo Spence. We move to them after a look at the self-images of the Victorian photographer Oskar Gustav Rejlander. Staunchly bourgeois but also astutely aware of the issue of self-presentation (a task that is something more than self-representation) Rejlander knew well what Coplans and Spence were to face. Fissures and ideologies: the fissures in aging bodies (Coplans and Spence do not spare themselves) play off against old histories recalled in these self-portraits, Coplans and the *kouroi*, Spence and a series of classic presentations of the essence of the beautiful. They spare the schools and histories no more than they spare themselves, no more than McCaffery spares modernist ideologies, and for precisely the same reasons: the refusal of those ideologies to acknowledge history's mutterings about old humanisms and their attendant transcendent selves. It is not only the ghost of Coleridge that listens in the wings; Descartes and Emerson hover there as well.

Photography, from its earliest phases, knew of that listening, knew the problems of fixing events that history had already fixed when one got around to fixing them in photographic images, knew what such fixings meant when one got around, inevitably, to putting oneself in the picture. Our reading of Cindy Sherman begins with a look at one of the earliest photographs, Hippolyte Bayard's self-portrait of the artist as drowned man—an impossible bundling of subjects and fixities, impossible yet feasible in a way Cindy Sherman rediscovers and develops. Her images are never self or not-self but each as the other's requisite Other, unbelieving, unbelievable, each the silvered background in which the other sees itself. Performance had emerged in photography's earliest phases and continues in the latest as though performance never stopped asking what it could mean for the making of images that once were used to memorialize the dead (compare Edward Steichen's early self-images, masterly modernist explorations of precisely such temporal questions). That there is a nostalgia in Sherman for an auratic potency of self (denied by her critics though covertly problematized) emerges in part in her play with the not-quite-presence of the never-quite-patent figure of the artist as young woman. The same nostalgia for aura appears in the photographs of Sherrie Levine, while the same sort of absence that is never quite fully itself appears in the poems of the late modernist Mark Strand, actively living out its impossibilities.

Much of Sherman's significance comes not only from her sense of what postmodernism is but in the counterprevailing issues that put her into a context more difficult and complex than any polemical reading can comfortably handle. That is true even of the polemics of Barbara Kruger, not always shrill and repetitive, a model figure in part because she bluntly positions herself at the opposite end of the spectrum from a figure like Gerald Stern, his centralizing impulses open to undoing through the fractional coherences emergent from the function of shifters. Where Sherman's ironies take the photographic self-portrait into the problematics of postmodern performance, Kruger's Benvenistian play takes the ironies of syntax into the always contemporary performance of the self as syntactical gesture; the self always a shifter evermore about to be, yet always, in every sense, the has-been of language.

All these readings argue what Thoreau had argued very early in his *Journal*, that "yes and no are lies." So are binary contrasts, as any modernism has inevitably to show, whatever its professions, as any postmodernism shows with glee and tenacity. Yes and no taken together as angry mirror images, or as angry photographs covered by a glass in which the viewer appears as part of the portrait within the image, grumble *sotto voce* at every point in this study, as much in Antin as in Schneemann and Sherman.

All such generalities need to be pinned down, reified by fixings, however tentative. That is the point of reading texts by Mark Strand and Sherrie Levine that set models for the positionings in the study that is to follow:

Keeping Things Whole

In a field
I am the absence
of field.
This is
always the case.
Wherever I am
I am what is missing.

When I walk
I part the air
and always
the air moves in
to fill the spaces
where my body's been.

We all have reasons
for moving.
I move
to keep things whole.

Mark Strand's poem is a well-known anthology piece, Strand himself an anthologist's instance of the surrealism of the Sixties. "Keeping Things Whole" is, in several senses, a phenomenologist's dream, a field of play for, say, the early J. Hillis Miller. It is a major exemplar of some of the tonalities of its time, a cultural phenomenon that offers distinct satisfactions. It satisfies partly because it seems to deliver itself in full acquiescence, its paradoxes embedded in a narrative that speaks through precisely phrased abstractions.

There are still other reasons for the significance of this lyric. It is a late modernist model of issues that have harried Anglo-European literature since the middle of the eighteenth century, issues of what is here and what is not, what can be said to be here even though it can also be said that it is not. Questions of presence have localized these issues from Blake and Chatterton through recent postmodernisms (Michael Palmer and Susan Howe are cogent examples). Strand is so aware of his place in the history of such localizings that his poem can be read as a commentary on that history.

Consider what it does with the sitings of absence, what the poem performs with places and spaces, the spaces that fill places, the spaces that places inhabit. "Keeping Things Whole" ponders the differences among spaces as well as their continuities. Spaces are never empty but always filled with that which comes after, that which is its own presence (*is*, not merely *has*). That which comes after ought also to be seen as the absence of what preceded it in the history of those spaces. Such a peculiar doubleness of being makes it impossible to define what inhabits a place as any one thing at all. Strand's speaker says he *is* an absence ("I am the absence / of field"), a thing as difficult to say as that he stands where he *is* (the latter is the way Thoreau put it, obsessively so). Presence and absence, then, are aspects and not just conditions of being. Strand's poem is thus about how we *are* in history, that point being rather less plain than the superficial and somewhat slick play with absence and presence. If the poem is also about negations, about the making of absence, it is particularly about how we take up absence within ourselves, making absence *and* presence—each, supposedly, the negation of the other—at home within our own spaces. Of course we too have been subject to negation, to being replaced by air: if this is a poem about loss it is about spaces losing us as well as our losing spaces. Strand's poem holds a species of nostalgia, nostalgia for oneself (we are what is missing in the places we inhabited), for where our bodies have been. In a sense, then, one is always subsequent, belated, the epigone of that which filled one's present space; and of course there is also a sense in which we are forever subsequent to ourselves. Yet we are always, at the same time, the possessors of what our predecessors left behind, their absence.

We are, then, peculiarly full. It is not only that we make things whole by filling up the absence of air and field with ourselves, but that we make ourselves whole by becoming another's absence as well as continuing (here more of history) our own indubitable presence. It is not, *pace* Descartes, that we are because we think but because we take in negations and keep them whole within ourselves as we move in and out of spaces. We are a collective, we contain multitudes. We are an anthology, a gathering of flowers that is, at once, absence and presence. As active and diligent centers we are coherent, cohesive, entire. Always on the move, we move to keep things whole in a wholeness we always possess, wherever we choose to move. We are peripatetic centers that bear our multitudinousness and add continually to it as we shift positionings.

Strand's poem argues that continual repositioning is what we *have* to do, the radical activity of our being-in-the-world. It is an activity connected with all that we have been as well as what we always are. That perpetual repositioning seems no danger to us because, the poem argues, we remain identical, whole in our completeness, as we perform the requisite shifting. It is surely because of our wholeness that we seem to do so well in keeping things whole. Imagine the ironies otherwise. (Coleridge imagined them well; so too did Poe. Rilke understood them as well as anyone). To put it another way: if there is a sense in which we are always reformulating ourselves, reconstituting ourselves, there is another in which the centrality that makes this activity possible is always-already-there; it cannot be erased and its origin cannot be known. Whatever this lyric's concessions to fracture and loss, whatever its narrative of our incessant repositioning, it exemplifies the romantic-modernist insistence on our infrangible ability to turn absent stuff into our own unshakable coherence.

More specifically, this poem offers a late modernist reading of the conditions under which we position ourselves in the world, a lyric-as-allegory of how and why we so move. "Keeping Things Whole" is a manifesto, in several senses a position paper. That it manifests itself in a lyric has its point and propriety, given the pivotal role of the lyric in the romantic-modernist tradition, given that tradition's reading of the lyric as affirming the private centrality of selfhood (an affirmation that occurs even when the center lies in ruins; Coleridge, once again). We heard that affirmation in Rilke's poem on the panther as well as in those on Buddha. Yet we cannot be too careful in making claims about romantic-modernist claims, in what we say they say. Even so programmatic a lyric as "Keeping Things Whole" refuses to make absolute distinctions between absence and presence. If that sounds as though the "self" informing Strand's allegory has aspects about it that speak of (speak as) a postmodernist "subject," that only means that *both* terms (not just "self" alone, as is usually the case) properly belong within quotation marks. Precisely that uneasiness about absolute demarcations informs the readings that follow: if this text begins with Gerald Stern and ends with Barbara Kruger, that does not imply an inflexible spectrum.

Still, Strand's lyric holds a pertinent, precise, and comprehensible link between genre and positioning, the import of which *requires* a centering of self, an assertion of its wholeness, whatever it leaves behind, and that within a genre designed to emphasize precisely such centering. Of course this finally says that Strand is a subtle reader of the history in which he partakes, that "Keeping Things Whole" is a reading of its own history. So are the poems, performances, and photographs whose material forms the substance of the chapters that follow. That Strand's poem has special potency comes from its obsessive focus on positioning, on thematizing the link of positioning to subjectivity and genre, on suggesting how action might reify those abstractions through the body.

Another way of putting the issues Strand raises is in terms of origin. The "I" who moves to keep things whole is the only maker of that complex of absence and presence which it alone inhabits. It is the locus of the beginning of the complex, though there is no perceptible time when beginning occurs because "I" makes a new complex every time it moves. Origin is no simple matter in this late modernist text which resists every rubber stamp we seek to wield upon it. Lost origins "exist" in the being of that which is no longer there, of that which is present only in the not-being-there that "I" takes into itself whenever it moves. All such origins are therefore reachable only through the "I" that fashions new origins whenever it moves. (Part of what this means is that a capitalized Origin, the Origin of origins, can never be reached, can, indeed, hardly be thought of. All that we have are its continually emerging epigones). Strand's lyric assumes the play on origin/originality that postmodernist artists have extended obsessively. This lyric "I" is original in the sense that however necessarily changeable its position, it is the only begetter of those contexts in those places. (One has to emphasize *those places*, the implicit geography. That too will be found in postmodern continuations). In Chapter 1 Gerald Stern will tell us that "no one can live in place of us," that is, in the place of us. Strand says that too, bringing out more openly what Stern's saying implies about authorial claims for the uniqueness of the work. Once again we hear the sounds of Benjaminian aura, what was supposed to disappear with the advent of mechanical reproduction but has in fact held on so tightly that such holding pervades the modernism Benjamin helped to define. Strand's lyric fuses dispersal and recentering within an aureole consistent in all its changes.

How, then, to handle another anthology piece, Sherrie Levine's *Torso of Neill*, an exact reproduction of Weston's photograph by the same name? Once again it is a matter of aura, of the grounding of the object in its uniqueness in the present moment, this time and place in history where no one else can stand. Levine has done more than break several copyright laws; she has fractured the auratic hold of the unique originator, Strand's "I" or any other that makes claims to being the exclusive owner, the only begetter. She breaks up the question of what Rosalind Krauss has called the originality of the avant-garde into a set of dubieties that find no center holding, no locus of beginning at which an originator stands, therefore no infrangible aura.[1] Most conjectures on original composition, at least since Edward Young's 1759 essay, assume a unique origin that stands as sole owner of all that it makes. Levine questions the ownership of any image, in part because all images have a long history, because, as Barthes says, there are no innocent texts. As Krauss tells us, quoting Douglas Crimp, in Weston's case that involves the *kouroi,* sculptured torsos of young men that lead back to origins we have no hope of indexing (169). We shall watch John Coplans parody precisely that history. But a topic of ownership is also a topic of positioning; those topics implicate each other in a perpetual finger-pointing. To question the one is always to question—threaten to unseat, remove, reposition—the other.

Strand and Levine argue for incessant repositionings but from very different assumptions, within very different frames. Strand's moves keep us going but keep us endlessly originating and fashioning ourselves. But repositioning as argued in a post-auratic framework urges that wherever we stand, whatever we stand to and make, we are always "afterward," always belated and secondary, not only because no one can stand in place of us but because we cannot stand in anyone's place but our own or even do more than point to what is finally merely another place. Whatever sense of the fractures of history Levine shares with Strand, her history holds only fractures, only the incompleteness of each place where an "I" stands, our own and every other. Strand posits a burden of consciousness that Levine could never accept because she could never accept such a reading of consciousness. The chapters that follow ponder those burdens and the credence they secure, what such burdens and credences have to do with what now seems a continual repositioning, impelled not only by history but the nature of the art we make.

Impelled in the lyric as in the photograph? Impelled, certainly, but in very different senses that have made the lyric the bugaboo of much postmod-

---

1. See Krauss's *Originality of the Avant-Garde and Other Modernist Myths* (Cambridge: MIT Press, 1985), 151–70. For comments on Levine, see 169–70.

ern theory, and the photograph the linchpin of many postmodern arguments. Given a hierarchy of genres that would take in several arts, the
photograph has supplanted the lyric as the genre that focuses most issues
of interest. We shall see in every photographer written up in the following
pages—Bayard, Rejlander, Sherman, and Kruger—an often subliminal
sense of the photograph as grounded in the making of those differences that
only history makes, that is, as complicit with history. Lucas Samaras, whose
photographs I shall be taking up in a later study, has worked obsessively
with Polaroid images because such images narrow the gap between the time
when the subject stands before the mechanism and the time when the
subject begins a process of Othering that can only increase in scope. In
Samaras's case there is a nostalgia for immediacy that matches his lyric
narcissism, putting his handling of the photograph into terms any late modernist could understand. Greenbergian claims for an autonomous timeliness
fizzle before any sense of the photograph's positionings, their place within
the play of its modes of involvement in history.[2] Overtly or subliminally
that sense has always prevailed in readings of the photograph's habits, whatever the modernist arguments, whether pictorialist or purist, for the "fixing"
of the image. That sense of positionings within manifold histories is the
inescapable subtext of every photograph, implicit in every reading, explicit
at many points throughout the art's development. Some of the earliest
photographs fascinate for the ghostly presence of those who walked through
the scene while the light was fixing the image. We see photographs involved
in history in a way we have never seen any lyric to be so involved: the
photograph's early task of fixing images of the newly dead put the point
precisely and engraved itself permanently into our reading of the medium.
The Renaissance lyric's argument for immortality through verse slips into
affectation before the photograph's daily claims.

The burdens of temporality involved in any photograph suggest positionings, repositionings, peculiar to the art, the complexities apparent in photographic self-portraits of the O. G. Rejlander sort. Rejlander's meditations
on the medium and on the making of self-images are as infused with a sense
of the image's ways of Othering as any our time has produced. Photography
has always suggested such speculations, suggested them as early as Hippolyte
Bayard. What it suggests to presence-haunted late modernist performers

2. Greenberg as bogey man appears routinely in polemical essays and collections of postmodern
art theory, for example *Art After Modernism: Rethinking Representation*, ed. Brian Wallis (New York:
New Museum of Contemporary Art, 1984).

like Allan Kaprow and Carolee Schneemann puts Rejlander's speculations into formats he might have guessed at. His self-portraits in dress-up suggest what performance artists made the issue of their work.

That is another way of indicating the differences between the romantic-modernist lyric's handling of absence and that of any photograph, Weston *or* Levine. Strand's reading of lyric as the site of collectivity, a point that contains and renders the acts of other points, counters the allegory implicit in Levine's co-optation, her tale of a dispersal that is pervasive and unshakable. And yet the peculiar consonance of meaning and mode seen in Strand's lyric echoes in the import of the counterpart coalescence in Levine's rephotograph. Her argument for the distancing of the act of origination resonates within a medium that mirrors the argument at every possible aspect. Photography puts that question with peculiar directness, the photograph's ways of being (or better, not-being) collocating precisely with such implicit geographies. The play of positionings implicit in every photograph makes photography fascinating for all postmodernisms, for Barthes, for the longings of Sophie Calle, for the pain and sardonic eroticism in the work of Jo Spence. Levine plays out her version of repositionings, of the play of belatedness, within a medium that reflects the consequences of such moves. Of course it is a peculiar belatedness, one that, it can be claimed, comes late to a party that never was: it has been argued at least since Benjamin that there are no original photographs, only original negatives.

Levine regrets missing the party. That much comes clear not only from the commentaries of critics, sympathetic and otherwise, but from her surprisingly frank reading of her own practices. Thomas Lawson's remarks on Levine are as jaundiced as his others on postmodernism: Levine, he argues, has given up on creativity, now rendered impossible, and has turned to appropriation: "Like any depressed victim she simply steals what she needs."[3] It is perhaps that "victimhood" which leads Lawson to speak of how her work holds "an almost romantic poignancy as resistant to interpretation as the frank romanticism of her nemesis" (161). A curious linking/likening of both sides of the argument persists despite the tendency of one of the poles to speak *sotto voce*. Lawson's remarks are exaggerated and ill-termed; "poignancy" is not quite to the point though closer to the point than some might want to acknowledge. Ann Hoy's more carefully tempered remarks more accurately describe Levine's appropriations: "Longing for art's

---

3. See *Art After Modernism*, 161. Lawson's social insensitivity ("like any depressed victim") would be remarkable for any time, more so for 1981, when this was first printed in *Artforum*.

old promise of transcendence and resignation about the current lack of faith blend in her rephotographs; they inspire mixed feelings of awe and irony."[4] To put it another way, whatever Levine's sardonic arguments against claims for originality her practices put out a further, unexpected perspective, a nostalgia for the times when such making was conceivable, when one could, like Rilke, speak of Buddha's centrality and what it means for the making of poems. Nostalgia holds the pains (*algea*) of homecoming (*nostos*), or rather, of insufficient *nostos*, *nostos* impossible. Levine's subtextual *Heimweh* opens out to the surface in remarks quoted by Hoy: "I choose pictures that manifest the desire that nature and culture provide us with a sense of order and meaning. I appropriate these images to express my simultaneous longing for the passion of engagement and the sublimity of aloofness" (122). These are feelings possible only to epigones, continually repositioning as origins grow more obscure. Harold Bloom's high romantic obsession with epigones confirms the history and increases its ironies.

The studies that follow pursue a spectrum of desires ranging from parodies of Barthesian *jouissance* in the work of Steve McCaffery to versions of that nostalgia Levine is almost alone in openly acknowledging. Positioning, then, is never without passion. It is also never without some sense of perspective, some sense of that which one is positioned in relation *to*; that which is, most often, the object of the passion. Positioning is always a mode of relation. The telling of positioning is the relation of a passion. It ranges from attempts to speak a Buberian "thou" (by Rothenberg most openly but also by Antin in front of his audience) to subtextual mumblings of the sort we have heard in Levine, speaking within a space that some see as a vacuum but is a speaking nevertheless.

The encounter of Strand and Levine suggests a continuity that is sometimes heard in that speaking but never above a whisper. That the continuity also involves a profound awareness of fracture is only one more irony endemic to that context.

---

4. *Fabrications: Staged, Altered, and Appropriated Photographs* (New York: Abbeville Press, 1987), 122.

1

Places of Lyric Occasion:
On Gerald Stern

In the section "Exclusions" in his alphabetized autobiography Roland Barthes describes his reaction to chancing on a bourgeois wedding:

> Walking through the Church of Saint-Sulpice and happening to witness the end of a wedding, he has a feeling of exclusion. Now, why this faltering, produced under the effect of the silliest of spectacles: ceremonial, religious, conjugal and petit bourgeois (it was not a large wedding)? Chance had produced that rare moment in which the whole *symbolic* accumulates and forces the body to yield. He had received in a single gust all the divisions of which he is the object, as if, suddenly, it was the very *being* of exclusion with which he had been bludgeoned: dense and hard.[1]

1. *Roland Barthes by Roland Barthes*, trans. Richard Howard (New York: Hill & Wang, 1977), 85–86.

Separated as secular intellectual from any such religious ceremony, separated as homosexual from any such bourgeois conjugality, Barthes is overwhelmed by the revelation of the stance he is compelled to take, a stance he understands full well but the essence of which comes over him, this time, heavily, weightily. The degree and extent of exclusion were such that they exposed exclusion itself, as though there were nowhere he could go where there was no exclusion.

To put it another way, there was no speaking he could do that was not the speaking of exclusion. If the intellectual finds himself outside such ceremony, that is partly because there are limitations to his language, codes that he cannot muster, genres that are beyond him; and he makes it known immediately that there are intimate relations among where he is and what he is and the modes through which he speaks:

> . . to the simple exclusions which this episode represented for him was added a final alienation: that of his language: he could not assume his distress in the very code of distress, i.e., *express* it: he felt more than excluded: detached: forever assigned the place of the *witness*, whose discourse can only be, of course, subject to codes of detachment: either narrative, or explicative, or challenging, or ironic: never *lyrical*, never homogeneous with the pathos outside of which he must seek his place. (86)

To stand in any place is not only to be granted the codes possible to that place as well as the language attendant on the codes; it is also to assume the genres that emerge from those relations. The connections of code and genre are surprisingly rigid, surprisingly involved with where one *is* in the world. As maker and wielder of language (and how much of a maker is he, given the authority of codes?) he finds that language cannot be separated from where it is uttered or from the genre or mode in which it is uttered; and none of these can be separated from who he is, intellectual, homosexual, perpetual on-looker at these and other ceremonies, these and other collectives. Outsiders speak in narratives, insiders speak in lyrics. Lyricists speak in terms of fusion, homogeneity. They sound the specific pathos associated with the specific ceremony, acknowledging that fusion of group and feeling in which the ceremony is as much part of us as we are part of it.

It is clear that self, genre, and place are not only intimately attuned (perhaps the only collectivity the narrativist can know?) but that the nature and conditions of each have the profoundest effect on the nature and conditions of the others. It would not be difficult to argue that each *is* the others, different only because we are inspecting from different perspectives. This is not to textualize the world (Barthes never did that) but to argue for the coupling of text and world in conditions that can produce an unusual *jouissance*. It is also to argue against some classical readings of the lyric and the narrative: the lyric has long been associated with the stance of the outsider, his separateness and aloneness, whereas the narrative has long been associated with the stance of the insider, who knows of what he speaks and tells of what he knows, no matter how much detachment he has to summon to do that telling.

But Barthes is not through with these issues. As though his intellect has emerged to save him from obvious pain, he continues in the next entry to pore over the nature of lyric, and comes finally to argue that it has no viable nature:

> Writing subjects me to a severe exclusion, not only because it separates me from current ("popular") language, but more essentially because it forbids me to "express myself": *whom* could it express? Exposing the inconsistency of the subject, his atopia, dispersing the enticements of the imaginary, it makes all lyricism untenable (as the utterance of a central "emotion"). Writing is a dry, ascetic pleasure, anything but effusive. (86)

It is now writing as such that keeps him outside (or more precisely, that shows him to be irrevocably outside). That is not, however, to say that he finds another position. There is no central place where the "him" sits, outside or anywhere else, because the subject is grounded only in atopia, that is, nowhere at all. The subject is therefore dispersed and inconsistent, the consequence of which is that there is no central emotion that would be felt by a central "him." So exits the grounded self-centrality that is one of the basic tenets of the romantic-modernist lyric, from Wordsworth to Croce and far beyond. The lyric, Barthes argues, is untenable, impossible, a genre with contradictions built into its bones. Of course he continues to state that there are intimate connections among self, place, and genre: this partisan of the text's erotics never denies these intimate connections, only their traditional modes. If there is no consistent position for the subject and therefore no consistent subject, the lyric, too, can never be consistent with its claims. Barthes does not argue that the lyric does not exist but that it cannot work.

Barthes's comments are a rereading of literary history, an undoing of the central genre of romantic-modernist poetry, partly through a redefinition of the relation of the lyric to collective experience, partly through a rethinking of the nature and positioning of the lyric subject. He illuminates the condition of figures like Thomas Chatterton (as isolated as any but posing as a tribal bard), various stages of Yeats, and a number of contemporary figures who have ridden the romantic-modernist tradition into days when its viability is in pervasive, perpetual doubt. Questions of collective pathos fuse with traditional lyric positionings in poets as different as Gerald Stern and Jerome Rothenberg, partisans of very different modernisms but equally concerned with the intimate relationships of self, genre, and place. In Stern these issues are especially obsessive.

II

The fourth poem in Stern's *Lucky Life* is the last of an introductory set whose purpose is to map out the contours of what follows. "The Power of Maples," "The Last Self-Portrait," and "At Bickford's" had explored, in turn, the Roethkean thrust of local nature, a Rilkean sense of the mutual reflection of persons and possessions as they age together, and the place of Manhattan in Stern's personal history—a history which shows that he is now "finally ready for the happiness" he had argued against in his youth.[2] "One Foot in the River," at the end of the set, draws all these issues together in a series of couplets that shows him commenting on the current poles of his world. Because his house in Pennsylvania abuts the river he can dip into the water's darkness when he wishes, his white hands exploring the black sands. He slips easily, effortlessly, into empathy with all that moves there, his personality so flexible that it can take up a place among aliens and sense their own fullness of self, that fullness a counterpart to his own: "I am able to live for days in a cold state / beside the catfish and the bony shad." That "bony" is purely Keatsian, its pristine clarity putting us inside the fish we are lying next to in the water. Our place is, after all, multiple, our selves are capable of exploring that multiplicity in all its elements, in every secret corner. Yet it is not as though this selfhood has no character of its own, no place of its own to be. As he works through all these gestures,

2. *Lucky Life* (Boston: Houghton Mifflin, 1977), 3.

he knows that his self's placement is sure, whatever the shape of the butch-
ery that the world is certain to bring: "I always know where I am when the
struggle begins." Those words about place, self, and struggle in fact do
double work. "Going to New York," he had said in the previous couplet,
"I carry the river in my head / and match it with the flow on 72nd Street
and the flow on Broadway." The matching of the two flows blends them in
his head; his mind is, like the riverbed, a conduit. But in his mind the
streams merge so fully that for the rest of the poem every flow involves
both, the flow of the river and the flow of the New York streets. To complete
the sentence I quoted in part: "I always know where I am when the struggle
begins / and a butchered face goes by me in the water." The wholeness that
happens in his selfhood happens, he suggests, in his poem as well. Self and
text are interchangeable sites for his maneuvers with place. In the poems
of Gerald Stern the borders of self, text, and place are porous, receptive.

And so too are the borders of the times he knows. Stern's is a fiercely
temporal world, particularly in the play of the old Stern and the new, that
self which emerged from a series of crises in his forties.[3] He hugs the immediate moment as one hugs a tree in a storm but his past in Pittsburgh and
Paris and New York never leaves him—partly because he needs to give the
present moment a clarity of context, partly out of nostalgia and some guilt,
mostly out of his sense that his selfhood is a forum, a town meeting, a place
of incessant debate between all that he has known and been and all that
he is now. With all of its complications the coupling of places like Easton,
Pennsylvania, and New York, New York, is only one of the kinds of straddling Stern performs.

That performing did not come easily, whatever the fluency and suppleness
of his later work. *Rejoicings*, Stern's first book, shows him struggling for a
voice and attendant language that would give the purest possible rendering
of the conditions of self, a way of speaking that would also be a way of
being.[4] What he sought in *Rejoicings* was what he said, in a later poem, he
had come to admire in Piaf, "the mixture / of absolute sadness and absolute
cunning, the voice / that lived on sound alone, that lived on anguish."[5]
He needed such focusing on, such distillation of, all that remained to him
before he could pull times and places together. Stern's first book shows that
focusing at active work. As he points out in "Some Secrets," *Rejoicings* is

3. For Stern's account of these crises, see "Some Secrets," in *In Praise of What Persists*, ed.
Stephen Berg (New York: Harper & Row, 1983), 256–66.
4. Originally published in 1973. I cite the reissue (Los Angeles: Metro, 1984).
5. "The Voice," in *Paradise Poems* (New York: Vintage Books, 1984), 40.

the name of the tractate on mourning in the Talmud (265). That quirky relation of title and content pervades the poems in *Rejoicings* and all that were to follow: he cannot separate mourning and rejoicing because he has within himself that which can never be divided. His selfhood holds not only his old and more recent feelings but all of the times and places that have engendered those feelings. *Rejoicings* shows him seeking the language he needs to handle that fusion. It stands as a portal to his later work, a corridor that leads toward his maturity and, at the end, puts us there. It puts us into a place where immediacies are pregnant with all that has been, where the things of his past and present are so profoundly intertwined that his brain can fool him into thinking that one is the other, as it does in "Blue Skies, White Breasts, Green Trees" from *Lucky Life*:

> What I took to be a man in a white beard
> turned out to be a woman in a silk babushka
> weeping in the front seat of her car,
> and what I took to be a seven-branched candelabrum
> with the wax dripping over the edges
> turned out to be a horse's skull
> with its teeth sticking out of the sockets.
>
> (2)

"Psalm," also from *Lucky Life*, shows Stern so conscious of his ways of working but also so confident in his skill that he can play with his predilections and turn into a conceit:

> I thought of the rabbis of Brooklyn bent over their
>   psalms.
> I thought of the tufts of hair and the bones and ridges
> and the small cows eating peacefully
> out on the open slope or in the shadows
> while the forehead wrinkled and the gigantic lips moved
> through the five books of ecstasy, grief and anger.
>
> (58)

He contains within himself the Brooklyn where the rabbis read as well as the Tennessee he drives through. His poem rejoices at all his worlds as well as the embrace of his words.

That supple interplay of locus, language, and self-as-collective gave Stern what he particularly wanted, a point of coherence in consciousness. It was a place from which he could work, make poems. It had all sorts of connections with his place beside the river in Pennsylvania, itself a place from which he had learned to work. That literal positioning is the "here," his place in Pittsburgh or New York the literal, touchable "there"; but he sees these literalities, too, as places within consciousness, points at which he can straddle the place where he is and those places he can conceive of in Marietta or Brooklyn or Berkeley. They are also straddling points for excursions in time, those personal and ethnic remembrances that are always ready to haunt. Stern has many ghosts, many he never knew, remnants of other histories that are also part of memory's lair.

He often needs to make a door to that lair, a place from which it can be opened, which causes it to open. The language Stern has come to, the places he has come to, come together to work on the door. He explores the textures of local things and the textures of a language that, simultaneously, sees and renders and judges. In "The Red Coal" the door opens with his blue chair and then takes in, for two sharply realized stanzas, the sink where he studies his hands as well as the hands themselves:

> I study my red hand under the faucet, the left one
> below the grease line consisting of four feminine
> angels and one crooked broken masculine one
> and the right one lying on top of the white porcelain
> with skin wrinkled up like a chicken's
> beside the razor and the silver tap.[6]

Stern plays with blue and red and white and silver, the sight of wrinkled skin, the sense of the razor's blade, to bring forward the place and its contexts and give the whole a density of being on which he can depend. He needs a fully realized point from which to reach into the lair and take on the vastness it holds. I want to call these points "places of occasion." They are places where occasions occur, occasions that, for Stern, are always leaps of the soul; and they are also the places that occasion such leaps. In a poem like "No Wind" the straddling is extreme. A homespun piece of Pennsylvania becomes the Archimedean point that every place of occasion is:

---

6. *The Red Coal* (Boston: Houghton Mifflin, 1981), 68.

> Today I am sitting outside the Dutch Castle
> on Route 30 near Bird in Hand and Blue Ball,
> watching the Amish snap their suspenders at the
>   sunglasses.
> I am dreaming of my black suit again
> and the store in Paradise where I will be fitted out
>   for life.
>
>   (*Paradise Poems*, 43)

Fact infused with wit prepares for the leap of feeling as "a small girl and I recognize each other / from our former life together in Cordoba." Standing among "the plastic tote bags, the apple combs and the laughing harmonicas," they weep for the memory of "the marble forest / of the Great Mosque / and the milky walls / of the Jewish quarter." In eight hundred years, he says, he will see her again. It will need "at least that much time / before we lie down again in the tiny lilacs / and paper love houses of the next age." The lair holds tribal memories, that which he could never see but can think of as a place for living and loving, perhaps even a place of occasion. The reach into the lair is not always as deliberate as it is in "The Red Coal." In this poem it comes as a surprise, though in no sense against his will.

Sometimes, however, there is the intensest sort of compulsion, less, perhaps, with people he meets than with elements of the lair, elements which reach out for him just as, on other occasions, he reaches out for them. Sometimes he finds the door to the lair open and facing his way. In "The Shirt Poem" the door is literal, the place of occasion a closet whose door he has to open "an inch at a time" to ease out some angry shirts. The past thrusts itself upon him in the person of shirts he has not seen for years, shirts he associates with the old days of the Left, "the dream / of brotherhood, the affectionate meeting / of thinkers and workers inside a rented hall" (*Red Coal*, 28). But the folding chairs are gone, there is no more "sacred locking of elbows under the two flags," and he is here beside the river in a peaceful and cushier life, loving that life yet touched enough by nostalgia to ask the dead for forgiveness. But these are surrealist shirts and they will not stay still.

> When I come home from New York City I stand outside
> for twenty minutes and look out at the lights.
> Upstairs the shirts are howling and snapping,

> marching back and forth in front of the silver radiator.
>
> .   .   .   .
>
> they are like prehistoric birds,
> half leaping, half sailing by.

Only when they wear themselves out do they give in and go back to their closet, standing there

> in place, in back of the neckties,
> beside the cold plaster, in the dust
> above the abandoned shoes, weeping in silence,
> moaning in exhaustion,
> getting ready again to live in darkness.

Wherever else the past is, it is always somewhere within him, hanging in the lair "in back of the neckties, / beside the cold plaster." On occasions he has to open the door a gingerly inch at a time to give air and reverence to the old forces inside.

And yet for every poem of straddling there is one of intense immediacy, exultation over the occupants and textures of this place. Stern cherishes the touch of the local, digging his fingers into the dirt of a flowerpot, pondering the details of a leaf that has taught him to live for love, listening to "the fish gasping in the underbrush / and the duck's heart beating twenty yards away" (*Lucky Life*, 29). That local world is largely rural, much of it a garden, all of it a place where he is surrounded by diligent lushness. Though he sometimes talks about the people near him—"the German farmers swearing in the underbrush" (14), his wife and daughter or an occasional friend—the main denizens of the place are those who spring up in it or fly through it. In poem after poem he ponders the feel and look of their presence as well as the contours of their relations to him, relations ranging from the subdued to the high-pitched, always pinned down to the textures of local conditions.

These are poems of encounter, the meeting of his middle age with the garden's immediacies. Middle age is, as much as the garden, the place he has come to and is surrounded by. He is at home (as much as he can be) in and with the self—centered, seasoned, packed—that he and life together have made for him. Poem after poem renders the meeting of that home which he now is (not just *has* but *is*) with the home places around him, the places of his rhododendrons and juncos, the dead turtle and the blue stones he seeks to lift, "[His] eyes bulging from the weight, [his] painful cries / floating through the wild flowers and the weeds" (*Lucky Life*, 14). The density of his self-presence meets and matches the equivalent density of this place in Pennsylvania. Yet that same sense of encounter with the plethora of presentness can occur elsewhere as well. Near the end of *Paradise Poems* he says that "Easton, where I lived, / has two small floating bridges in front of it / that brought me in and out. I said goodbye / to them both when I was 57" (*Paradise Poems*, 66). There follows a series of poems on other places where similar encounters can occur, in Tuscaloosa ("Red Bird"), the Arizona desert ("One Bird to Love Forever"), and a place beside an Iowa river ("Two Trees"). What he now is he will be wherever he is.

Still, with all this compulsive turning to the touch of immediate life Stern is never so fully focused on the things at his feet that he stands there single-selved. No part of himself is put aside solely for immediacy, however intense the concentration in the moment of focus. Wherever he is, whatever he does, he always sees himself in context. Too much has happened, too much has been read and felt, there has been too much love of Spinoza and the rabbis, there have been too many sorrows, both his and those of others. Curiously, though, it seems that immediacy can cure the attacks of memory. Even more curiously, the stuff of intellect can lead toward the healing afforded by the touch of immediate life. In "I Need Help from the Philosophers" (*Lucky Life*, 9–10) Stern's powers are fully at play. "Haggling over [his] youth like a tender dealer," he finds in a single moment of presence all sorts of images of the past, a friend "stuttering through his father's old jokes," Olive Oyl sobbing once more "behind a fence in Brutus' thick arms," his own neck "fresh from the barber, [his] chest bursting." Like the speaker in Lawrence's "Piano" but with far more defensive power he is drawn toward that which has thrust itself forward; and yet, again like Lawrence's speaker, he knows its capacity for damage, the cost of sentiment and nostalgia. Dante and Proust cannot help; only Spinoza can. Attacked by that which now lives only in the lair he turns to another part of memory to fight off those warm and unwelcome images from his oldest days. Then, in an unforeseen turn that it takes the whole poem to explain, he begins to talk of a trip to Long Beach Island, where he goes "to lie down with the sand dollars" and watch the Philadelphians convalescing, "lying in rows breast side up." He too will convalesce but in his own way and place. The scope of the content that obsesses him is met and matched by the scope of his acts. Those acts can handle not only the old times of Pittsburgh and the current ones of this island, not only philosophers and comic-strip characters, but various modes of focusing and the various modes of language that make the focusings work. The first half of the poem is packed with proper nouns, specific as proper nouns are, yet distanced in the way that things must be that exist only in the mind. Most of the nouns in the second half are not proper but generic—pigeons, jellyfish, fleas, "the crab's thin shell"—yet, unlike their proper predecessors, they point to that which can be touched, which is densely, pointedly present. Names that specify speak only to the past; names that generalize speak to that which is at his feet. The halves of the poem make up a package of mirror images, that package a patent whole. That whole is finally the wholeness of the life of Gerald Stern, but it is also the wholeness of complementary modes of language that Stern has mastered in order to come to terms with his life.

At the end of the poem Stern brings it all deftly together, his touch subdued and expansive. Fleeing the pressures of personal origin he enters the phylogenetic place where the whole show began, Spinoza, Olive Oyl, his haircut. In a gesture repeated throughout his poems he lies down in the water and studies what is there. He fixes on present specifics in order to make a place of grounding from which he can move to the ancient, immutable. He enters "the sea wrack itself to get as close as possible to the trenches":

> I lie in the middle of the egg capsules and the lettuce.
> I fish through the skeletons.
> With all my heart I study the crab's thin shell—
> like a prostrate rabbi studying his own small markings—
>   so I can rise for one good hour like him
> into a second existence, old and unchanging.

Stern turns the things at his feet, the capsules, the lettuce, the shell, into the stuff of a place of occasion, a place that occasions a major moment of his soul. He becomes like one of those rabbis he thought of in Tennessee; yet his text is not the Talmud or Spinoza or words of his own ("his own small markings") but the markings on the things of this world. To read the inscriptions on the crab's thin shell is to cure, to purge. To read in these conditions is to rise for a while into a way older than memories of early haircuts, older than Dante or Spinoza. When he stares at the sea's junk, the sort of stuff one walks through on the way to somewhere else, Stern finds in the facets of detritus all the inscriptions that he needs.

Two of Stern's comments can help us here:

> When I look at the statement I made to *Contemporary Authors* a few
> years ago, I see I emphasized my attraction to weeds and waste places
> and lovely pockets and staking out a place that no one else wanted
> because it was abandoned or overlooked. . . . I have always loved
> the secret places that were just beyond the reach of our penetrating
> minds. ("Some Secrets," 265)

> It's pockets of secrecy that I've always been searching for. Things
> that no one else wanted. . . . Things that are ignored or overlooked;
> weeds. It is amazing what is passed by.[7]

If his reach takes in Spinoza and Pittsburgh, it also extends to the webs
of the spiders that live "on the iron bridge / going across to Riegelsville,
New Jersey" (*Lucky Life*, 78), the "hard green daffodils growing / in clumps
beside the stone wall and the cesspool" (*Red Coal*, 21), the "kind of sun-
flower, / only smaller and less demanding / on a side street in Phillipsburg /
faced away from the truck fumes and the air horns" (*Paradise Poems*, 13).
Such places and objects contain not only refuge but text, a place to hide
and something to read while one is in that place. Such places are, he says
in the essay, "a perfect location for my own emotions." If they are places
for the self, they are also places that the self takes into itself, just as we
take texts into ourselves, take in the inscriptions on things. The "hard
green daffodils" next to the cesspool "go with the melancholy and the cold
rain / with the black trees and the frozen seedpods" to make a landscape in
which the lamb once more "drops his red blood / on the dirty ice." Fighting
the drain of the icy season he holds himself open to the occasion, turning
the waste and secret places of the world into the stuff of his private joy.
One part of the result is that he transforms himself into his own pocket
of secrecy:

> The sun goes off and like a white eye
> watching. I wake up singing,
> floating, bursting, inside my sweet shelter.
>
>   (*Red Coal*, 21)

Pockets of this sort turn up often enough in the poems to complicate
(though not, finally, to contradict) the image of Stern that emerges from

---

7. From an interview with Mark Hillringhouse, *American Poetry Review* (March–April 1984):
26. The interview took place in April 1982.

reviews and jacket blurbs. He has been called our Whitman because of the expansiveness, the ebullience, the exuberant openness of voice. His stance and gestures classically Whitmanian, Stern turns himself outward to the world, accessible, ready, hungry, and warmly generous. Such openness is a gift of himself to the world, given outright in love and compassion; but it also permits an absorption of all that his exuberance lights on in the places he inhabits or conceives. Openness is a two-way street. At this level Stern seeks for poems of pure relation, relation defined in terms of the feelings emergent from him and put out into the world, whether ecstasy, woe, love, the hatred of Nazis, shame.

The play of these gestures comes through as much in his syntax as in his statements. Never quite conversational, his speech has some of the openness of conversation, its unforced transitions, its habit of moving from one main clause to the next or of working through a series of parallel clauses or phrases. Here is the beginning of "Climbing This Hill Again":

> This is a feast, climbing this hill again,
> snapping thorns, rubbing a little blood on my ankle.
> I know every tree on the hillside,
> every stump and runner.
> I lie on my back again as I always do,
> stretching my legs out and entering the blue world.
> Over my bed a 30,000 pound stone sits
> supported by a lump of grass and a few flowers.
> I draw little figures in the flat spaces
> with my round eye, as I always do,
> and make the shadows out of the sun's roots.
>
> (*Lucky Life*, 41)

His language makes itself available to that of which it speaks, just as he does. Modifying phrases pile up, each adding more to his actions and our seeing, each opening more of the world as it gives the world more fact and density. Consider what Ashbery would do in a similar situation: while adding more to the seeing he would add even more to the stock of that which is held back, not quite spoken. Each offering would increase mystery, the unspoken growing as the spoken did, because the spoken did. Stern makes other kinds of mystery, other modes of making mystery. The syntax in this passage supports a way of speaking that promises to show all that can be shown and to stride toward it directly without evasion or delay. Subject and verb get swiftly to the point, that swiftness speaking of, promising, sincerity, an opening-out. The vision is urgent, compelled. What we were taught in grammar school to call first-person-present-indicative-active forms the essential pattern of this and many Sternian passages: "I know . . . I lie . . . I draw . . . [I] make." When the action moves to the future (many of his poems offer a covenant for future action, a covenant of the poet with himself but also with his reader) the same pattern often holds. Here is the final stanza of "Hidden Justice":

> I will put my small stage here
> under a thick leaf
> and I will eat and sleep and preach right here
> and put my two dogs there
> to keep my two guards busy
> with prayer and feeding.
> I will live completely for the flowering,
> my neck like a swan's,
> my fingers clawing the air
> looking for justice;
> year after year the same,
> my fingers clawing the air for hidden justice.
>
> (*Paradise Poems*, 16)

The immediacy and directness, the emphasis on his fullness of presence in that place and time, are the same in this future tense as in his discourse of the present: "I will put . . . I will eat and sleep and preach . . . I will live." Here is part of the first stanza:

> This is where I'll go to breathe
> and live in darkness
> and sit like a frog, and sit like a salamander,
> and this is where I'll find a tiny light
> and have my vision
> and start my school.

Parallel phrases and clauses pile up in rapid sequence, no room between them for crannies that might divert the movement as it works through the point. Stern so reads his stance in the world that he can assume his fullness of presence even in moments not yet made.

One of the by-products of such syntax is our sense that he has found his place and his way of working within it, and that he plans to continue in both. The *settledness* of self comes through as much in the language as in what he says about Easton.

Yet to offer oneself in such openness does not mean that there are no mysteries, no pockets of personal secrecy. Stern's persistent claims for a packed density of self (it is so certain that he can promise its substance to future actions) means that there is also a language of the hidden—sometimes of that which cannot come fully into the open, sometimes of that which is none of the open's business, the language working to show only that something is there. We saw how Mark Strand seeks for a pure sort of absence in which the presence of self is described as the absence of something else. Strand can thus achieve a wholeness that is complete and yet composed in part of what is not there. Stern asserts another sort of wholeness in which the presence of one aspect claims—implies, affirms—the presence of another. He is so aware of his own latent content that he is bound to produce meetings that involve tonalities other than those of intensest openness. Whatever his settledness into place, Stern knows from his own history, from the Pennsylvania seasons, that there can be no settledness without the emergence into the scene of radical diversity. Multiplicity is thus not only the knowledge he has come to but in fact an essential truth. This means that however frank in their forceful stride, Stern's gestures of openness cannot show all that a context holds. In "Hidden Justice" he will find a place for his small stage in the forest and lie down on it under a thick leaf, but the justice for which his fingers claw the air will be hidden, and may always be so. The existence of justice is not in question; what is in question is whether his clawing will succeed. And look at that word "clawing," which appears twice in the second stanza: whatever the settledness on one's stage in one's own forest there are places within him that have never yet been settled, whose urgencies impel them up from the darkness where they sit and simmer. "Clawing" speaks for those dark places, for their mysteries and secrets that a driving urge toward openness may never fully undo.

Because these are Gerald Stern's dark places, surrealist shirts will continue to push out of closets and dance their urgencies before him, dance them until the urgencies are undone and the shirts can go back on the rack. The echoes of surrealism that can be heard in *Rejoicings* and *Lucky Life* are sounding here too, but they have become more supple and subtle. They are most distinct in some of the *Paradise Poems*, "Picking the Roses,"

"Steve Dunn's Spider," and "One Bird to Love Forever." Stern's surrealism, though wryer than that of the early Bly, touches some of the issues that the deep image touched. Surrealism is one of Stern's ways of speaking secrecy, the mysteries that reside in the openness, with it and sometimes within it. The thrust of that which seeks to push up and out, to have its way with the contours of consciousness, can turn up in his garden or in the landscape around Easton or even in the Arizona desert.

In "Picking the Roses" the roses he picks (chooses, plucks, probably from a catalogue) are for the spring, the order made "in early February / before the ice cracks and the island gets back its dignity" (*Paradise Poems*, 6). The interstices of the house are stuffed to keep out the alien chill, "a towel against the front door / to keep the wind out / and newspapers squeezed into the holes / so we can have good reading for the bright wasps." He knows most of the landscape, the "hot slope / where the strawberries used to be," the place where, when the roses arrive in corrugated paper, he can "stop for a minute to hear the words skip / on the water or collect like mice behind the garbage cans." What he cannot touch in familiarity is that which may be lurking outside the cabin in February: "If there is a boar, he is outside snorting. / We will need him for the bleeding and regeneration to come." And indeed they do use him, the boar and Stern together becoming the chorus at the unfreezing of the turf. When the time comes, Stern will "tear the ground with [his] shovel / and bark with pain," his barking escalating into primal speech which blends with that of the boar who must die so the season can live:

> Then for two blocks up and two blocks down
> my screams, and the screams of the boar,
> will mix together.
> There will be talking afterwards and sobbing
> and touches of cynicism and histrionics
> in the living rooms by the river,
> and single voices wailing in the tradition
> of the old Orient, and choruses of flies
> boring everybody with their small details,
> crash of bone against bone,
> mixture of broken weapons and falling shadows.

And then the moment of spasm subsides, slowly but perceptibly, into a passage of pure directness: "I will sleep . . . I will be rocking . . . I will collect." The lengthy passage is fleshed with phrases that build the spring-to-be, stems and clouds and buds and trees. Like the surrealist shirts the boar had come forth in his time. Stern can only guess at its existence in February (if "there is a boar") but in the spring it emerges and screams along with that within the shoveler which had lurked within through the winter but now emerges screaming. That which had lurked within him emerges in the openness imaged in the long striding rhythm that takes the poem to its end. Passion and the rush of wit carry his frankness into the spring, his own and the world's openness meeting and matching for half the year.

Stern ends his first four books beside the water. In *Rejoicings* he is the water. That book concludes with "Turning into a Pond," the long siege of language finally successful. His desire to place himself is so deep ("All I need is one foot in the mud / to keep my sanity") that he wants not only to root himself into the mud but to be that which the mud supports. The poem puts us into the frame Stern would develop in *Lucky Life*. That book concludes with "Something New," the title telling plainly of inconclusion. At the beach, playing with sand castles, Stern discusses with those beside him "the simple pleasures." At the end he imagines himself, a year gone by, standing in the same place, "whispering words of greeting . . . to the little Greek genius / inside the hill of sand that used to be our castle." He imagines that she will dare him to give himself to the waves as she did, to simplify and discard and then to live by the sea as she does, "under the buried notes and the combs / singing and humming and sleeping." Whatever the rootedness in the book, at the end there is only an imagined future in which he still has not settled in, still is open to challenge. *The Red Coal* concludes with "Here I Am Walking," and the poem ends with him saying that he will sit on the black rocks at the edge of the beach, "just where I was / twenty-five years ago," still unloading the lair's baggage, dreaming, "finding a way to change, or sweeten, [his] clumsy life." Still no ultimate rooting, no progress from the end of *Lucky Life*. *Paradise Poems* concludes with "The Dogs" and an elaboration of place, the textures of home. Strolling up and down the river he stops on the catwalk, the river's spray in his face, the landscape dense, the sky "dark and heavy," the island "rich and empty." The weight of all these endings is a comment on the work, an ultimate clarification coming from the need to put it just right.

One of Stern's master similes is his sense of himself as a plant, fixed in this garden to which he has come. He is part of that which gets rooted whenever he does his springtime digging. He is linked to the place through likening, a perpetual *imitatio*, the result being another version of that obsessive pondering of wholeness that informs every part of his work. But plants cannot be Jewish: if he exults in that which his poetry always celebrates, if he sings his way through much of *Paradise Poems*, he often turns to his ancient sadness when he has taken care of his world. In "Bee Balm" he plants flowers for the hummingbird whom he loves to watch and entice to his lips. Then, his world settled into its comfort, he will lie down on his couch, letting the yellow light go through him "so [he] can last the rest of the summer on thought, / so [he] can live by secrecy and sorrow (*Paradise Poems*, 33). All of the music and dance, the ecstasy and celebration, have to share him with a sense of something still to be achieved, something beyond that sorrow. Whatever the rooting, there is a need for still more watching and waiting:

> I mean that my one chance for happiness
> depends on wind and strange loyalty and a little bark,
> which I think about and watch and agonize over
> day and night,
> like a worried spirit
> waiting for love.
>
> (*Red Coal*, 55)

Whatever the settledness, the lushness, his is a qualified plenitude, its contrary still open and waiting to be filled: the last words of *Paradise Poems* are "rich and empty." It is because of that waiting that all of Stern's books end with an encounter with the primal, the place of beginning which is also the place of ultimate seeking, beyond singing and secrecy, celebration and sorrow. This poetry loves and fears the past, exults in the present and glosses its pain. Being next to the primal sea in a state of full realization would be the purest rooting of all, the ultimate achievement of desire. The reach toward that absolute locus is one of Stern's radical gestures.

III

Stern's first four books had photographs on their covers but *Lovesick*, his fifth, does not, showing instead an etching by David Hockney from an edition of the Brothers Grimm.[8] And where the other covers had been relatively sedate—old postcards, an old photograph of Stern, a more recent one, an unspecified image from a building—this one manages to mock and define itself at once. Titled "Riding Around on a Cooking Spoon, 1969," it shows a grotesque two-dimensional figure straddling an enormous three-dimensional spoon, the whole spoon twice the length of the figure, the spoon bearing an immense bowl at its front equal in size to the figure's trunk. The cover blurb on the paperback edition, just below this image, says that "Gerald Stern is the most startling and tender poet to emerge in America in a decade," but though there is surely tenderness elsewhere in Stern's work it is glaringly absent from this phallic fantasy. Just above the image is the book's title in red, which has somewhat more point in relation to the image but takes most of its effect from this characteristically ironic, impertinent juxtaposition. None of the previous covers is quite so self-defining, none shows the confidence this one does. His mode now settled and secure, recognizably his own, Stern's place in the contemporary poetic scene has become increasingly clear.

Some remarks in "Knowledge Forwards and Backwards" can open a reading of that place. His mind, he says, is "a kind of purse, nothing / is ever lost (Lovesick, 67); such storage is surely the basis of knowledge backwards. With that knowledge one is on the way to becoming ("accumulating") a demon, developing a power, a look, sight, cunning; this, clearly, is the capacity for knowledge forwards. And yet it seems that only self-engendered knowledge can accumulate in this way because "no one / can live in place of us." We are for ourselves and to ourselves, our being all and only our own, very much in the high modernist mode, much as Rilke's Malte reads the being of a pot cover or Edward Weston reads peppers. We are in our own places; indeed we are those places, requisitely so. If "no one / can live in place of us," that means that we must occupy those places and that no one else ever can, a set of conditions with which Stern lives happily. "No one / can live in place of us" shows how Stern continues the tradition of Shelley (whom he resembles more basically than Whitman) and of recent figures whom he admires like Richard Hugo and James Wright. ("A Song for the Romeos," in Lovesick, is dedicated to "my brothers Jim Wright and Dick Hugo.") Stern has spoken to me of his dislike of David Antin's talk-

---

8. Lovesick (New York: Harper & Row, 1987). An earlier version of this material on Lovesick was printed in Poetry East 8 (1988), which was devoted to Stern and which contains a good deal of valuable material.

poetry, and one can see why he dislikes it, given the radically different workings of genre and speaker in Stern's lyrics and Antin's stand-up "improvisations." As much as anyone in our time Stern stands as a model of the late modernist lyric poet.

If no one can stand in our places, that means not only a kind of privacy and even aloneness but a profound sense of one's presence to oneself, as well as the sense that such self-presence defines a center where one is at. In "I Do a Piece from Greece" Stern is lying on the bed in his Pennsylvania house, playing a violin in a wild caricature of success: "I raise the bow / above my head and bend a little, my hair / is hanging down. I am at last the musician / my mother wanted" (*Lovesick*, 4). Around him, sitting on boxes, are fantasies of his aunts and uncles, "sobbing and sighing." Though Stern finds it a joy to be here, his ancient relatives howl; but that howling and that joy are not so far apart because his playing, he says, is "the only way I have of weeping." More, it is his way of joining with those he has loved, harmonizing with them in sounds that end as shrieks. Stern's throbbing, aggressive, present-tense syntax sets us insistently into this immediate moment, centering on its upfrontness, making it the temporal locus where he and the old ones meet. But it is not only relatives that so meet: toward the beginning he speaks of "the streamlined body / we dreamed about in the thirties," toward the end he reaches back to talk about thirteenth-century singing. That this moment of collection can only be temporary is clear from Stern's obsession with what is no longer here (his aunts and uncles) as well as what he has come to (his success as a musician). This moment too, however tuneful, shall pass. It is a moment of time's abeyance, an instant of pulling together, of harmony at all levels, musical, personal, temporal; but what happens within that occasion is no more than the acts that fill a pause.

The place seems more than itself, if only through the allusions studded throughout: he does a piece from Greece, puts on a California tie, imagines himself lying "under the sea of Azov" (the northern arm of the Black Sea), wants the moon to shine on the Allegheny, speaks of certain kinds of singing as done "in parts of the south." As he joins up disparate times, so does he pull in diverse places; and as those times cluster now, so do the places cluster here, beside the moonless Allegheny River. But we can center still more specifically. The poem begins by locating the piece from Greece not in Greece but in him ("I haven't done that / for three or four years"); and that, too, is where the uncles and aunts are, the boxes on which they sit more within him than without, the harmony of violin and voice perceptible only within himself. He is the temporal center, the geography primer, the ultimate site of all this multileveled, multitextured immediacy.

To put it another way, he is the place where the knowledges forwards and backwards meet, their center, their focal point. But his role is far more complex because he is not only the center but the instrument of centering, the point of convergence and the converger as well. None of this intersecting is an accident, an unforeseeable epiphany, but a willed singing into being, an act that could not have happened had he not been fully confident that he is himself a hub and can therefore offer himself as the locus for such events.

Events of that sort happen in a poem like "There I Was One Day," where Stern figures himself as a series of large birds. Standing on one foot in a church parking lot he is "a giant whooping crane / with my left ibex finger against my temple / trying to remember what my theory of corruption was" (Lovesick, 26). He wants that theory because he remembers his parents, "immigrant cranes," whom he shocked when, in his teens, he yanked the tablecloth off the table. That scene grounds the poem in complicated pain. Neither mitigated nor deflected by the self-mocking image of the bird, the pain is, quite the opposite, directed into the poem by his bizarre vision of himself meditating on the sense of the scene that was. Passion and the grotesque had already joined on the cover, within the image by Hockney and in its play with the language around it. Neither negated the other then, nor do they do so in this poem or anywhere else in Stern. The same can be said for the silliness of idea ("I thought I'd trace the line of pure decadence / to either Frank Sinatra or Jackie Gleason"), which finds its own place within the poem's multitudes. All of these are possibilities within Gerald Stern, himself the locus of a bundle of tonalities, a mix of foolishness and "anger and righteousness," of "the stuttering of violent justice." Still— and this is Stern's major point—the mix is not a discordant, noncohering jumble of elements. What we see are shards and disjointed fragments but facets of a totality that can only be called Gerald Stern. I say "only" because of the ending of the poem:

> Just a walk for me
> is full of exhaustion; nobody does it my way,
> shaking the left foot, holding the right foot up,
> a stork from Broadway, a heron from Mexico,
> a pink flamingo from Greece.

Nobody walks this way, no one else can do quite this mix of birds, this bundle of (elsewhere) incongruous facets that add up to himself. A unique concatenation, he not only centers this diversity, he *is* this diversity. The singular frame that holds the whole, he is also the whole's content.

At once, then, center and circumference, he is also a kind of collective, concentrating the substance of the knowledges forwards and backwards. Stern is so omnivorous that he wants all that he sees, not only all he knows is still hanging around inside but all he can put together. That has to do with more than species of long-legged birds. It takes in the variousness of places and times, as in "I Do a Piece from Greece," but it also takes in the variousness that he brings into a place, simply, it seems, by entering the place. In "Stopping Schubert" (*Lovesick*, 9) he is driving from Newark to Oberlin. Halfway there, nearing his home town of Pittsburgh, he stops the tape of Schubert, puts some paper on his comb, makes his old humming sound and bangs the "swollen dashboard," thinking of his past and the Schubert songs that once raged on his trombone. Schubert was then and is now ("I still love Schubert / most of all"), and therefore Stern was then and is now: Schubert has always been present to him as he has been present to himself, and each continues to be so. Since there are no breaks in Stern's love, there is therefore a consistency (continuity, wholeness, whatever the losses, whatever the knowledge) in himself as well: "I am not that different / even today." Which is not to say that he sees no incongruities here: his current Schubert had been "roaring and groaning / halfway there, the violins in the mountains, / the cellos in the old state forests."

Playing around the scene of such anomalous juxtapositions is Stern's Surrealist heritage, not so evident or prevalent as in his previous work but still emergent at appropriate moments, such as this one on the road. Part of Stern's attraction to Surrealism had surely been its capacity to interlock the disparate, to convince us of the rightness of their mutual presence even if the reasons are so mysterious that they never come quite clear. In Stern and the Surrealists such assemblage is a version of montage, the major modernist device from the Cubists through Eliot and Eisenstein and beyond. That the echoes of Surrealist montage appear less often in *Lovesick* shows that Stern has learned to make that kind of interlocking work in his own terms. If he needs no more than himself to show this mode of montage at work, if he can put his surrealism aside except for an occasional nostalgic look, that shows not only his current mastery but what that mastery built on, his personal predisposition to do things in this way. If he can do it well enough now (Stern's later uses of montage make a major mode in *Lovesick*), he could do a version of it even in his trombone days. That is the point of the poem's last words:

> I have kept it a secret for forty years,
> the tortured composer from central Pennsylvania,
> Franz Schubert.

That too is what he means by "I am not that different / even today."

The relationship of montage to Stern's sense of self-presence appears not only in his concern with time but his concomitant concern with the most intense immediacy. Stern has an eye and passion for detail, for the nuances of an experience, the facets not only of himself but of the contexts he encounters. "Nobody Else Living," the first poem in the book, sets these patterns going for the collection that follows:

> Nobody else living knows that song as well as I do.
> On bad days I fill the tub with hot water
> and rest my head on the freezing porcelain.
> I fill the courtyard with sounds.
> They come through the frosted glass,
> they come through the transom. All that wonderful
>   pity,
> all that broken bliss, for twenty or thirty minutes
> now rich and reminiscent and warm,
> now cloudy and haunted.

The poem as a whole plays out an oxymoronic context, a reaching for elements that differ in how they define experience. If there is the quasi-binary play of hot water and freezing porcelain—each touched by, touching on, different parts of his body—there is also the combinatory (not nearly binary) play of pity and bliss, emotions not obviously related yet clearly not contradictory. Those emotions beget descriptions of two quite different ways of gazing, rich-reminiscent-warm, cloudy-haunted. The set of hot and freezing emerges from sensuousness ("feelings" defined in terms of the sensory), the set of pity and bliss from emotions ("feelings" defined in terms of passions). The set of adjectives has to do with differing tonalities, ways of describing those emotions which, themselves, generate emotions.

And where is Stern in all this? He is where he always is now, at the center concatenating. (In fact from all we have seen we can conclude that he *is* all this). The elements in that canny business with the hot water and freezing porcelain, each touching different parts of his body, are discussable together because they meet in him. Only as they so meet does their pairing have any meaning. Further, because it is first in the poem, that pairing sets up the meaning of the other pairs that follow, where import comes partly from relationship to himself. Yet it is not such placement alone that generates the ultimate gist, for all of this takes place within "twenty or thirty minutes," not the forty years of "There I Was One Day" or the equivalent in "Stopping Schubert."

Consider, then, these components. A variety of contrasts meet in this immediate moment. In that moment they meet within him as the organizing center and therefore bestower of meaning. Because he brings them together he makes them present to one another. Because he is the field where all this variety meets and moves him to sing and feel, these moments serve to make him even more present to himself, more intensely aware of himself as the locale of collection that makes significance possible. (In several senses he is the maker of the poem's meaning.) "There I was One Day" shows Stern to be, at once, center and frame. "Nobody Else Living" begins with a counterpart assertion ("Nobody else living knows that song as well as I do"), confirming him not only as unique concatenator but as a fascinated observer of himself being himself at a variety of levels, thus of himself most intensely present to himself. That self-presence is hardly neutral or without consequence, for this, we are told, takes place "on bad days," so the sense of intense self-presence comes out to be a cure for what ails him at that moment. Late modernism rarely gets as pure as this, as definitive of its desires.

Stern's basic mode runs radically through every phase of his work. A poem like "Washington Square" appears to contradict Stern's comment about our requisite self-presence, but it does not:

> Now after all these years I am just that one pigeon
> limping over towards that one sycamore tree
> with my left leg swollen and my left claw bent and my
>   neck
> just pulling me along.

> (31)

That sounds like Keats's remark about watching a sparrow peck around in the gravel: "or if a Sparrow come before my Window I take part in its

existince [sic] and pick about the Gravel.'"⁹ But where Keats seeks to evacu-
ate selfhood in order to become that Other, Stern's pigeon is his avian
surrogate in the world of Washington Square, Gerald Stern with wings, the
wounded, limping poet who *will* manage to get through: "I remember the
one pigeon / fighting his way through the filthy marijuana, / sighing." Stern's
poem is closer to Wordsworth's "Resolution and Independence" (his bird
doing the work of Wordsworth's old leech-gatherer) than anything Keats
ever did.

The rarity of the Keatsian in Stern's work explains another of his tenden-
cies. Several times he speaks of his aloneness, once of his "loneliness," but
he uses the word without the unnerving connotations of profoundest pain.
He begins "Grapefruit" with his usual urgency and calculated awkwardness,
the juices of the grapefruit threatening to wet his chest and stomach (*Lovesick*, 58). Outside in his garden are the "wavy tree" with "pitiful leaves,"
the "useless rhubarb" with its stalks "too large and bitter for eating," some
lettuce and spinach too old for use, a thin tomato plant that yields puny,
pinched tomatoes. This, he says, is the way the saints ate, "only they dug
for thistles." At the end, in another customary practice, he exults in what
the earth brings, though this time he speaks, unusually, in the rhetoric of
open prayer. In the middle of the poem is this: "Oh loneliness, I stand at
the sink, my garden / is dry and blooming." Ironically inappropriate, "loneliness" of that sort has more to do with "aloneness" (he is the only person
on the scene) than with longing for company. Warmed by the generosity
that creates this untasty multitude, awed by the completeness the scene
offers, Stern envisions a saint's possibilities of life and also lays out his own.
He routinely enacts the desire for an inner world so capable of knowledges
forwards and backwards that it needs nothing more than itself and what it
can readily find. Stern's positive capabilities serve his obsessive self-
centering, the focusing and framing through which he makes his world.

Those acts have myriad meanings and effects because he and his multitudes work skillfully together to enlarge each other's dimensions. In "No
Longer Terror" he describes a day's meditation on light, inside and outside
his house (62). He ends by saying twice "though I am alone," referring to
how he still dresses for dinner and eats his meals course by course. Now we
know how to take that point. His stance is precisely the same whether he
is surrounded by multitudes, as in his worn-out garden, or whether he *is*

---

9. From his letter to Benjamin Bailey of 22 November 1817. See *Selected Poems and Letters*,
ed. Douglas Bush (Boston: Houghton Mifflin, 1959), 259.

multitudes, acting as a collective. Whether plants or persons or places, the multitudes meet in him, with him, because he alone makes the meanings they have in relation to one another. Yet we cannot reduce these conditions to a routine uniqueness. Stern cannot make the multitude's meanings unless he is first present to himself, aware of himself as a place. Only then can he be aware of himself as the sole place where these components can converge and gain their particular coherence, their unique concatenation. But such moves are reciprocal: Stern becomes most present to himself (most aware of most of himself) when he convenes the collective and works out its ultimate import. If he cannot center or frame unless he is tightly, broadly, confidently, present to himself, the performing of those processes gives him an even more intense sense of presence to himself. That reciprocity goes far toward making the Sternian mode possible.

The question is less what to do with other modes of mediation than it is what to do with mediation itself, working in the middle ground with modes that we call media, with texts and the acts that perform them. What to do, for example, with Jerome Rothenberg? He argues for the kind of public mediation exemplified in the ethnopoet, argues against the private romantic-modernist lyric mode that Stern effectively models; yet he also argues for a self-presence at moments of making that is as intense as (though far more fleeting than) any that Stern claims. What to do with David Antin, who grounds his stand-up talk poems in the firmest self-presence and immediacy in the moment, yet goes on to work out modes whose distancing from that moment grows as the modes continue? Steve McCaffery responds to Sternian claims through the person of a ventriloquist whose voice is never quite placed; yet nothing so neat as a spectrum runs from Stern to McCaffery. Nothing in the middle is as assured and self-consistent as what stands at either end.

2

The Histories and Poetics
of Jerome Rothenberg

"Thought," said Trista Tzara, "is made in the mouth," a comment Jerome Rothenberg finds so useful and pertinent that he quotes it quite often, especially when discussing orality and performance. Yet if thought is made in the mouth it is also made in history, out of it and by it, in terms of what history does, subject to its conditions. Rothenberg knows that too, and in the introductory remarks to "New Models, New Visions; Some Notes toward a Poetics of Performance," he combines the comment from Tzara with a reading of the order of history that puts the question within the frame of a basic phenomenology. Establishing an image that opens what Geneva School critics have called a *point de départ,* he speaks of history in terms of an oxymoronic figure at once confining and unrestricted: "The origins we seek—the frame that bounds our past, that's set against an open-ended future—are no longer Greek, nor even Indo-European but take in all times and places."[1] One can read Rothenberg's image in terms of a late modernist

1. In his *Pre-Faces and Other Writings* (New York: New Directions, 1981).

mode like Geneva phenomenology because it is typical of the images the Geneva School sought out, images that define the point at which experience begins, that determine the contours experience is to take. Yet there are modernisms and modernisms, a multiplicity encompassing not only origins and phenomenologies but modes as different from Geneva as Schwitters from Bachelard or Pound from Poulet; modes that influenced Rothenberg's claim that endings are non-sensical, quite literally beyond any sense. Indeed they would have to be, given not only the open-endedness of Rothenberg's image of history but his remarks at the end of an interview that "I don't like to see fixed ends. I like to see the thwarting of ends" (*Pre-Faces*, 223–24). Rothenberg's Dada heritage is clear, his grounding in the practices of late modernist performance equally clear. Yet it is misleading to take his work only in terms of issues like *points de départ* or the quest for origins or the quest for what Henry Sayre has called "metaphysical wholeness."[2] Those points and quests are there but so is a set of counterurgings that turn Rothenberg's work into a many-faceted field everywhere beset by difference.

Among other things this means that Rothenberg's reading of history cannot be confined to the image we saw. If at times he envisions history in terms of a determining shape based on a point of radical origin, his instincts may also move him toward a reading of historical time that finds it open everywhere, ultimately without the orderliness of any linear sequence. In a dialogue with William Spanos in which Spanos wonders whether Rothenberg "disregards the imperatives of human historicity," Rothenberg answers that his reading of history finds an exact analogue in one of modernism's most exalted phases:

> I see the process in time as non-linear & multichronic (including but not dominated by dream-time), though synchronic and simultaneous in consciousness: i.e. the mind bringing together a large number of elements from culturally & spatially separated chronologies. That's a way to deal with time, as cubism dealt with a multiplicity of spatial perspectives without, I think, denying roundedness.[3]

This mode of reading space is a way of dealing with history, giving it legibility; but at the same time it protects a shape ("roundedness") that

2. Sayre, *The Object of Performance* (Chicago: University of Chicago Press, 1988), 183. Sayre used the phrase not only in terms of Rothenbergian oral poetics but of American poetics as such. It is certainly pertinent for Rothenberg's work and reflects other comments made about him, comments usually skeptical about both "metaphysical" and "wholeness."

3. "A Dialogue on Oral Poetry with William Spanos," *boundary 2* 3 (1975): 537–38.

Rothenberg acknowledges in cautious negatives but that stands there beyond denial, a figure of a different desire. The balance is tricky, a way of having determinate form (Bachelard has an essay on the phenomenology of round-edness) and not quite having it, both at once.[4] Searching for such balances, seeking to define not only a way of reading the world but—more radical and, in fact, causative of that reading—a way of seeking to *be* in the world, is characteristic of Rothenberg. That intricate play of positionings goes far toward explaining Rothenberg's understanding of performance as well as the ethnopoetics in which he sees performance grounded. It also helps to explain an equally intricate interplay of self-making and text-making which runs through all his writing and substantiates his significance within the contemporary context.

Rothenberg's varied readings of temporal process speak of multiplicities, histories nestled within histories, histories of different sizes and sometimes of different shapes. Ethnopoetics argues for a global history, what Paul Christensen has called "a Jungian universe of mind" peopled with "arche-typal heroes."[5] History so encompassing has its center everywhere and its circumference nowhere (the relevance of that old phrasing tells much about Rothenberg's ties). That is another way of putting the ethnopoetic reading of history as multidimensional and peopled with practitioners of perennial activities, a community steeped in recurrent acts of communion. The sha-man's up-front chanting is one of those acts that make history a series of repetitions, but that series is without sequence since the acts are always the same; history, in this reading, never progresses. This is part of the ultimate import of the "roundedness" Rothenberg speaks of in the dialogue with Spanos.

And yet there is far more to the textuality of Rothenberg's sense of history, for within that roundedness, that "non-linear & multichronic" process in time, runs a rigorously linear narrative, a more private and specific fable emergent in, for example, the connections between *A Big Jewish Book* and *Technicians of the Sacred*, between *Poland, 1931* and *A Seneca Journal*.[6] It emerges most specifically in the *New Selected Poems*, where

4. See Gaston Bachelard, "La phénoménologie du rond," in *La Poétique de L'Espace*, 5th ed. (Paris: Presses Universitaires de France, 1957).

5. Paul Christensen, "Some Bearings on Ethnopoetics," *Parnassus* 15 (1989): 147, 153. For similar comments and others that extend into issues of global health and politics, see Gary Snyder's "The Politics of Ethnopoetics," in *The Old Ways* (San Francisco: City Lights Books, 1977), 15–43.

6. *A Big Jewish Book*, ed. Jerome Rothenberg with Harris Lenowitz and Charles Doria (Garden City, N.Y.: Doubleday, 1978); *Technicians of the Sacred: A Range of Poetries from Africa, Asia, Europe and Oceania*, ed. Jerome Rothenberg, 2d ed. (Berkeley and Los Angeles: University of California

Rothenberg draws from a series of earlier works to bring out an implicit narrative, what he calls in the "Pre-Face" "a single long poem or sequence that the individual books . . . may have tended to obscure."[7] If in one sense that fable emerges in a poem like "Cokboy" ("saddlesore I came / a jew among / the indians"), in another the syncretism of that and similar phrases ("silk of his prayer-shawl bag beneath / cover of beaverskin above") obscures the immersion in linear time of an exultant and bitter narrative that sometimes sounds like an ironic reading of romance, with a set of traditional figures such as magicians and wanderers. Cokboy, Rothenberg says, *came* as a Jew to the place of the Indian, the phrase rejecting stasis for movement within history. (One of his related poems is "Esther K. comes to America," another is "Galician Nights, or a Novel in Progress.") If Rothenberg's universalism is rounded and radically timeless, his vision also holds an intensely timeful fable that revels in its motion from the shtetl to the Indian village with a half-way stop in the Lower East Side. His remarks in the "Pre-Face" to *New Selected Poems* show that this fable is not a collection of sporadic and occasional comments on ancestral and recent doings but a stubbornly persistent strain whose point is as much in its linearity, its record as a spiritual journey that goes from there to here, as it is in any time-transcending likeness of Jew and Native American.

Still, the fable presents a series without sequence in the sense that we have seen: the same types of figures, performing the same functions (again, the primacy of act and therefore of history), appear in a multitude of places. Given the syncretism built into ethnopoetics, given the continuities that such syncretism asserts, such figures will always be up-front in their worlds and in Rothenberg's work. Other functions and figures turn up repeatedly in his histories. In "The Suicide of Dada," which appeared in *That Dada Strain* and in *New Selected Poems*, Rothenberg refers to his "ecstatic Dada father," speaks of how

> still marching to that Dada strain
> the procession of the fathers enters for the last time
> the caverns of the cabaret
> become a disco now.

He tells later in the poem how

Press, 1985); *Poland, 1931* (New York: New Directions, 1974); *A Seneca Journal* (New York: New Directions, 1978).

    7. *New Selected Poems* (New York: New Directions, 1986), vii.

last week I saw
in boundaries of New Pascua
still alive
old clown
old Yaqui fat face
the man I would address as father
mean and fat

and tells earlier in the same poem of those

who once watched the Dada kid
strut before hundreds
saw him hitch tie up to adam's apple
his heavy collar fallen to his chest.
(*New Selected Poems*, 116–18)

Allied to these "ecstatic Dada fathers" are the rabbis and tzaddiks of Poland, magical father figures. Allied also, in a different way, is Esther K., the figure of Rothenberg's mother. All fall into a familial pattern taking in more than a confrontation with strong precursors. The Pre-Face to *That Dada Strain* is especially elaborate on the "fatherhood" of the Dada figures. It tells how the authors of Dada "have passed, as Blake would have said, into 'eternity,' to become the fathers of imaginal acts done in their memory," how "the DADAs appeared to me both as children & (in a reading of their name that they denied themselves) as fathers—literally the generation of my own father."[8] Rothenberg's linking of personal and literary progenitors is rarely so specific. It openly suggests some of the deeper reaches of his familial pattern. Insofar as he defines these figures as familial Rothenberg builds a set of relationships and, for himself, a place within those relationships. Insofar as he defines them, then, he defines himself as well: by making a genealogy he makes a self and creates a private myth. (Figures like Blake and Hölderlin should be read precisely this way. Rothenberg's relation to Blake involves more than some obvious echoes.) That makes his fable a text, a tissue of weaving where he works in a place for himself within the patterns he is working out. Penelope undid her web so as to remain ever

---

8. *That Dada Strain* (New York: New Directions, 1983), vii–viii. For comments on the influence of Dada on Rothenberg, see John Zalenski, "Rothenberg's Continuing Revolution of the Word," *North Dakota Quarterly* 55 (1987): 202–16.

Penelope; her actions were designed to sustain old relationships. Rothenberg weaves so as to uncover all that he is, which means all that he belongs to (here, too, there are old relationships) as well as all that to which he can never properly belong. In that sense his fable is an autobiographical act, though never as openly personal as the autobiographical gestures of artists like Duane Michals or Lucas Samaras.[9] But if Rothenberg sometimes sounds like Samaras—his acts of self-constituting often based, like those of Samaras, on his fabricating of others—he is more openly historical than Samaras has ever been, more aware of himself in a context of actual places and persons, however fabulous he makes them. There is no place in Rothenberg's work comparable to Samaras's apartment, the purpose of which is to define a secluded, private space within which Samaras can explore the shapes of subjective spaces.

As counterpart of these figures Rothenberg's private and specific fable also occurs in a series of associated places; it has a geography of locations and events and the linkages among them. Such places speak histories, in this case what happened to several of those tribes that have their being outside the mainstream of white Anglo-European Christian culture. In *Poland, 1931* (the year of Rothenberg's birth but not the place of his birth; the title weaves his history into the history of a tribal whole) the places speak of passions and pogroms. In *Khurbn and other Poems* they speak of the whirlwind that set off the ultimate pogrom.[10] But this is only part of his canonical map. Rothenberg's geography includes places like Salamanca, New York, and communities of Native Americans, who, on the face of the matter, have nothing special to do with Jews, though the relations of both groups to the mainstream culture have many (often unfortunate) similarities. Rothenberg's writings argue for very precise linkings of these very

9. For a contrary view, which seems to suggest that Rothenberg's major work eschews the autobiographical, see George Economou, "Some Notes Towards Finding a View of the New Oral Poetry," *boundary 2* 3 (1975): 662. Economou argues for Rothenberg's submergence of ego in the role of a sort of "communal or tribal poet," but that makes Rothenberg's position seem more categorical than it actually is. Economou's essay offers a number of useful speculations on the relation of older oral poetics to contemporary practice in figures like Rothenberg and Antin.

10. *Khurbn and Other Poems* (New York: New Directions, 1989). Despite his arguments, in the Spanos interview and elsewhere, about the shape of history as "non-linear & multichronic" Rothenberg reads the history of the Jews as markedly linear and continuous, as witness to not only *A Big Jewish Book* but its recent successor, *Exiled in the Word: Poems and Other Visions of the Jews from Tribal Times to the Present*, ed. Jerome Rothenberg and Harris Lenowitz with commentaries by Jerome Rothenberg (Port Townsend, Wash.: Copper Canyon Press, 1989). For a useful study of Rothenberg and "ancestral roots," see Kevin Power, "Pack Up Your Troubles in Your Old Kit Bag and Smile, Smile, Smile, from Diaspora to Galut," *boundary 2* 3 (1975): 683–705.

different clans, not only in the occasional cracks about the ubiquitous Jewish peddlers but particularly in the person of Rothenberg himself: he stands in this context as a centering figure, a collective. We saw that part of the reason for Rothenberg's figurings of fatherhood is to devise places for himself in relation to Central and Eastern European culture, places artistic as well as tribal, the Cabaret Voltaire and the Polish synagogue. Dada spaces enfold a kind of primal scene that engenders the history of an alternative poetics. The dead communities of Eastern Europe speak another history, clear and unbearable. Here Rothenberg takes on, takes up within himself, certain common memories and a memorable ambivalence. Yet, as he makes clear through the figure of the old Yaqui, another of those whom he would address as father, the linkages are not only among paternal figurings but also among the histories in which each father figured. Here the continuities become more than uncommon and almost certainly unique: How many Jews whose forebears came out of anywhere in Eastern Europe have been adopted into Native American tribes? Rothenberg was when he became a beaver in the Seneca nation in 1968; his wife and son became, in the same ceremony, blue herons (*Seneca Journal*, 2). The move from the shtetl to the reservation (keep in mind the analogy of the reservation to the Pale of Settlement in Poland) forms a purely linear history that may be peculiar to one man. But it is not as though Rothenberg has exchanged one tribal past for another; he added on to what he has. He has developed a kind of con-centering; a multiplicity meets in him in what to many would seem a most unlikely relation.

This is still another way of saying that much of Rothenberg's fable is autobiographical, an act of self-constituting. In this fabulous text he in-scribes his own lines of descent as well as those to which he is allied, to which he seeks alliance. But those simultaneous lines ought not to be taken as suggesting that his fable is static, its history fixed and whole. Consider, again, Penelope, and all that her weaving shows of the relations of texts and transience. Consider, too, Rothenberg's multiple readings of history, one of which takes history as synchronic and everywhere open, the other of which shows it as full of the movement and price of time. Both readings appear in the fable of Jew and Native American. In one of its aspects the fable expresses the universal wholeness ethnopoetics argues for, expressing it in part in a journey as archetypal as any of Rothenberg's repeated charac-ters. But the fable also enacts another way of history, a series of specificities that show experience to be changeful and unique, momentary and particu-lar. That reading emerges in Rothenberg's remarks about the substance of

"an American present that was itself haunted by multiple languages &
identities" (*New Selected Poems*, vii). We ought to take Rothenberg's
"haunted" to mean that we are obsessed not only by "multiple languages &
identities" but by multiplicity itself, a context of specificities that seem
always to slip away from suggestions of ultimate coherence. Though Rothenberg seems to argue in the Pre-Face to *New Selected Poems* that such events
are ultimately concrete universals, his work as a whole *also* asserts a flux
and diversity as immersed in the movement of time as the practices of
ethnopoetics are in timeless repetition. The play of positioning that seeks
to handle, at once, edges that have no end and a roundedness that remains,
has counterparts in other positionings (but surely they are all the same?)
that has other oxymorons to hold in perpetual restlessness.

Take, for example, his relations to Charles Olson. Rothenberg frequently
refers to the distinction Olson makes in "Human Universe" between "language as the act of the instant and language as the act of thought about the
instant."[11] Olson's instantaneity has finally to do with how modes of making
poetry relate to modes of being in the world: at the beginning of "Projective
Verse" he says that his essay will suggest "a few ideas about what stance
toward reality brings such verse into being" (*Selected Writings*, 15). Whatever Rothenberg's echoes of Olson's momentariness he has a set of problems
different from any Olson shows, for Rothenberg also deals with those requisite repetitions of essentially the same act, performed in the same stance,
fulfilling the same roles, that appear in every version of ethnopoetics. What
persists in the work of the ethnopoet is more detailed and elaborate, more
specific and concrete, than what Olson suggests at the beginning of "The
Kingfishers" when he remarks that "what does not change / is the will to
change" (167). What persists in Olson is a Heraclitian potential. What
persists in this aspect of Rothenberg's work is not only a potential for change
but a set of recurrent gestures whose stability marks them as the acts of
the ethnopoet.

It is precisely at that point that Rothenberg's different readings of history
link up to his understanding of how texts work. Olson's comments on
momentariness and change echo in a number of remarks throughout Rothenberg's work, not as frequently as Rothenberg's statements on the acts
of the ethnopoet but sufficiently to show that the playing-out of difference
is more than subtextual. Near the end of the interview in which he suggests

---

11. In Charles Olson, *Selected Writings*, ed. Robert Creeley (New York: New Directions,
1966), 54.

the thwarting of ends he argues that "the only absolutes for poetry are diversity and change" (*Pre-Faces*, 223). He makes similar points elsewhere, some of them dealing with movements within texts, others with the movements of texts. Take, for example, that point in the dialogue with Spanos where Rothenberg reads Gershom Scholem as saying how "every stabilization in the text [of Torah] would hinder and destroy the infinitely moving, the constantly progressing and unfolding element within it" ("Dialogue," 515). Rothenberg brings in Scholem to support his argument that the act of writing-down, however beneficial in preserving the tradition of oral commentary, is inescapably pernicious. Writing-down counters that within the text which incessantly changes, which finds its meaning in change, which (to put it in Barthesian terms Rothenberg is unlikely to use) makes that bundle of words a text rather than a work. Rothenberg counts himself among those who think of poetry as "linked to, as that very process of unfolding & changing" ("Dialogue," 515). His language suggests that it is not only orality that resists the freezing of fixity but poetry as such. Writing-down becomes a thwarting of desire, a closure without completion, a concluding without conclusiveness; and that brings round again the grounding image with which Rothenberg figures history, the radical phenomenology that posits a frame at one end and openness at the other. Closure, it is clear, ought to occur only where it cannot be avoided, in that framing which encloses the point of origin. From that point on, Rothenberg's "poetry of changes" begins its refusal of fixity.

That refusal means, finally, a refusal to acknowledge the *full* viability of any bundle of words outside the moment of its making. In "New Models, New Visions" Rothenberg rejects the idea of the masterpiece, of the text so deep and definitive that it stays on as a monument, fixed in its place and condition: "There is a move away from the idea of 'masterpiece' to one of the transientness and self-obsolescence of the art-work. The work past its moment becomes a document (mere history)" (*Pre-Faces*, 168), and a work is only more than a document, only has its fullest being, in its moment. This is Olson's concept of "language as the act of the instant"; the work beyond its moment becomes, in Olson's terms, "language as the act of thought about the instant." Once out of its moment language suffers a fracture of that fusion between word and occasion which makes the artwork the channel (and locus?) of momentariness, the work slipping into a state of "self-obsolescence." The change that Rothenberg, citing Scholem, saw occurring *within* Torah—that change revered and channeled insofar as Torah is oral but fixed and therefore attentuated when Torah is written down—

has to be put into conjunction with the change *of* texts, their requisite, self-generated obsolescence. The perniciousness of writing-down lives in inverse ratio with the privileging of orality, for orality, by its nature, creates works-for-the-moment.

Other remarks by Rothenberg suggest that among those momentary works is the "subjectivity" that appears in the oral moment and makes that moment's texts. Sometimes Rothenberg sounds as though the life of the artist comes into fullest being in those moments of performance: "The performance or ritual model includes the act of composition itself: the artist's life as an unfolding through his performance of it" (*Pre-Faces,* 169). He puts it only slightly less categorically a few pages earlier in his remarks on Tzara's readings of his own and primitive poems: "the process of a life and its emergence as performance in the soundworks and simultaneities of the dada soirées" (166). The life that unfolds in the performance unfolds because of the performance and perhaps as the performance; that is, the self (subject) is not only performative but maybe, itself, performance. We see the *possibility* of drawing on Olson to conclude that the self, too, may be "the act of the instant," may be, then, a subject.

John Erickson's reading of Dada makes several relevant points:

> It is true that Dada sought to unfetter the self from tradition, but it also sought to unfetter the self from self, to free it to act, unimpeded by convention or self-consciousness, wholly committed to the present moment, guided only by absolute spontaneity and chance in combination with the artist's specific perceptions.[12]

Dada performance cuts up all sorts of continuities in order to be "wholly committed to the present moment." Consider the image of Hugo Ball performing in his Tin Man suit. As Ball wields that gesture, it insists on its own immediacy, its being in and for the moment, in and for and as the performance. The performance, then, is act and occasion *as* each other; and if we pick up Rothenberg's suggestions about the self in its performative moment, it comes into fullest being in and as this occasion, whatever else it may be at any other time in its history. In other words, in its moment Ball's *Lautgedicht* referred only to its own utterance and its private possibilities, what it could be before it became anything else (referential, for example). That is, Ball explored his language's up-frontness, its capacities

12. *Dada: Performance, Poetry, and Art* (Boston: Twayne, 1984), 115.

in and as that moment; but there is more to the occasion, for he explored them in an act in which the consciousness wielding that language simultaneously explored its own immediacy, what it could be and do (being and doing always seeking to become the same) in the context of that occasion. The Ball performance had so stirred Rothenberg that he used the famous photograph of Ball in his Tin Man suit on the poster for a conference on Performing Language held in Binghamton in 1987. Echoes of Ball's performance sound all through Rothenberg's work, particularly as the subtext of his comments in "New Models, New Visions" on "the artist's life as an unfolding through his performance of it."

These echoes of Ball go far toward explaining much of what Rothenberg sees as the poet's requisite positioning. In *Symposium of the Whole* he speaks of how "the oral recovery involves a poetics deeply rooted in the powers of song and speech, breath and body, as brought forward across time by the living presence of poet-performers."[13] In an illuminating set of interviews with Gavin Selerie and Eric Mottram which clarify his links to classic modernism, Rothenberg speaks of the shaman and the poet in terms of such presence. "The function of the poet," he says, "is through his own person," and that positioning goes for the shaman as well: "The person, the personality, the presence of the poet, like the shaman, is extremely important. . . . The person of the shaman is the catalyst that makes it go. . . . [He is] definitely a presence."[14] Earlier in the same interview, during a discussion on sounding poems, Mottram referred to "the sense of it being as you say the public place but also the physical presence of that poet and more often than not very close to you—not a long way off on a platform but on the same level and in the same acoustic with you" (9). In his response to Mottram Rothenberg speaks not only of how he sought, using instruments such as rattles, to involve his whole body, but also of how "that concern with re-physicalizing the act of poetry, both in performance and composition," is "what the whole Projective Verse thing was about" (10). Nothing can be more immediate than immediate physical experience, which comes into being the moment its moment begins and goes off wherever it goes the moment its moment has passed. Rothenberg's more-than-Olsonian urge to physicalize his art is his way of bringing the fullest possible immediacy into those moments as they occur.

13. *Symposium of the Whole*, ed. Jerome Rothenberg and Diane Rothenberg (Berkeley and Los Angeles: University of California Press, 1983), xiii.
14. *The Riverside Interviews 4: Jerome Rothenberg*, ed. Gavin Selerie with Eric Mottram (London: Binnacle Press, 1984), 23–24. For more on the shaman and "presence," see 32.

More precisely, one should speak of the fullest immediacy the poet *needs*. That, in turn, comes down to a question of who or what is immediate at that moment which is also place and therefore also occasion. In the dialogue with Spanos and, later, in the Riverside interviews, Rothenberg fine-tunes one of his most intricate positionings, seeking to work out his stance in several strands of history that often have dramatically uneasy relations. With Spanos, Rothenberg sketches certain modernist readings of the visionary. With Blake and Whitman as precursors, modern poetry has, he says, "gradually abandoned generality (including the subjective, lyrical kind)," going, instead, after "the particulars of *this* immediate experience, & (or because) the experiencing 'self' is itself in a continuous process of change ("Dialogue," 513). Zukofsky and the Objectivists have linked "I" and "eye" in such a way that "the return to the object . . . also implies a 'seer'—an *I* through which subject & object are joined." (Rothenberg also finds such joining in Rimbaud and Copper Eskimo shamans.) Then, quoting Olson's remarks in "Projective Verse" about getting rid of "the lyrical interference of the ego," he argues that, nevertheless, "none of this denies a 'seer' so much as it refocuses our attention on the object of sight—its purpose and the process by which it occurs."

Rothenberg wants to vacate what he calls subjective lyricism in order to focus on the object seen. Yet he argues at the same time that there can be no seeing without a seer who is clearly the point of origin from which seeing begins. Whatever one's own "continuous process of change," it seems that we have to have a site of inception, the location of that aspect of "I" which is also "eye." And in fact, speaking to Spanos, Rothenberg posits precisely such a point, establishing thereby a classically modernist reading of self, a quasi-Cartesian model with which figures as different as Rilke and Steichen would be very much at home: "Just as the (modern) poem derives from a particular vision (an experience deliberately mediated by the *I*), it takes shape in a particular structure & a particular language, with the *I* again at center" (514).[15] He further confirms this geography of self by insisting, again, on how "the poem emerges from the linguistic patterns of *this* experiencing self," the poet's action "coterminous with that of anyone who recognizes his own immediate relation to the world & speaks it." *This* self in *this* moment, unique but not lyrically subjective, private and personal because

15. With this argument for a mediating center Rothenberg parts company with Olson, who speaks in "Human Universe" about "the inherited formulations which have helped to destroy [man] (the notion of himself as the center of phenomenon by fiat or of god as the center and man as god's chief reflection)"; see Olson, *Selected Writings*, 59.

particular yet without "the lyrical interference of the individual as ego": that is the complex and difficult balance Rothenberg seeks in this passage.

Once again self and text are shown to be homologous: "the idea of the oral" is "of a source of forms renewed in each instance," just as the self is so renewed ("itself in a continuous process of change"). At once a point of origin and an open-ended entity, the Rothenbergian self turns out to have precisely the same shape as that Rothenbergian reading of history with which we began: "The origins we seek—the frame that bounds our past, that's set against an open-ended future." With history and self as homologous as self and text, Rothenberg's world looks more and more like the absolute contrary of any subjective lyricism. The self, in its turn, seems more like that anomalous self/subject we have already seen in that world.

That contrariety continues in another passage from the Riverside interviews. Referring to a remark by Diane Wakoski that his muse takes the form of "old Indians and Hasidic Jews," Rothenberg argues that it is sensible to think about the muse as "that *other* person, that *other* situation, that one addresses in the poem—in the attempt to direct it away from the self" (13–14). Putting an other in his poetry would be one way of incorporating "that which is *not* the lyrical subjective voice. The 'lyric' on its own seems to be a very limited instance of what poetry can do—but so pervasive we have to figure out a real resistance" (14). And in fact radical elements endemic in Rothenberg's work, so formative that they determine much of the mode of the work, go along with the question of the other to direct attention away from the lyrically subjective. Collage and translation, he says, do such other-directing performance too to a certain degree, as does any mode in which we merge with place and occasion. Most important for Rothenberg, though, is the suggestion that ethnopoetics as such negates the pull of lyricism: "The concern overall with peoples, with cultures, with other poets, with the history of poetry at this time—all these are ways of bringing other voices in." He agrees with Eric Mottram's suggestion that "your relationship again between the poet's self and a very recognizable and researched ancestry is another way that you stop the lyric soulfulness of the ego, and that kind of arrogance, from dominating the poetry."

One can read such issues back through Olson's comments on the ego's "interference," ending at Eliot's remarks on the flight from personality (ironic given Rothenberg's antipathy to Eliot's work); yet there is far more in play here, far more at stake, than any single line of literary history can hold. Paul Christensen argues that the ethnopoem should be, among other things, "a transpersonal, I-negating testament of consciousness" ("Ethno-

poetics," 156). Part of the point of the unlyrical is to achieve such transpersonality, more precisely, a reading of personality that evades the merely
personal; and that achievement puts the Eliotic impersonal into a credible
continuity of attitudes. Transpersonality moves into other areas as well,
other histories, some much less susceptible to centralizing persuasion. For
example, what Rothenberg finds in Olson and knows full well in Eliot
appears in a different version in *Technicians of the Sacred.* He quotes Jung
on the I-Ching's involvement in acausality ("the moment under actual
observation appears to the ancient Chinese view more of a chance hit than
a clearly defined result of concurring causal chain processes"). He then
relates that observation to Jung's ideas on syncronicity and the problems it
raises about "indeterminacy & the observer's part in structuring the real"
(*Technicians,* 567–68). If there are Eliotic impersonal centers that serve as
active catalysts, there are also the decentered transpersonalisms of John
Cage and Jackson Mac Low. Rothenberg cites those two in the context of
acausality, a context granting the largest sovereignty to that which transcends persons as well as personality.

He continues his discussion of these issues with a quotation from Tristan
Tzara's *Manifesto on Feeble Love & Bitter Love.* After arguing that one can
make a Dadist poem by cutting words out of a newspaper, shaking them in
a bag and lining up the words in the order in which they left the bag, Tzara
ends with an assertion to "copy conscientiously. / The poem will be like
you" (*Technicians,* 568). One will be the co-maker of the poem because one
shakes and empties the bag in which chance has aligned the words. The
poem will be (not just be of) that particular occasion because a new random
shaking will make a poem for the new moment. If, then, as Tzara says, "the
poem will be like you," the "you" will also be *of* the moment's occasion, *be*
that occasion. Unlyrical because it omits what Mottram calls "the lyric
soulfulness of the ego," such a self shuns all that one means in speaking of
poetry as expression. Central for that occasion, it is personal because the
poem "will be like you"; yet the "you" the poem will be like transcends any
personality through its links with chance and the acausal. Rothenberg's
prevalent sense of the homology of self and text argues that the self itself
derives in considerable part from chance and the acausal, argues, finally,
for that anomalous self/subject.

A compulsion to put the subjective above mere personality links his
reading of ethnopoetics with his sense of the acausal and his antipathy to
lyricism. That same distancing stance extends to his own ethnicity, that
aspect of oneself defined through one's status as capitalized noun, Jew or

Native American. Rothenberg regularly refuses to define himself as Jew in any way that would determine his conduct or require that he think contemporary politics in messianic terms. Yet his historical definition as Jew has always obsessed him, his place in that long sequence of death and beauty, laceration and passion. He seems always to have felt Other within the sequence even as he accepted his own place within it. That is why the line from the shtetl to the reservation comes through as rigorously ironic: though it carries him along with it, he is, at once, on it and off it, never singularly either. Further, that mode of self-positioning which seeks several sites at once takes in still other elements, including, with particular emphasis, Rothenberg's place within the histories of alternative poetics. From the earliest points of his work he has complicated the romantic-modernist assertion of the poet as Other to the mainstream world by arguing stringently for alternative modernisms, for other ways of understanding the place of language in the world than those afforded by any mainstream line. To this opting for other poetries one has to add his taking-on of membership in the Seneca nation, a voluntary assumption of still another Otherness. Already Jew and Alternative Poet, his status as Seneca complicates and intensifies his sense of simultaneous aloofness and participation. Since this condition could be seen as everyone's status—an irresistible point, given his arguments for universals, given, further, the prevalence of that stance in his work—ethnopoetics becomes, in this reading, an allegory of experience.

Victor Turner puts one reading of that positioning in his review of Rothenberg and Benamou's symposium on ethnopoetics: "In his seminal 'Pre-Face to a Symposium on Ethnopoetics,' Jerome Rothenberg (who invented the term and the genre) sees *ethnos* as the *other* who is nevertheless *we*, or as Schechner puts it, the *not-not-me* beyond the *not-me*."[16] That *not-me* rings right out of Emerson's *Nature*: "All that is separate from us, all which Philosophy distinguishes as the NOT ME, that is, both nature and art, all other men and my own body, must be ranked under this name, NATURE."[17] That which the ethnopoet defines as *not-not-me* never fully enters the *me:* it is always holding back even as it gives itself out. Yet neither is the *not-not-me* ever entirely Other, without some claim on part

16. *Symposium of the Whole*, 338.
17. *Emerson, Essays and Lectures* (New York: Library of America, 1983), 8. For comments on ethnopoetics in an Emersonian context, see Hugh J. Dawson, "The Golden Day at the Golden Doorway: An Emerson Theme in Veblen, Sullivan, and Dewey," in *The Green American Tradition: Essays and Poems for Sherman Paul*, ed. H. Daniel Peck (Baton Rouge: Louisiana State University Press, 1989), 111–12.

of me, as part of me. That Other which we address in our poems in order to avoid addressing the self comes, finally, to not-not-be us, the ethnopoet's way of having and not having all that we are and are not. We define ourselves substantially in and because of a context that contains a bundle of strangers. Turner phrases that stance in terms of his well-known concept of the "liminal . . . a 'threshold' position, a betwixt-and-between state" (341).[18] That is cultural anthropology's way of putting Rothenberg's reading of one's situation in the world.

Rothenberg's poetics refuses tidy binary choices because such choices assume a rigorous track as coercive as it is constrictive; and if there is one thing Rothenberg learned from the Dada fathers, it is not only that everything is possible but that everything possible can occur at any time.[19] The simultaneous readings in the Cabaret Voltaire were, in that sense, the definitive Dada sport, and Rothenberg's continuation of that practice in joint readings with Jackson Mac Low argues for his understanding of their meaning for his work. But to a poet-theorist like Rothenberg simultaneity also involves not only acts in history but how subjectivity emerges in history. Distinctions that are comfortable in artists as different as Stern or Barbara Kruger (they are not, of course, the same distinctions) never quite fit into place with aspects of Rothenberg; and the fact that they are different distinctions tells something more about Rothenberg's anomalous place in contemporary positionings of the subject. In a paper Rothenberg delivered at the meeting of the Modern Language Association in Washington in December 1989, he argued that

> "I" & "other" are also false, are traps to keep us from the poem.
> Or put it in a different way: that "I" becomes or *is* the deepest "other": that inner thing you can't touch, the life that always gets away from you.

This reading of self finds a place in a poetics that *also* argues for a subjectivity fullest in the immediate moment, one that finds itself beset by an unceasing

---

18. For other comments on Rothenberg and the liminal, see the important study of Rothenberg in Sherman Paul's *In Search of the Primitive: Rereading David Antin, Jerome Rothenberg, and Gary Snyder* (Baton Rouge: Louisiana State University Press, 1986).

19. Note also the following, from the comments on Jung and the I-Ching: "That modern physics at the same time moves closer to a situation in which anything-can-happen is of interest too in any consideration of where we presently are." *Technicians,* 567–68. Thus does an "alternative" poetics find space within the center of the mainstream.

play of difference as immediate moments come and go. In fact that play appears even in this reading: what Rothenberg says about "the life that always gets away from you" is another speaking of slippage, of that which surely is us yet always just evades our touch.

Rothenberg's poetics is thus, at all points, dialogic but not dialectical (however much dialectics is grounded in history, it implies a wholeness of relation foreign to all the divergences in Rothenberg's work). As a practicing ethnopoet Rothenberg performs an act that is, because recurrent, a fitting participant in an organic universe; yet "organic" also means "transient," up-front for the moment in which one's fullness of being emerges, descending into (mere) history as that fullness deflates. To speak of any performance only as archetypal because it enacts once again the shamanic way with language is to argue for a discourse of analogies and counterparts and there-fore of continuities; a discourse that discloses metaphors because of the likeness of the acts, that also discloses metonyms because any one of the acts does the same within the whole as any other of the acts. Rothenberg implicitly rejects such an unqualified poetics. To argue as he does for the slippage of up-frontness into the fixed tenuities of history is to suggest unbridgeable fractures in the continuities of being, to suggest proximate states involving diverse conditions of being—states whose relation to one another may be deeply affected or, more drastically, effected by difference.

That is why problems appear when we speak of Rothenberg's work only in terms of "metaphysical wholeness." Those problems emerge when the matter of Rothenberg as metonym is taken incompletely, without qualifica-tion, when metonym and metaphor are seen without the difference that characterizes them as much as any likeness does. Every ethnopoetic act is inscribed in every other, which makes ethnopoetic time the time of *illud tempore,* the time when all time is present. But there is still another sense in which the ethnopoetic act can be seen as metonymical, a sense that takes the act out of *illud tempore* and puts it into history; and Rothenberg reads history in terms of what is not there as well as what might emerge. His performances acknowledge not only the Otherness of those whose acts he is continuing but, as his remarks on "mere history" suggest, their palpable absence from his own immediate scene. His acts locate ancient presence in a gesture that is at once indicative and broken off. Rothenberg's awareness of both the intensity of immediacy and its irrevocable transience makes any immediacy insular. It is surrounded by absences that jut up against it and barely give it a space where it can come into being, be itself for the time it has before it becomes as one of them, before it, too, slips into "mere

history." If his is a world of separate, unique centers, those centers perpetually shift, slide from one focal point to the next, absence behind and before
them. All of this is as true of the ethnopoet himself as of those he indicates.
In Rothenberg's acts the ethnopoet is always indexical to himself, those acts
pointing back not only to his precursors but to himself as absent precursor to
himself. His own previous slippage into the mereness of history is part of
the context in which he functions as metonym.

Any reading of Rothenberg's ethnopoetics as only absorbed with achiev-
ing "metaphysical wholeness" is an incomplete reading that risks sentimentality. But that patent inadequacy ought not to lead us in the opposite
direction, toward defining such performances only in terms of the Benjaminian auratic, the uniquely personal grounded in its historical moment.
Whatever its capacity for aura, every ethnopoetic performance is tied in-
eradicably to a forever absent Other, an Other who is oneself as well as every
other who did those things one is doing now. Presence in such conditions is
profoundly qualified by difference, always referring back to something pre-
ceding it that can never be recovered but can only be continued in an
open-endedness that can never be resolved.

No single frame can hold all that Rothenberg's poetics knows about the
positioning of the subject. That poetics speaks in a plurality of voices, which
makes the taking of its utterance in any single way an incomplete taking
that attempts to install closure where closure can, in fact, find no credible
place. To argue thus is to argue for a discourse that qualifies all analogies
through radical, generative difference. That much comes clear from the
introductory poem to A *Seneca Journal*:

Salamanca A Prophecy

(1)

> a city on
> a turtle's back
> a longhouse
>   /
> was like Jerusalem
>   's temple resting
> on a whale

(2)

> impossible to bring it all
> together.

3

David Antin:
The Boundaries of Talking

The table of contents of *talking at the boundaries,* Antin's first book of talk-poems, takes us rapidly, incisively, into the heart of the sort of work he does. Five of the eight titles have to do with location: "what am i doing here?"; "is this the right place?"; "talking at the boundaries"; "a private occasion in a public place"; "a more private place."[1] These titles obviously offer a set of instructions for reading, but they also suggest some of Antin's basic obsessions. What we are to read is a kind of geography: specifying a "here" always makes a place called "there," defining the boundaries at which he talks lays out the contours of his current being, speaking of public and private places colors his map with varying hues invoking modes of relationship to places. Specifying, defining, speaking are therefore acts of mapping that create a geography. Antin's poems mediate, and enact, the way things happen as well as what happens. In fact, the "way" is so much of the "what"

---

1. *talking at the boundaries* (New York: New Directions, 1976), vii.

that they come close to being identical. Antin's poems are the performances of a surveyor. They are as crucial to the performer as to the place where he performs because these poems map, enact, his ways of being in the world. In "a more private place" Antin says:

> theres nothing can disturb my life except   i
> dont know whether im in one place or another.
>
> (*talking,* 261)

A few lines earlier he points out that

> the sense that theres a track in back of you is what makes your self.

Making tracks, defining and clarifying trails and spaces for the self, become essential gestures in the texts of these poems, elemental parts of their textuality. Whatever else they are, they are acts of self-constituting that end by being acts of self-locating. In fact, locating and constituting appear to be the same act seen from differing perspectives.

Those acts also, necessarily, inspect a context. They probe a milieu that takes in the voice that talks, the place that encloses the talking, and the audience that fills its spaces; but the milieu also includes the way these elements work together to seek a definition of what it means to *be* then and there. William Spurlock, a student of Antin's work, argues that it continues the tradition of site-specific art.[2] In the condition from which it begins, in its status as a performance, an Antin talk-poem is as situational as any earthwork by Robert Smithson or draping by Christo. Yet unlike pieces by Smithson or Christo, Antin's ordinary forms grow out of the temporal immediacies of the occasion. When the occasion is over, the poem becomes something else (however temporary Christo's work it lasts for more than the time of draping). Antin recognizes this occasionality and thrives on it. In a piece called "diderot's hieroglyph," performed at Binghamton, New York, in October 1985, he began by picking up the comments on postmodernism made by his introducer, worked quickly into a crack that "from the modernism you want you get the post-modernism you deserve," and then eased into the subject of his performance. The printed version of "a private

---

2. From a comment by William Spurlock in *Dialogue/Discourse/Research* (Santa Barbara, Calif.: Santa Barbara Museum of Art, 1979), 4.

occasion in a public place," from *talking at the boundaries*, begins with Antin
speaking of the sound equipment behind him on the stage. He then asks his
audience to come closer because he uses as little paraphernalia as possible, in
fact no more than what he calls "this micro bit of equipment," probably
referring to his tape recorder (211). After these gestures—which knit the
people in front of him to the equipment behind him as well as to himself
as speaker and the specifics of his system of speech—he moves with ease
into the subject the title suggests. Many of Antin's beginning gestures are
as shrewd as this one, fomenting a dialogue among the elements of the
scene. The performance drives that dialogue to the end of the talk-poem,
moving with and co-fostering the changes in pace and passion that push
and define the piece. In *tuning*, his second book of talk-poems, Antin makes
plain his awareness that he is dialoguing with the occasion:

> i thought if i came to a place   and had no words in my
> hand or mouth   but only my historical disposition to speak
>   in a particular way   out of whatever particular background
>   i had   that whatever I said and did would have to relate
> to this place.[3]

In "a private occasion in a public place" in *talking at the boundaries* he made
the point more generally, tying it to an old definition of the lyric:

> i consider [poetry]   in this case
> coming with a kind of private occasion to a public place   i
> mean youre all here   and its a public place   and im addressing
> a public situation   and im doing what poets have done for a
> long time   theyve talked out of a private sense   sometimes
> from a private need   but theyve talked about it in a rather peculiar
> context   for anybody to eavesdrop.
>
>   (212)

Antin alludes here to a traditional reading of the lyric as the sounds picked
up by an eavesdropper, in John Stuart Mill's well-known "eloquence is
heard, poetry is *overheard*."[4] Antin's insistent emphasis on dialogue and

---

3. "how long is the present," in *tuning* (New York: New Directions, 1984), 84–85.
4. See René Wellek, *A History of Modern Criticism*, vol. 3, *The Age of Transition* (New Haven: Yale University Press, 1965), 133.

occasionality is designed not only to tie together self, text, and place, as he understands them, but also to define precisely his own mode of such tying. To do so he specifies what it is that he does not do: he does not set up those conditions for eavesdropping which, to Antin as much as to Rothenberg, limit the possibilities of poetry.

Most of Antin's beginnings probe such definitions and conditions, sometimes explicitly, as in his regular discourses on method, always implicitly in how they take account of the occasion. The implicit speaks for history in a way the explicit often rejects: for example, his practice of using the specifics of the scene as a place for departure puts his poems into a tradition of meditative poetry that goes back to the religious meditative lyrics of the English Metaphysicals.[5] The practices of the mode include how the poem begins with the composition of place, goes on to meditate on the meaning of that place in the life and times of the meditator, takes off from those specifics into transcendent speculations inspired by the place, and at the end returns to the scene from which it began. The meditative poem renders a circular journey of the spirit in which self, place, and text take up all manner of intricate relations with one another. Antin's talk-poems have similar shapes and desires that take meditative practices up to his own position in history, the place where he stands and straddles some of the riper habits of late modernism and some of the moods and modes of a restrained postmodernism. Antin is never transcendent, and his own poems show how he abhors the rounding-out that ends so many meditative lyrics. None of those is so openly indeterminate as any of his works, none has such sudden, slam-bang, conclusions without conclusiveness. And yet the mode of his talk-poems comes patently, powerfully, out of the meditative line, performing the same sort of pondering on what it means to *be* in that place at that time, moving out from that meditation wherever it sends the speculations of this intensely immanent self. Antin's attacks on lyric conventions, attacks so radical that they tackle lyric in some of its fundamental gestures, take their place within poems whose workings go back to some of the lyric's most magnificent models.

---

5. The classic definition of the mode is in Louis Martz's *Poetry of Meditation* (New Haven: Yale University Press, 1954). That tradition continues into what Meyer Abrams has called "The Greater Romantic Lyric." See *From Sensibility to Romanticism: Essays Presented to Frederick Pottle*, ed. Frederick W. Hilles and Harold Bloom (London: Oxford University Press, 1965), 527–60. If many of the poems in the tradition show a greater uneasiness about the relations of self and place than Martz and Abrams suggest, their descriptions remain the basis from which further work develops.

He never openly acknowledges these generic affiliations, preferring to leave them as a subtext working its way with silent inscribing to define the geography of genre. Antin's more overt concerns have to do with the need to define his own turf in relation to that of others, especially those others who take up the central spaces of modernism:

if robert lowell is a

poet i dont want to be a poet   if robert frost was a

poet i dont want to be a poet   if socrates was a poet

      ill consider it.

(*talking*, 1)

He considers not only the way he differs from such poets but also the way he differs from his earlier self, when he was, like the two Roberts, the poet as writer-down. He begins "a private occasion in a public place" (in *talking at the boundaries*) by stating that he could have come there to read from a book

and it would be a little bit like

taking out a container of frozen peas   warming them up and

serving them to you from the frozen food container.

(211)

But he will not "cook or / recook anything for anybody." Frozen peas are the product of a different present than this.

That point spells itself out in several passages in *tuning*. He used to do poetry readings, he says, and enjoyed reading out loud because poetry is, like music, "most / real in performance" (147). (This equation of reality and immediacy is precisely analogous to Rothenberg's Olsonian argument for the poem as the act of the moment.) But even reading will no longer do because it has become more and more difficult to make the written-down come back to life. There is a difference that cannot be bridged over, a sense of the always-already-other about that which is written down, an otherness to the occasion. As he puts it in a passage from *tuning*:

i began to hate being the servant of

a previous impulse   being an actor.

(148)

Reading one's poems is not enactment but reenactment, not a local and immediate move but a gesture of remembering. In Rothenberg's terms it is a working with "mere history." For Antin it is an impersonation, a feigning, a fiction. The self one seeks to extract from the black marks on the page is a stranger, its voice no longer one's own. That which resides in the text is not that which stands in this place, fronting this occasion.[6] Antin moves logically from these remarks to recalling the taping of a piece that was "a meditation on beginnings" (148). In effect he argues that to pry origin and occasion apart is to falsify the occasion's conditions, to act rather than to be. This is no nostalgia for lost origins—Antin's irony would permit no such taking-in—but an insistence that any beginning is sufficient only to its own occasion, that it can never fit in the contours of another beginning's occasion.

He puts it in a related way somewhat earlier in *tuning,* in a passage where he is less concerned with what reading cannot do than with how it undoes his awareness of immediacy:

<blockquote>

                                    my sense
     of the present disintegrates for me as I read [. . .] i lose
     track of anything i would call the present   and i have a taste
     for the present [. . .] i have a very strong commitment
         to the idea of the present.

                                                        (84)

</blockquote>

This commitment is so basic to Antin that it appears in both books of talk-poems and continues in later pieces, such as, for example "what it means to be avant-garde."[7] That poem touches on issues of temporal space, one of Antin's long-standing interests. He makes the most of the opportunity afforded by the occasion by telling two related stories, one that he heard from a friend and one that had happened to him. In a lecture at the Folger Library, Marjorie Perloff had been reading from her work on Antin and John Cage:

---

6. As Antin put it in a letter to me of 25 January 1985, describing how he came to make talk-poems, "I got to feel afflicted by the texts of the poems I was reading, as if an anterior state of mind was exerting a kind of tyranny over my present, and I experimented in a number of ways to get out of this situation."

7. In *Formations* 2 (1985): 53–71.

                                          and whatever differences
there may be between cage and me   and these are considerable
    we were both obliterated by the righteous wrath of harold bloom
        who had hardly heard more than our names when he denounced
        the proceedings as ridiculous and us as nonpoets and stormed
off the stage.
                            ("what it means to be avant-garde," 57–58)

Antin goes on to tell about his performance at the Folger, somewhat later
than the time of Bloom's tantrum, and what happened after he spoke. As
he and the audience stood around the punch bowl after the performance
he was asked

                                                          what do
    you think of harold bloom?
                        i said im sorry   i dont think
    of harold bloom
                        they said but could you think of
        harold bloom
                    i said i could think of harold bloom   i said
    i could think of harold bloom if i wanted to   you want me
        to?   all right   ill try.
                                                          (59)

After reporting what he said to the group at the punch bowl about Bloom
and the Eastern literary establishment Antin turned to speculations about
Bloom's theories of influence. He shows how Bloom holds an "inverted"
idea of the avant-garde, and he gives a parodic but accurate summary of
Bloom's "early and late comer" idea from Anxiety of Influence.
    Consider the intricacies, ideological and temporal, of what Antin has
just performed. Standing before his audience, the one that has just been
listening to a series of talks on the avant-garde, he tells what happened at
the Folger during a lecture on his work, and what happened at the same
place after his performance at a later date. In both of the reported cases
the subject of Harold Bloom, unrelated though it may seem to the subject
of the present performance (the meaning of the avant-garde), becomes, for
a moment, the main focus of interest. Antin shows that the issue of Bloom
is not tangential at all because Bloom is profoundly preoccupied with the
very questions of time and presence that occupy Antin, Bloom pursuing

the effect on late-coming poets of the still potent presence of their predecessors. The ironies are neat, sardonic: the report on Bloom's tantrum and on the audience's memory of that occasion leads Antin to pull Bloom into the subject of his present performance, to make Bloom a theorist of an inverted avant-garde and thus grist for Antin's mill. And Antin does all this in a context whose structure evokes the intricacies of presence in his work. There are three stages at issue here, three occasions involved. However close their relation they have to be kept distinct in order to open up the intricacies of Antin's play with a presence that is always, equally, absence. The first stage is that in which Bloom was present (and then absent); the second the occasion when Antin performed at the Folger and was asked, after the performance, to think about Harold Bloom; the third the time of the performance of "what it means to be avant-garde" when he reports on those past events and then draws the theories of Bloom into his immediate orbit. Adding to this temporal network Antin refers, just after the comments on Bloom, to some remarks Richard Schechner had made "just a moment ago" on the current state of the avant-garde. The spectrum of time and presence/absence, even within these few pages, has expanded so elaborately that it can take in, coherently, even the themes of a moment ago. Antin's gift for finding likeness in the most disparate circumstances (egged on, in this case, by the two appearances at the Folger) leads to an elaborate instance of that obsession with presence, its absoluteness, its gradations, that drives and radically determines every element of his work.

But the exercise of his gift for aligning situations does not end with the absorption of Bloom. More precisely, the absorption of Bloom does not end with the comments on his theories because Antin goes on to examine, through several statements and stories, other aspects of presence. His penchant for building casts of characters by telling relevant stories about them develops a context for Bloom that meticulously puts him in his place. Building on his comments on Bloom, Antin argues that the notion of the avant-garde

                                    turns itself from a discourse
          into a tradition   whose members worry about its decline in
      a threatening future   and maybe thats why im such a poor
          avant-gardist because im mainly concerned with the present
              which if i can find it might let me know what to do.

                                                                    (64)

And it is the present which, he says a few lines later, he wants to occupy; that is, if he can find it. Commenting on rising unemployment and how

> if for a long time i didnt know what it meant
> to be haunted i begin to know it now in the present

he reads from his hometown newspaper, the *San Diego Union*.

He begins by reporting on a story about two old men killed by a falling fire escape. Then, as he continues to leaf through the newspaper, "looking for the present," he comes on two letters to Dear Abby, letters "relating to the problems of the tradition." The first, he says, could have been written by Harold Bloom, Antin putting Bloom in his place by finding him a place in Abby's daily melodrama. He had pointed out earlier how Bloom phrased his theory in terms of a "seedy freudianism," a father-son struggle for poetic power. This is not, Antin argues, a true theory because it cannot be tested and in fact explains nothing; but it *is* very funny (tradition backs you into a corner like a Kafka cockroach or a Beckett character) and it has a comic likeness to the theories of Clement Greenberg

> in which the
> brilliant achievement of one artist closes an avenue to
> the next.
>
> (62)

He compares Bloom to Kafka, to Beckett, to Greenberg, each comparison a step deeper into silliness. He reaches bottom when he finds Bloom in a letter to Dear Abby. The writer's parents are divorced, she says, her mother remarried. The writer wants a traditional wedding (a wedding with and within the tradition), but she wonders which father should give her away, which father should put her into the tradition. She loves them both, she says, and "this is giving [her] an ulcer."

The second letter, Antin points out, "is a little more like me." Caught within a mode of tradition that cannot seem to catch up with the present, this writer takes her dilemma with more self-amusement than Bloom takes his. She was a second wife. Her ex-husband's first wife was named Sue, and her mother-in-law persisted in calling the writer Sue even though her name is Joan. The ex-husband now has a new girlfriend, Jean. The mother-in-law calls Jean Joan, still a step behind the present though at least a step ahead of where she was before. Antin's comments on these quirky relations of being, presence, and place seem surprisingly resigned, though from what he says elsewhere in the piece we know they are not. Tradition will resolve in the present for Joan and for himself. All we have to do, he says again, is find the present, a seeking that is another of Antin's defining acts.

With that shrewd and graceful transition he slips into the final movement of the piece, one of those long personal stories that characterize his conclusions. He tells of moving his mother to San Diego because she was having problems at home, "losing her grip on the present," which meant little to her (68): "she loses hold of the present about as soon as it goes past" (70). The piece ends with Antin telling about phoning his uncle in Miami, whom he had spoken to just recently after a twenty-year gap, and hearing from his aunt that his uncle had been killed by a car (recall the old men crushed by the fire escape) just after they had last spoken:

> now i hadnt counted on
> the presence of fort lauderdale or miami   or my uncle
> who had appeared on the telephone and then disappeared
>   nothing within the horizon of my discourse could have
> prepared me for the moment with my aunt fanny   who had just
> lost the husband shed lived with for over forty years and was now on
>   the telephone
>   and it seems to me that if you cant respond to
>   that youre not in the avant-garde.

(71)

The performance ends right there, these last words left to be developed by the readers (so that the piece, in effect, never ends, because there will always be more readers, and it will always end differently because there will always be different readers). Antin and Bloom and the writers to Dear Abby, his mother and uncle and his newly widowed aunt, the audience at the lecture at the Folger and the audience at his performance there, presence and the avant-garde, tradition and the future that will become the present and find us: all these come together at this point, their import just beginning to be understood as the piece comes to an end. The crisscross of echoes and contacts is extraordinarily multiple, impossible to sort out. Its multiplicity is mirrored in all those tonal shifts, which took this talk-poem from mockery to shock with all sorts of stops between, from the abstruseness of literary theory to its modal contrary, the tense and piercing pain of sudden recognition. What Antin recognizes as he speaks to his aunt is that, at this moment on the phone, he has indeed found the present which he says he always looks for, the place which, he says, he always wanted to occupy. But it is truer to the scene to say that it has found him; in several senses whose relation is bitterly ironic, it occupies him. As elsewhere in his work he is jarred suddenly, forcibly, into a sense of the present as the moment we are *at,* its immediacy surrounding us, compelling us to acknowledge the fullness of the moment's existence and its hold on us.[8] But there is more to be known. The abruptness of the ending leaves Antin's audience/readers with an experience modally similar to the moment on the phone. The sharp, intense awareness of the poem's unexpected stop shocks us into recognizing the touch of immediacy, the moment we are at just now, with the piece just over, and its reverberations just begun. That moment of fracture is also a moment of the fusion of experiences, a linking of speaker and milieu in a way none could have foreseen.

Antin's reverence for the present comes in part from his recurrent sense of the inadequacy of remembering.[9] It comes also from his compulsion for address, especially for a view of address that sees it as, finally, dialogue. "Real discourse," he says in an interim section of *tuning,* "is dialogue" (28). Part of that dialogue, he continues, involves an encounter with the material, part an encounter with himself, part an encounter with the audience which is and listens. All of the elements in this multilogue in which Antin is the central figure occur at the same time and scene, the moment of this occasion. His audience works actively as busy but mute participants in the performance, but are probably unaware of their participatory role. At the beginning of "dialogue," the piece in *tuning* which follows the interim section on discourse, Antin remarks that he has never thought of himself as doing monologues, that his talk-pieces involve "engaging with people" (219). In his essay "Talking to Discover" he argues that "in all language acts there is always an other, even when it is only the self alone."[10] And in an interview in France, published in *PO&SIE* in 1983, he agrees with the definition of modernism that sees it as a "rupture avec le langage de représentation" but adds that he situates himself not with a sense of rupture but with a sense of social contract: "C'est vrai, il n'y a plus de rupture. *La*

8. Compare the striking comments on presentness in "how long is the present," in *tuning,* 95–99.

9. See particularly "the sociology of art," in *talking at the boundaries.*

10. In *Symposium of the Whole: A Range of Discourses Toward an Ethnopoetics,* ed. Jerome Rothenberg and Diane Rothenberg (Berkeley and Los Angeles: University of California Press, 1983), 459.

rupture, c'est fini!"[11] He works with and within the sense of immediate community that comes with the idea of "social," and he also works with the sense of engaged connection built into the idea of "contract." For Antin the making of art is a communal performance, the acting out of a compact made at the moment and place of the occasion, and for itself alone. However much he is at the center—and it is mostly his voice we hear—everyone at the occasion takes part in the working out of the whole.

That is one of the basic reasons why he, like Rothenberg, abandons the traditional idea of the lyric as private speech that we can hear only by eavesdropping (recall Mill's comment that poetry is overheard). He is the primary instigator of a communion with a group that unites in its moment and speech, much like the work of Rothenberg's ethnopoet, much like the communal performances in Alan Kaprow and Carolee Schneemann—all of them ways of making art that were inspired in great part by the communal modalities of the sixties and seventies. Antin's conception of his art as dialogic is different by design from that of the Frosts and Lowells who are not poets of his kind. It also works in ways very different from the poems of Michael Palmer or the poems and performances of Steve McCaffery. Their sense of irreparable fracture between artist and audience, as well as within the artist himself, makes such communal dialogue the subject of ironies; the ironies, for example, of McCaffery's Chinese Ventriloquist (whom we shall look at in the next chapter). Antin stands openly, patently, between the modernists who preceded him and postmodernists like Palmer and McCaffery, sharing elements with those on either side of him, however uneasy he is with both. His positioning is based partly on his rejection of the modernist lyric; partly on the obsessive sense of presence that informs his work; partly on a self-centering that claims a Cartesian wholeness and coherence as firm as that of any modernist lyricist; partly on his sense of the interworkings of audience and performer, a sense compatible with neither romantic-modernist lyricism nor the postmodernist sense that such communion seems impossible for our (perhaps any) time. Antin shares with Rothenberg, Kaprow, and Schneemann, but not with these other figures, an intuition that the moment of making art is always identical with the occasion in which it occurs and the community to/at/with and within which it occurs.

Antin takes such conceptions beyond those of many performance figures by including not only the occasion in its time but that coming together for

---

11. "Conversation avec David Antin," *PO&SIE*, no. 25 (1983): 38.

dialogue which is the occasion's intent, perhaps its reason for being. The concept of "tuning" that he develops in his second book of talk-poems emphasizes not only the differences among the elements in the occasion but the acts that seek to bring them into some sort of harmony. In "gambling" he lays out the basic encounter, the radical gesture in the contract from which the talk-poem is to emerge:

```
                                         coming as i do
from a different direction and at a different pace to this place it
     is only "more or less" the same place to which youve come by a
different way at a different pace       because we have a different
     sense of it       and consequently it has a different sense       for
each of us / [. . .]
                    [. . .] / now the point of doing these pieces
     for me       is that it gives me a chance       by a kind of subtle but
ordinary human concentration             to get a sense of where youre
     coming from and how             and to allow that sense to put some
          pressure on my own way of moving       to bring me into
          somewhat closer range of you       close enough to compare our
ways of moving             our sense       with each other       and in this
situation i find a fundamental human act       this negotiation in
     a common space.
```
(tuning, 167)

The act of dialogue is itself an aspect of tuning, perhaps the principal aspect, perhaps even the tuning itself.

All of which comes to mean that it is only in the situation of performance that the potential of the talk-poem can be fully realized. Only when he has a live audience to address can Antin work out the unique relations of mode and positioning of his genre. That is why the concept of address, that putting-forth which is, at once, challenge and courtship, turns up often in these pieces, always with a sense of the communal aspects of the performance. At least three times it turns up in relation to his working at a typewriter. In the poem "talking at the boundaries" he complains that going into a closet to type is an "unnatural language act": a closet is no place to do addressing and there is no one to address (talking, 56). He says much the same thing in "how long is the present," pointing out that he not only finds it difficult to imagine the people but

> a present at all
> while i sit at a typewriter   so part of the issue of this
> talking is my sense of address   my sense of trying to address
> something and someone at a moment   when they are here
> for my own
> convenience   for the sense of urgency i get out of it.
>
> (*tuning*, 88)

In "tuning" he expands these comments into a framework that includes literature, the tradition's written texts. Literature, he says, has for long been in an "artificial hermetic closet," one in which Antin himself has written things, "confronting a typewriter and no person." Thus literature as written text has neither urgency nor "need of address" (105). But it is precisely that need that Antin feels so urgently, precisely that need which his mode of making poems both frames and meets. In fact, "address" implies for Antin a corresponding response, whether articulated or not: the address cannot be completed until it is in some way returned. Address can work only in a dialogue. In "dialogue" Antin tells of a friend who became a minister. His friend felt that the minister of God

> should address the
> religious spirit of the people   and bring it to address itself to
> the world.

But Antin's friend would have difficulties with such multiple addressing in places like Elizabeth, New Jersey, because

> what view
> would they have of him   this guy who had a calling and was
> calling on them to respond to his calling.
>
> (*tuning*, 225)

A call that is not answered is talk that will never become a talk-poem. Even if Antin's audience never speaks up (there is no reason why it should), its response to his putting-forth—its noises and shuffling and staring, its giggles and tense attentiveness—intensifies the address, which in its turn responds to the response. It is in such constant adjustments at every stratum of the occasion that the act of tuning takes place.[12]

Sometimes that adjustment becomes a major part of a talk-piece. In at least one case it becomes the central subject. If tuning cannot be fulfilled by Antin sitting in his hermetic closet, addressing himself to no one, it gets even more difficult to handle in a far trickier context, performing on the radio. "whos listening out there," delivered in San Diego over KPBS, worries that issue through. Antin thinks of his invisible listeners as separate from one another, alone or in groups, "a lot of little private audiences" which know nothing of one another (tuning, 270). And he is also separate from them: each is within an occasion only partly shared with the others. Antin seeks to establish dialogue by imagining an audience composed of people he has known, playing a desperate game to foster the response he needs for the piece to work at all. Because he has known those people he can guess their response and therefore, he hopes, keep the dialogue going. This is the talk-poem that ends tuning, and its critical placement shows the importance of these issues for the book and his mode as a whole. That he ends with such an ambiguous, equivocal scene, showing himself in an urgent seeking, reveals the continuities of his need as well as its refusal to accept less than all.

That need, that seeking, occurs everywhere in Antin's work, at every stage within it, from performance to written-down text—that is, from its originary condition to its final state. But even before the beginning Antin looks for every hindrance, anything that could stand in the way of the address. In the performance at Binghamton to which I referred he removed a screen at his side and a podium in front so that there would be nothing between him and his audience. There was only, as there often is, a table on which he placed his tape recorder (photographs of other performances show a similar setup). He wandered around from behind the table to the side and sometimes the front, each move outward reestablishing a communal space that he shared with at least the first row of the audience. The moves that took him behind the table again were less an undoing of this newfound directness than a show of confidence in its strength. But when he moved once again to the sides or in front of the table something else was happening:

12. "Tuning" also includes the place of one's immediate talking in the discourse that precedes it. As he puts it in "Talking to Discover": "Through tuning you're seeking some kind of agreement with some previous utterance, some image of previous utterance or some image of intended utterance, and to this degree you're making use of language-discourse habits and patterns" (459). Antin edges close to Barthes at just this point; at this and surely no other.

by making such moves anew he would reconfirm the directness, as though the time behind the table had gone on a bit too long and had to be countered once again. He danced our mutual space, and through this dance inscribed himself in space and turned the spaces of the occasion into a text the audience could read, into which the audience itself was written. If the performance is the text of the occasion, made by and in the occasion, such gestures are part of Antin's way of making a place for himself and us in that text, writing himself and us into the scene. Of course we inscribe ourselves when we shuffle our feet, cough, and mumble; but Antin inscribes us even further by establishing spatio/kinetic relations that move beyond the relations of performer and audience to become finally the relations of co-participants in the scene. Though his gestures may well be unconscious they show the significance of the kinetic in his work, its way of moving in available space. No tape or written text, not even a video, can reproduce the audience's (largely unconscious) awareness of those moves which take the talk-performer up to and sometimes into the audience's space. Of course all of this happens while his speaking is working its way, its immediacy confirmed by those bodily moves that weave him into the spaces of the occasion.

Space and spaces preoccupy Antin. Their variety has to do with the odd kind of thing the talk-poem is: in part an oral, largely spontaneous utterance within a communal scene; in part pure sound, when the poem gets to its taped form; in part a play of black and white when it gets to be a written-down text. What to do in space and within it, the question Antin has to ask himself, is matched by a question his audiences implicitly ask: What kinds of space does a talk-poem occupy? The answer is neither single nor simple, since it has finally to do not only with the successive stages of the poem but with how Antin conceives his acts and the sort of art they make.

At the time of the performance there is a plethora of spaces, each of which absorbs him in different ways, to different degrees. There is, of course, the original physical space—the room, the auditorium—that enfolds him and his audience, the "actual" locale in which the performance occurs. It is analogous to the page on which the words are written down because it is a fabricated enclosure that cuts off and defines. The rest of the performance's spaces are not visual or physical at all. There is the space created and occupied by the subjective interplay of Antin and his audience, an invisible, impalpable space to which he is highly sensitive. That is the interpersonal space in which the engagement with the audience occurs, a space that continues to gain in content as the performance goes on but

necessarily disappears (whatever we keep of it in memory) when the performance ends. Interpersonal space begins and grows within the physical
space of the scene but is not identical with that space. Yet events in the
physical space inevitably affect and effect those in interpersonal space.
Antin's gestures in physical space, those dances of the body around the
table, are designed to affect and effect the interpersonal space and to keep
its actions tense. In fact this question of spaces goes back well beyond such
play, to the moment of the performance's beginning or just before it. When
Antin enters the spaces of the room he comes, as he says, with several ideas
in mind "but no particular words in my mouth" (talking, v). That is, he
enters the spaces of the room and then the interpersonal spaces with certain
possibilities for discourse in his mind. The opportunity to perform gives
him the space within which to test his ideas, to probe them and unfold
them as the self-generating discourse of his piece begins to develop. The
interplay of all these spaces—the physical, the interpersonal, the spaces of
possibility—carries him through the performance and the spaces it now
occupies. One of his difficulties with the radio piece came from this business
of space: what possibilities are open to him when the physical and interpersonal suffer such clear limitations? Which is to say what now seems clear,
that these questions of spatiality have a great deal to do with the question
of address, for address needs all it can get of all these kinds of spaces in
order to go about its business.

But with all this talk of spaces it has to be kept in mind that only the
space of the auditorium has any kind of sustaining presence, that the other
spaces are made at the time of the performance and disappear when it is
over, abiding only in interstices of memory that gradually grow clogged. In
"the sociology of art" Antin punctures the "illusion of spatial form" that
comes with the ability to flip the pages of a book back and forth. That
illusion generates a "synthetically derived memory," the result of our forgetting that the mind has itself constructed this space and the "imaginary
configuration within it" (talking, 190). There is no such illusion concerning
the spaces of the performed poem: all parties involved recognize that they
have made every space but the physical one, and that at the end it is the
only one that can still be immediately known.

Those mind-constructed spaces do not end with the performance but
follow Antin's text to its appearance on the page. Yet even before it gets
there its phenomenological condition—what it is, where it is, the kinds of
spaces it occupies, what we perceive when we perceive a text—has been a

momentous question. In his prefatory comments to *talking at the boundaries*
Antin says that

these

talks were worked out with no sense of a page in mind

the texts are not "prose"   which is as i see it a kind

of "concrete poetry with justified margins"   while

these texts are the notations or scores of oral poems

with margins consequently unjustified.

(v)

"Unjustified" is a multileveled pun with multiple effects. Whatever else a
page is, it is a demarcation in space, and the paper's edge is the line defining
where the world ends and the page begins. As I noted earlier, the page is
roughly equivalent to the room in which the performance takes place, the
physical space that becomes the site of the mind-controlled spaces that
come into being with it. The text, oral or written, has to have such demarcation in order to exist at all. But when Antin speaks of the page in these
prefatory remarks he does not mean the page as object but what we put
onto that place, the visual layout of the text; and given that definition he
can reject what prose calls pages, not only for the reasons put in these
remarks but for others as well. Some of those others appear in comments
quoted on the back cover of *talking at the boundaries,* where Antin puts the
question of pages in terms of a struggle for power. The space, then, becomes
a question of turf and how we define it: "as an improvisation is not in
'prose,' which is an image of the authority of 'right thinking' conveyed
primarily through 'right printing'—justified margins, conventional punctuation, and regularized spelling—this book has been printed without recourse
to such appeals." "Appeals" is crucial in this context: as we shape our pages
we are in fact appealing to the audience to accept our way of thinking, in
effect to accept our authority. Spacing is part of the appeal to our readers
to consent to that self-serving condition of contraries in which we would
like to exercise power and also do the wooing that is central to "address."
Of course Antin is making his own kind of appeal by rejecting the margined
layout, the conditions of "right printing" in which prose appeals occur.

He rejects that layout in other ways as well, ways that also seek to avoid
the making of mind-forged manacles to which every text is susceptible.
Justified margins continue the sharp defining of space that the edge of the
paper began. But if the shape of the leaf of a book is a requisite straitjacket,

the shape of the margin, in fact the margin's existence at all, is certainly not inevitable. However we choose to put it, the margin needs no justification. Once that point is established Antin can then go on to define his own kind of authority through the kind of visual layout his printed texts take. It is an authority based on openness (closure makes that authority uneasy, challenges it, defies it); on the refusal of predictable layout (we know what the next prose page will look like even before we turn it over); on the flow of visual rhythms that take their shape not from an imposition from without but (in good organic, romantic-modernist fashion) from the needs of what is being said. Antin's spaces punctuate the text in ways that seek to get closer than commas and colons can to the actual rhythms of the words. Though those spaces can be seen as a kind of negative space they are no more unoccupied than the minutes of so-called silence in a piece by John Cage. The pauses created by those spaces are occupied by the memory of the words that reverberate through and around them, by the echoes in our minds of the words we have just experienced, just as the pauses are so occupied during the moments of performance.

And yet they are not quite the same as those pauses, the analogy holding only to the point where spaces of apparent emptiness are shown to be not what they seem. Those in-between moments that the audience goes through as it listens to an Antin or a Cage are fuller than any spaces that appear on any page. Further, they are foreign to fixity. The spaces on the page may claim the same sort of foreignness but their claim cannot stand against the facts of their condition. The refusal to define margins or use conventional punctuation is an attempt to fight off fixity on the pages of the written text. But even as these gestures seek to undo immobility they show themselves to be as locked-in as their opponents, as tied to what and where they are as any comma or justified edge. We can always turn back to those pages and find them as margin-less and comma-less as they were when he wrote them down. Of the spaces connected with the performance, the only one that remains, as we have seen, is the physical space of the room in which the audience partook of (took part in) the performance. That is, spaces of several sorts come into being during the performance, most go back out of being when the performance is over. But the spaces on the page, whatever their status as counterparts to the pauses in the performance, never go out of being, never cease to make their statements against the discomfiting lies of fixity, even as they are, themselves, irrevocably fixed. The paradox is patent, it is potent, and it points to ambiguities that pervade Antin's work. These questions ultimately urge us to compare talking and writing, what each is and can do, how each faces up to fixity and address and other concerns of Antin's art.

"writing," he says at one point,
                                    is about anxiety   trying to hold some-
            thing still.

                                                                (talking, 192)

What one tries to hold still is the presentness of a beginning, of self in its momentary context responding to the calls of the occasion; but such holding cannot succeed for

                                    books are   imperfect recordings
            of transactions that occur in real time.

                                                                (tuning, 54)

That comment is worth all the pondering we can give it. Everything that occurs during the performance of a talk-piece (all that happens, spoken and unspoken, that is experienced through every sense, between Antin and his present audience) is the transaction of which he speaks. Talking is the instrument that makes the transaction possible, that pulls the elements together to create the occasion. It is not, like writing, an act of recording but that which the act, taped or written, seeks to preserve. It is not imper- fect, like writing, because in the world of the talk-piece only recording is imperfect. The fullness that results when talking makes all of the elements concur is the perfection from which everything outside of the occasion, every other stage in the process, falls away.

Antin's sense that talking causes such perfect occasions is essential to his conception of what he is about. In "a more private place," a piece from *talking at the boundaries,* he talks near the beginning about talking to himself, moves from that into wondering where the self can be said to be located, then moves from that speculation (none of these moves is innocent) into discussing a scene of fruitless talking where people would mutter and shout but "nothing would happen." Then, finally (and precisely to the point), he moves to the casual but crucial comment that "talking is making something happen" (241). Talking is cause, the agent of transaction; the transactor of, for example, the self's emergence in the moment. When he wondered where the self is located, he worked over the idea that the self is what comes out when he says words like "out": "as i say it it comes out and i suddenly see it / out there" (241). What happens when he says "out" is what happens in every talk-piece. The occasion becomes the place where self locates itself, not only the site where speaking occurs but the scene where self is spoken:

the only way
    that   i can conceive of myself   as a personality   is by
an act   of memory   by an act of interrogation of my memory
    which is   also talking   the self   itself   is emergent
in discourse   in some kind of discourse   it is probably available
    but it comes up under dialogue   and the dialogue   is
conducted with it   and then the self emerges   even though the
    self   may not have been there until you called upon it.

(talking, 10)

That too is what talking makes happen. Antin compels us to add "talking" to our concerns with "reading" and "writing." Talking, too, is a mode of inscribing. The occasion it causes to happen is the text that contains the inscription, the scene where our selves our inscribed.[13]

The occasion is the primary text, the point of origin. There are three texts or states or conditions at play in Antin's pieces, raising the question whether the talk-piece is one thing that goes through three successive stages or three things bound together by common material or origin. Though the first of these choices seems preferable, an argument can be made for both. The first state is the occasion in which the talking occurs, the second the taping of the sounds of the occasion, the third the printed version of the shape of those sounds, that stage where they become black marks on a white page. The original performance is beyond all reproduction, always-already-other even as it is happening. At its most complex the occasion takes in a lavish variety of the experience possible to it, visual, verbal, oral, aural, even tactile and olfactory; as well as the tense, ineffable awareness of the presence of others in a self-generating dialogue. Even a video of the performance could not take in a large part of what actually happens. The taping is the first recording, the first stage (depending on how one reads the totality) that shows either a loss of the occasion's immediacy, a decline in the sense

13. In "Talking to Discover" Antin speaks of "those linguistic acts of invention and discovery through which the mind explores the transformational power of language and discovers and invents the world and itself" (451). Later he comments that "the invention of the self is an outcome of talking to discover, the outcome of a discourse genre" (457).

of presence, or else a move toward a new immediacy, a new sense of presence. Because the visual is lost (we no longer see Antin perform or the
audience respond), the auditory comes into intenser play at this stage,
singled out from the ultimate whole. Because of that singling-out the hearer
becomes especially aware of Antin's intonation, his characteristic rhythms
of speech, the pauses and turns by which he shifts into new ground as the
piece develops. And of course the tape can be replayed, *that* version of the
piece performed again and again to help us do what we cannot do with the
original performance, grow familiar with all its details. The taping stage is
useful for those approaching these pieces from the final state of the text,
the second recording stage, the black marks on the white page. A hearing
of the tape makes it possible to provide (through hearing an image of
Antin's voice speaking inside of one's head) those slides and intonations,
the characteristic shifts of pitch, which the words and spaces by themselves
can never fully provide. Yet the written text can go back to what the tape
can never offer. Through his rejection of margins, through his use of spacing
on the page to do what punctuation tries to do, through the further use of
that spacing to reproduce in another medium some of the cadences of speech
one heard in the original performance, Antin recovers a version of the
visual as he gives up the auditory. It is as though the taped and written
versions were mirror images, each able to offer what the other has to give up.

Still, even with both together, listening to the tape while reading the
text, one still feels the loss of that *Gesamtkunstwerk* which is the original
performance. Antin argues, once, that each stage has its own sense of
the present; each is therefore different and other and owes obeisance only
to itself:

<blockquote>

                                                        it would
  be a great mistake to believe that my love for the present
only occurs when im talking   because once ive established
  my love for the present through my talking i dont give it up
    when im writing   when im sitting in front of the typewriter
  i feel like im sitting in front of a typewriter   and ill be
  damned if i am going to feel a profound sense of obligation to
another moment that now no longer exists.

(*tuning*, 94)
</blockquote>

Yet this remark is an anomaly, a requisite but passing recognition that the
moments at the typewriter also exist in real time. The remark cannot be

squared with his contrary comments on writing and address, or with the difficulty he mentions, in precisely the same piece, of imagining a present while he is sitting at the typewriter (88). Antin's one-time comments at this point counter not only his other remarks but his obsessive concern with what he argues to be the absolute presentness of the performance.

That is one way of looking at the relations among the stages but it is not the only possible assignment of privilege among the stages. In fact the ways are so multiple, the claims for each stage so firmly based in Antin's concerns (for instance, his refusal to defer to a previous state of being), that the relations among the stages, the matter of priority or privilege, the ultimate question of locating where the talk-poem actually *is*, cannot finally be fixed in any certain and dependable form. And that, obviously, is just the way Antin wants it. It makes for a perfect alignment of meaning and mode.

Part of that alignment comes from Antin's choice of mode, his desire/ compulsion to begin with oral performance. In "the sociology of art," a long and important piece on the different mappings of the world available to oral and written cultures, Antin argues that oral societies are always changing and fluid, but written societies are necessarily fixed (*talking*, 190). But his firm rejection of fixity takes in technique as well as mode, aspects of the way the mode works itself out: that is, the rejection determines how his talk-pieces come about as well as what they come to mean. Consider the spaces of possibility. Antin approaches the performance with no fixed plan but with material that may well be appropriate for the occasion. As he once described it to me, it is like a pianist approaching a Mozart cadenza. He knows that he will touch on certain matters here and here and here, but he has no worked-out scheme on how he will get from one place to the next, and is not absolutely certain that he will get to all the places. At every stage of the talk-poem we can watch him probing for breakthroughs, testing ideas and incidents to see if they can clear the way to the rhythm that will make the whole cohere and carry him through to the end. Thus he comes to the performance with an openness to possibility that settles in only during the performance, sometimes near the beginning, sometimes only after considerable probing. That refusal of fixity extends to the way the pieces end, not only in the original performance but at the printed stage as well. Slow or rapid, probing or assured, the beginnings are locked into the occasion in the manner of the meditative poem and in a way that would surely please the most devoted Aristotelian. The middles, though often the result of some tense and difficult circling, usually step out confidently. But the endings never accede to the insistence on coherence that

drives the Aristotelian plot, never round out the occasion with the conclusive return seen in the meditative poem or the Greater Romantic Lyric.
Abrupt, often puzzling, frequently a comment on the stories with which he
likes to conclude a performance, the endings are an apt undoing of any
expectation (his play with beginnings and middles seems to foster such
expectations) that the piece will close off in any conclusive way. Antin
begins the piece "how long is the present" by touching on the (Rothenbergian) question "whether poetry is inherently oral" (*tuning*, 83); "and when
i say poetry," he says, "i mean poetry in the large sense," that is "any work
that one can think of as a significant / attempt to take possession of the
world" (84). The world the talk-poem seeks to possess shapes and is reflected
in the poem that seeks to possess it. If his refusal of traditional coherence
brings Antin to that sort of consonance, that is only one more of the ironies
in these poems that hate to stand still.

It is precisely in such refusal of traditional coherence that the question
of Antin's canonic positioning—the positioning of the self/subject within
his work, the attendant question of the positioning of his work among the
works of our time—gets most intricate, most subtle. Whatever difficulties
Gerald Stern has accepting Antin's work, whatever difficulties Antin has
accepting the lyric centricity of Stern's poetry, Antin's talk-poems partake
as emphatically as any art in our time of the sense of the up-front self,
intensely present in the moment of the poem's origin. When Antin stands
in front of an audience and gets the talk-poem going, there is an extraordinary plenitude of presence. (Stern's "no one / can live in place of us" goes
as much for Antin at the occasion of making the talk-poem as for Stern at
any point.) Part of that has to do with his sense of the emergence of self
in the immediate moment, one that echoes a similar sense we have seen in
Rothenberg's work. Sometimes it takes a form we saw in one of the talk-
poems, where he speaks of the self as "emergent in discourse," coming up
"under dialogue," even though it "may not have been there until you called
upon it" (*talking*, 10). At the end of another talk-poem, its pondering of
selfhood among the densest in his work, he ends by saying "im here to /
define myself" (*talking*, 231). Sometimes he argues a different but comparable point, a version of which I quoted at the beginning of this chapter:
"the sense that theres a track in back of you is what makes / your self," a
Lockean remark about the necessity of continuity in order to establish identity. However Antin puts it, the immediacy of the moment of discourse is
dense with the presence of all that surrounds him and all that is himself.

And yet there is a sense in which the talk-poem contains multitudes, a move from the immediacy of the occasion to greater and greater distancing, a move whose track and contours are obsessive in our time. If Antin's passion for presence (his "very strong commitment / to the idea of the present") sends out late modernist sounds that have never ceased speaking in our time, his awareness of how texts distance themselves from their originating occasion sends out very different sounds, the sort that speak more bluntly, ironically, in the work of Steve McCaffery. Antin's tape recording looks forward to McCaffery's, but where McCaffery begins with that secondary, mediated stage, as in his performance of the Chinese Ventriloquist, Antin emphasizes a primary, originating stage whose overwhelming immediacy dominates all that follows it. What Antin knows and puts there for us to know, to see in its making, to know as being-made, McCaffery sees as forever beyond any awareness we can muster. Antin stands, then, as a kind of test case for our time, the wielder of a spectrum whose primary allegiance is to where the spectrum begins, the point of the self's emergence into the immediacy of the moment's discourse. What we shall see in the next chapter in the pairing of Schneemann and McCaffery is suggested, bruited, in the stages of the talk-poem, what it knows, ponders, suspects.[14]

14. For important comments on Antin, see Charles Altieri, "The Postmodernism of David Antin's *tuning,*" *College English* 48 (January 1986): 9–26; Marjorie Perloff's chapter "No More Margins: John Cage, David Antin, and the Poetry of Performance" in *The Poetics of Indeterminacy* (Princeton: Princeton University Press, 1981), 288–339; Sherman Paul, *So To Speak: Rereading David Antin,* in his *In Search of the Primitive* (Baton Rouge: Louisiana State University Press, 1986); Henry Sayre, "David Antin and the Oral Poetics Movement," *Contemporary Literature* 23 (1982): 428–50, as well as the comments on Antin in Sayre's *The Object of Performance: The American Avant-Garde Since 1970* (Chicago: University of Chicago Press, 1989). Volume 3, no. 3, of *boundary 2* (1975), "The Oral Impulse in Contemporary American Poetry," is relevant to Antin throughout, and it contains his significant correspondence with the editors (595–652) as well as Barry Alpert's essay "Post-Modern Oral Poetry: Buckminster Fuller, John Cage, and David Antin," 665–82. *Vort* 7 (1975) is devoted to Antin and Jerome Rothenberg. See also Antin's essay, "Modernism and Post-modernism: Approaching the Present in American Poetry," *boundary 2* 1 (1972): 98–113.

4

Presence and Its Discontents, 1: Carolee Schneemann and Steve McCaffery

In the Barthesian text-as-body, the metaphor (metonym?) that grounds textual excitement in its varying degrees of pleasure and *jouissance,* the play of figures seems to spin out from figure to figure as each figure generates excess that spills into, becomes, another figure:

> Apparently Arab scholars, when speaking of the text, use this admirable expression: *the certain body.* What body? We have several of them; the body of anatomists and physiologists, the one science sees or discusses: this is the text of grammarians, critics, commentators, philologists (the pheno-text). But we also have a body of bliss consisting solely of erotic relations, utterly distinct from the first body: it is another contour, another nomination; thus with the text: it is no more than the open list of the fires of language.[1]

1. Roland Barthes, *The Pleasure of the Text,* trans. Richard Miller (New York: Hill & Wang, 1975), 16–17.

The figure the Arab scholars use for the text-as-figure is not only admiring but admirable: their contemplation (but that is too sedate a word for even their restrained expression) generates an anatomy that echoes those generic designations of certain texts as "anatomies." Barthes accepts the Arabian spillover and adds his own, the equation of anatomists and grammarians, all those who can work with their subjects only when they are treated as objects, acting out the counterpart dissections of bodies and sentences. No excess is permitted in those kinds of anatomies, which means that the restraint which holds figuration to this precise analogy allows none of the undoing of boundaries that Sadean-Battaillean overflow effects in its (ever imperfect, ever incomplete) quest for fulfillment. Somewhere behind these restrained analogies we hear their Wordsworthian-romantic version: "We murder to dissect." We also hear Barthes speaking of the text of pleasure, participatory in that it "comes from culture and does not break with it," exercising its hedonism within those constraints that make the fullness of pleasure possible (14). Another analogy, then, the result of another re-strained spillover that culture can still comfortably accept: anatomist, gram-marian, reader of texts of pleasure. It is clear that even our discussions of figures take place within, are guided and given form by, a master text within which all sorts of spillovers play themselves out. We may, in fact, find it difficult to get outside of texts, even when speaking of the body.

The entry on the Arab scholars ends thus: "Does the text have human form, is it a figure, an anagram of the body? Yes, but of our erotic body. The pleasure of the text is irreducible to physiological need" (17). The idea of text-as-body is confirmed once again, but now we can see that different aspects of the body belong to different attitudes toward the text: the body as a coherent palpable object, readable but not writable, belongs to the anatomists/grammarians; the body as coherent cultural object, to a certain degree writable, belongs to the text of pleasure; the body as erotic object (coherence makes it uneasy, defies it; it is therefore thoroughly writable) goes with the text of *jouissance*. The latter is the text of unrestrained spill-over, the text that "unsettles the reader's historical, cultural, psychological assumptions, the consistency of his tastes, values, memories, brings to a crisis his relations with language" (14). It is that aspect/attitude which seeks to destroy culture by bursting the restraints that bind—pleasurably (masochistically?)—the anatomies and texts of pleasure. In that unbinding the reader loses not only culture but "the consistency of his selfhood" (14), an undoing of himself as subject—implying that self/subject has edges, con-tours, boundaries, that it overflows through fractures as excess seeks exit. (That such activities suggest the work of the Id in its self-appointed functions within the classical Freudian model opens up other figurations with their own uneasy contours.)

What we have out of all this play of figuration, constraint, excess, reading, being, is more than body, then, more even than body-as-text and text-as-body. What we have is ultimately the suggestion of still another set of analogies, text-as-self, self-as-text; and it is put in such a way that artists as different as Carolee Schneemann and Steve McCaffery can see eminent sense in it, though the sense(s) in which they see it are largely, sometimes intensely, antagonistic. It is precisely those disagreements that Schneemann and McCaffery have performed. That the whole has always had to do with "meat joy" comes clear in any reading of Schneemann's collection of scripts and images.[2] But that the matter of meat joy can take perspectives dramatically contradictory to Schneemann's comes clear at every point in McCaffery's work and (as we shall see in the next chapter) in the play of photography and performance in the art of Sophie Calle.

Take, for instance, the dust cover of *More than Meat Joy*, which contains an image suffused with the blue-green of water (Fig. 1). Much of the image's force is lost in any coverless library copy because the version of the scene in the text (117) is black and white and more nearly square than the rectangular cover version. The scene comes from a variation of a performance called *Water Light / Water Needle*, which was given several times in March 1966 at Saint Mark's Church in New York City, and once again in May of that year at the Havemayer estate in MahWah, New Jersey (see 103–17 for notes, the score, and documentary photographs). In its Saint Mark's version, performers, secreted in cupboards, burst forth into a room in which heavy ropes cut through the air, their performance a series of moves around and over the ropes, which "enclosed or surrounded the audience seated below" (105). In its second version the structure was set up to be filmed, rigged in a grove of trees on the Havemayer estate. It is that second performance that generated the image on the cover (see 116–17).

The image shows four nudes bent over, facing away from the camera, the top ones' arms stretched over the others, their buttocks prominent. The effect is that of some strange aquatic plant, its "head" above the surface, its roots deep within the water, some multifoliate foliage made of fundamental flesh. Only one of the figures can be identified by sex, the figure on the far right by her left breast, though the hips and musculature suggest (without

2. *More than Meat Joy: Complete Performance Works and Selected Writings*, ed. Bruce McPherson (New Paltz, N.Y.: Documentext, 1979).

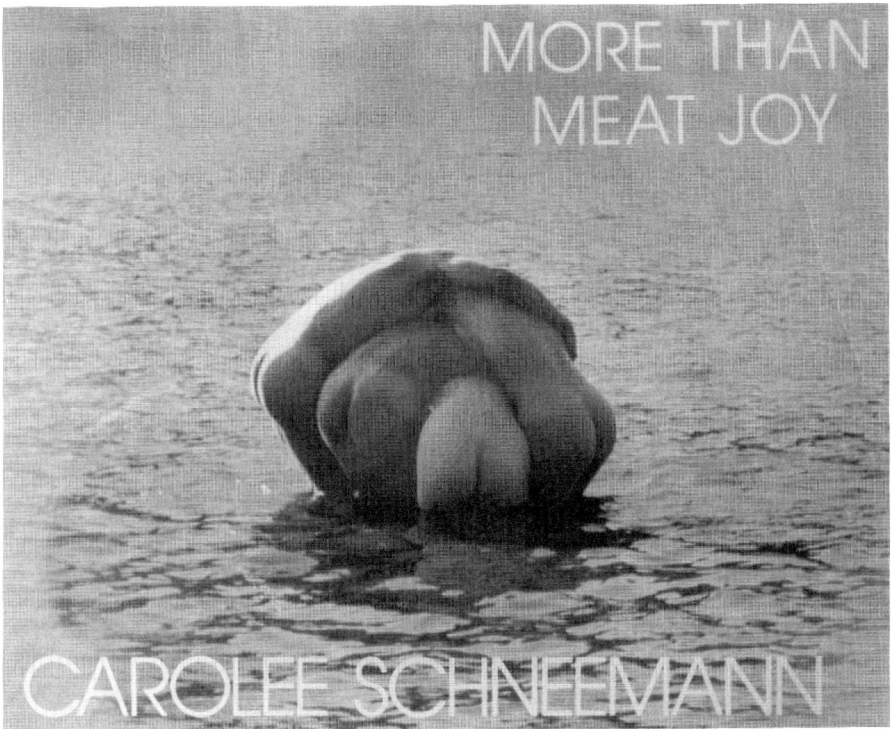

Fig. 1.   Carolee Schneemann, cover from *More than Meat Joy*

asserting) that both figures on the right are female. However, the black and white variant of the scene printed in the text shows no hint of a breast, and the overall glimmers of difference are considerably less certain. In both versions of the scene, the overt emphasis is on the generic, the human, indeed the radically human *just* emerging from formlessness.

The event at the Havemayer estate confirms the fullest meaning of the emergence from the cupboards, what Rochelle Owens has called this performance's way of "telling the story of the birth of the soul and linking together the forces of life" (*More than Meat Joy,* 270). Still, such comments suggest nothing of Schneemann's ironies, too easily ignored in her work's radical bodiness and occasional bathos. Consider, again, the scene in the water. Buttocks are as generically bodily as flesh can get, as fundamental as any part, the image of our meatiness, of the immediacy of our flesh. Her image flaunts the fullness of flesh, yet this is a special body art that seems to play down gender as the group performs our emergence from the primal element. Schneemann figures origin and suggests its sexual neutrality, its capacity, at that stage, for parthenogenesis. Yet there is the unstated suggestion of that ironic flattened breast, its *sotto voce* "yes, but . . . ," its sardonic looking-forward to what the words just above it on the dust jacket call "meat joy." In fact, the dust jacket enacts primal history as it moves through several stages of biology; and yet the full title is "more than meat joy," which means "meat joy and more," foreseeing what Schneemann later speaks of as "nonsexual physical contact" (187) but also suggesting what Owens describes the performers as doing: "drifting us along with them to show us passion and the essence of our being" (270). That interplay of essence and passion is seminal in Schneemann's work, crucial to its intent, its intentionality. Yet this is only one line in Schneemann's multifoliate art: steeped in self-awareness it seeks to resist the reductiveness of bathos. It is always alert to the surprisingly tentacular life of "the essence of our being."

Some aspects of this alertness appear in the cover image, in its play of essence and irony, of elemental being and basic mooning. That play is typical of Schneemann at her best. In one of its facets it comments on our stances in the world, inscribing a sardonic allegory of the self's positioning within its context in the world. That context includes a series of acts; or, from another point of view, it takes in various slants on the same elemental act, a celebratory rooting in waters which is also, at the same time, a celebration of ourselves, jointly and separately. The jointness is obvious. The separateness is asserted by that slyly flattened breast attesting specificity and difference within and away from the group. In fact, partly because of that breast, what is celebrated, finally, is our presence to ourselves as well as to the waters and each other.

It is precisely those multiple modes of presence (again, Schneemann as multifoliate) that she sought in her group performance work. She brought out possibilities of presence not only within the group but within each individual who takes part in (but simultaneously moves away from) the enfolding of the group. (Something of the same experience occurs in much of the work of The Four Horsemen. Its relation to the communal improvisation in New Orleans and Chicago jazz, our culture's defining version of the mode, needs to be explored.) In an early piece called *Newspaper Event* Schneemann instructed the other performers to cultivate risk and uncertainty, "randomizing processes, chance methods, and natural movement, where each person tended to realize instructions or tasks as an independent, self-reliant unit/entity"; but she also wanted a (not quite countervailing, something more than supplementary) commentary on that independence through "touch, contact, tactile materials, shocks—boundaries of self and group to be meshed and mutually evolving" (33). Schneemann wanted those boundaries to evolve both separately and together, presence to oneself and to others shown to be never fully distinguishable yet surely never the same. If that combination of modes of presence—to oneself and to others simultaneously—speaks of ways of the sixties and early seventies (as it also does in the work of Allan Kaprow), Schneemann's probing of presence explores it more subtly than most such speculations of the time. That probing also speaks for and of late modernism by finding ramifications of essence and presence without any counterpoised ramifications of absence—ramifications that some have shown to have an equivalent intricacy, contrary thrusts of the sort that postmodern artists like Steve McCaffery and Sophie Calle turn into the substance of their work. It is not only that Schneemann argues against lacunae but that she seeks out areas and conditions of presence where the question had not been broached, expanding the geography that presence can inhabit and performing that expanding by showing presence reaching out to new conditions, additional contexts. After she gave up her group works, Schneemann spoke of how she sought to effect "the thoroughness of our mutual awareness and the degree to which that heightened an 'ordinary self,'" a heightening that causes the self both to be and be part of (184). If her solo work puts her intimate, categorical, unequivocal presence up front in the world, much of the sense of that centralizing emerges from the contrary multivalence of the group works. What the separate self solos is all that much more solo because of the heightening of contextual understanding, the staking of further turf, effected in the group works.

And in fact that solo grows more emphatically solo because of the ultimate grouping in which it inevitably takes place. The dust-jacket image suggests aspects of that scene, not only in the fact of the water but in the blue-green coloration that bathes the image. As Schneemann puts it in an early notebook: "We are a part of nature and of all visible and invisible forms" (13). That same site and coloration appear early and late in *Fuses*, her well-known film on lovemaking, and to similar effect.

Schneemann's sense of organic relations as the locus for every solo sits comfortably, coherently, with the stress upon immediacy in a passage from Antonin Artaud that she cites in her preface. Theater, she quotes Artaud as saying, has to "steep itself in the springs of an eternally passionate and sensuous poetry . . . a poetry realized by a return to the primitive Myths." The mise-en-scène has the added task, Artaud continues, of "materializing these old conflicts and above all of giving them *immediacy*" (7), that is, up-front, perceptible, affective/effective presence. What Schneemann calls her "concretions" emerge in, intensify, and are intensified by such immediacies. Concretions intensify all of our faculties simultaneously, as well as all the areas those faculties can reach to. Once again Schneemann seeks every possible site for immediacy, the completest establishing of presence: "Perspective is the over-all immediacy in which each area partakes of every parameter open to it" (13). What occurs, then, is "movement of the immediate present" (14), movement, that is, not just *in* the present but *of* the present, temporality itself indistinguishable from the movement which carries it; and because that movement moves presence into every parameter, temporality and movement grow indistinguishable from the presence they embody. Daryl Chin has argued that throughout Schneemann's career "the immediacy of *presence* has concretized her concerns" (*More than Meat Joy*, 266); but in Schneemann's pioneering body art, presence is more than a mode of concretizing her concerns: it is itself the central concern, the end of her art as well as its means, what it seeks to find but also the mode of its seeking. Happenings, then, ought to own not only spontaneity but that sense of timeliness to the moment which is the moment's way of asserting its temporal presence: "Happenings: raw, direct, no intermediate crafting, fabricating"; and she goes on to a rapid series of distinctions among Kaprow, Dine, and others, their ways of opening up, and opening up to, the moment's immediacy (56).

What the moment opens to, Schneemann suggests in an early notebook, is precisely that sort of Battaillean overflow/excess we saw emergent in the Barthesian "erotic body," the pleasure of which transcends any mere "physiological need." In Schneemann's words, "Our best developments grow from works which initially strike us as 'too much'; those which are intriguing, demanding, that lead us to experiences which we feel we cannot encompass . . . [which] have the effect of containing more than we can assimilate" (9). Schneemann's pervasive eroticism, intense, intent, informing every aspect of her work (*Fuses* puts it in its purest form, as itself and nothing else), comes out to be a literalizing of this mode of being a text, turning that eroticism which in Barthes is always something more than metaphor into that which absorbs all metaphor into the (excessive) forms of itself. Her pioneering of contact improvisation seems, then, the fostering of ultimate writerliness, the inscribing of an ultimate text; and yet there is that in her work which Barthes would never endorse, a counterpart and contrary to the opening out of excess, a centripetal gesture essential to every humanism and many modes of modernism, early and late. As she put it in notebook comments in July 1963: "When I write the sympathetic dominates: central tension high, streaming from periphery to center, 'away from the world, back into the self': wrote Reich" (19). Barthes could never condone such centripety, which goes absolutely contrary to that radical openness, that refusal to congeal, that he saw as mandatory to any meaning of "text"; and indeed it seems likely that Schneemann is aware of such refusals, for she frequently speaks of, takes into her performances, conditions of textuality that she contradicts aggressively.

Which is not to say that those contrary conditions are excrescences, appendages, tangential escapades. They result from the excess of performance; their appearance is an ironic tribute to the possibilities of overflow. If the 1964 performance called Meat Joy "has the character of an erotic rite: excessive, indulgent, a celebration of flesh as material" (63), it also plays intensely with all manner of secondary effects which are not in themselves excessive (at least as Schneemann presents them; others think otherwise). Those effects stem from the impulse of the context to explore its own geographies, including the geographies' way of finding a place for contraries. (This means, of course, that the erotics of exploration take their origin from the text's narcissism, the erotic engendering the erotic in continuous self-begetting.) Three-minute discs of popular songs conflict with tapes of Paris street songs but, more significant, the audience enters to the sounds of a tape/collage of Schneemann's voice reading "the written notes formative to Meat Joy (so that the work is verbally revealed before it begins)" (64). The work, that is, enters with the secondary fully up front, and as soon as Schneemann can put it there (Steve McCaffery will take this sort of thing several steps further and turn it quite around with, among others, his Chinese ventriloquist). But the performance then shifts into some of the intensest immediacy in her work, the ultimate action of Meat Joy a "propulsion toward the ecstatic" (63). That propulsion is all the more privileged because we come to it through a precursor whose primary function is to lead to the propulsion, to prepare its way, and after the preparation, to stand as the memory of what the mediate is like (the secondary as John the Baptist).

In fact, it is precisely this sequencing that pits Schneemann's piece against any talk poem by David Antin, which begins in the immediacy of performance and works through to extremer and extremer stages of the secondary. Antin's explorations of presence point out the degree to which Schneemann labors dangerous games. Her mode might unearth aspects of the context that could threaten her persistent search for ramifications of presence. More precisely, what it might unearth could threaten her performance's certainty that in its self-made overflow it will find only further modes and conditions of presence. Because *Meat Joy* offers the secondary only as a channel, the potential in the secondary for contrariety and conflict (the emergence to the surface of the secondary's subtextual mutterings, its claims for its own authority) takes no open part in the performance. Instead, that performance seems patently to argue that ecstasy and the secondary can have nothing to do with each other, that the secondary can offer only a *report* about ecstasy because it only, necessarily, speaks about that which is absent. Schneemann never says anything less, even in *Fuses;* yet her irony seeks (if with mixed success) to counter the potential for bathos in her work, leading her to take what she knows are risks by introducing the antagonist of that presence she espouses. In *Ghost Rev* she incorporates "film as a material element . . . a material equation with the constructions" (97). Here she allows the secondary's mutterings to come up to the surface; the result is an intense sense of active contrariety (however material the film stock, the content of any film always speaks of absence). To win this war of contraries she proposes to dominate the films perceptually with physical activity. The performance presumed the films antagonistic, that the two performers would spread action in literal dimensions away from the fixed-screen illusions of image, depth, speed, rhythm, direction, duration. It was that or have a performance embellishing and ancillary to the films—and Schneemann could never accept ancillariness for the body (97 and 99). This play of positionality admits the subtext into the scene, lays the antagonisms out but (after all, it is *her* performance) puts dominance out of doubt.

And yet her irony continues to play out its potential. The body's erotics are always, in some sense, an erotics of presence. This may be another way of saying that presence itself is potentially erotic, a point that Barthes would never deny. To affirm the erotic is therefore to affirm presence; but this cannot be taken to mean that to play down the obviously erotic is in any way to deny presence or even, finally, to deny the erotic as such. In *Ghost Rev* Schneemann seemed to want an ungendered performance: she and the dancer Phoebe Neville wore painter's overalls "to de-emphasize our body shapes" (99). And yet the fact of their presence—it is the performance's point to assert that fact—put the erotic into the scene because, as Schneemann sees it, presence and the erotic inevitably affirm each other. In her terms each is an aspect of the other, as she had suggested them to be on the dust jacket of her book. This too is more than meat joy for the joy is a joy in presence as such. Thus, whatever the threats to the privilege of that presence she espouses, Schneemann continues to seek out conditions where the threat can be made and countered: whatever the conditions, she is confident that presence can never be put aside. Whatever else the joy, it will always be a joy in presence.

That is why Schneemann can turn out instances of the secondary at its most fluent, most florid, and still hold to that up-frontness which she sees as the point and purpose of her art. A 1977 work called ABC—We Print Anything—In the Cards is made up of a set of 315 boxed 3 x 5 cards, some text, some image, the whole relating a narrative of Schneemann's simultaneous affairs with two lovers.[3] She was putting together the text of ABC while she was living the experiences figured in the text—a practice significantly reminiscent of eighteenth-century epistolary fictions such as Clarissa in which the making of the story and the occurrence of the story are presented as simultaneous, perhaps even identical, acts. In these texts and in Schneemann's ABC the narrative is a gerund as well as a noun, a telling as well as that which is told. To put it another way, she tells the telling of the narrative as well as the tale itself. It is, then, in one of its aspects, a performative act, as well as, in another aspect, that which is performed, which means that it is, at once, primary and secondary. Still, despite ABC's patent resistance to categorical definition, Schneemann, as always (here she differs from the eighteenth-century models), persistently draws attention to the fact of the experience and therefore the strength of up-frontness, insisting on its primacy whatever the secondary does. It is precisely that insistence that makes Schneemann's work so different from that of Steve McCaffery, whatever the confluence of concerns. That insistence puts Schneemann in line with figures like Rothenberg and Antin, not only in terms of performative acts but in the simultaneous play of primary and secondary that characterizes some of the most complex late modernist performances—performances so multifaceted that even terms like late modernist, however generally valid, need significant qualification. In his analysis of ABC Scott MacDonald puts a related point this way:

[Schneemann] wants to use the making of a work to preserve, consider, and reorient the process of the emotion (and the illumination/confusion it brings) as she experiences it. . . .

3. For a reading of this work, see Scott MacDonald, "The Men Cooperated," Afterimage 12 (April 1985): 12–15.

> . . . This making of the work within and during the situation itself
> is Schneemann's means of making it function formatively and pro-
> gressively within the process of life. (12, 14)

Credible as far as it goes this reading is far too unitary; what it recognizes
is extremely important but is only part of the context. It is only when we
acknowledge the simultaneity of being and telling in *ABC* that the multifoliate character of Schneemann's text comes clear. The photographs were
being taken as the narrative worked itself out. Situated somewhere between
full presence and absolute absence, they were waiting to be absorbed into
a text whose ending was not yet in focus and perhaps not even previsioned.
No categories suffice for *ABC* or, in fact, for Schneemann that recognize
and play out all the ironies of presence. Those ironies include that dense
subtextual muttering which hints at discontents she is ready to acknowledge
because she is certain that she can keep them comfortably under control.

That awareness of multiplicity extends to Schneemann's sense of the
relations of photographs, film, and the body, an understanding too complex
to be encompassed in any single performance and which continues into
later work, including the work of recent years. *Up to and Including Her
Limits*, a performance of the mid-seventies, continues the use of ropes and
pulleys begun in *Water Light / Water Needle*. Schneemann, nude, swings
around the room on a cable, floating ecstatically while writing on a wall
onto which are projected film and video images of her life (*More than
Meat Joy*, 224–33). Temporality and presence, body and artifact, image and
ecstasy, intersect in a condition where no stasis seems possible, no fixing
final. In *Catscan*, a performance presented at Binghamton on 16 April 1988,
Schneemann projected images of love, destruction, and death (shots of her
and her cat mouth to mouth, images of a burning building, closeups of a
dead deer) onto a large screen and danced before the screen while, simultaneously, a soundtrack projected her voice commenting, in various degrees
of distinctness and indirection, on the images. The simultaneous play of
different positionings and therefore different conditions of self (in the image, on the tape, up front on the stage) continued the irresolution of *Up
to and Including Her Limits* in ways that undo any sense that Schneemann
can be easily categorized. That continuing also makes clear that whatever
the threats to the primacy of presence, Schneemann feels that she can
handle whatever comes her way.

Still, she is not the only one threatened in such contexts, not the only one to be aware of the tense interweaving of presence and the erotic, in texts and in bodies, textual bodies, the bodies of texts. The encounter of primary and secondary ultimately comes down to questions of authority, that is, of power, that is, of potential challenge to the Word understood as phallic. That challenge seems to some to multiply immensely when it appears in (as) the person of a young woman; yet the fracas has to do not only with gender and attendant roles but the authority many feel (and they are usually ambivalent about it) to be intrinsic to immediacy and presence. Consider the comments of a psychiatrist speaking of a conference in London with which Schneemann had some difficulty: "We didn't welcome a woman taking an equal space among ourselves, we distrusted a theatrical form, and we certainly didn't want a very young woman putting on a performance which incorporated our own words with a countering physicality" (151). Logophallocentrism is rarely so self-aware, so frank. Consider, further, a photograph of a group of nudes, one of whom "holds a sign across her body inviting you to the opening, because her husband has insisted her naked body—only ink on paper—not pass into public domain" (192). In so phrasing the husband's response, Schneemann exposes his sense of his wife's body as private property. Yet the situation is not nearly so categorical because by speaking of this sense of threat as responding to "only ink on paper" Schneemann denies the possibility of an indexical reading of photography, all that makes the photograph in Barthes a subject of the intensest eroticism as well as, simultaneously, the sign of an irrevocable absence. She denies, that is, the conditions of an exemplary postmodernism whose ironies match her own in intensity but differ dramatically in design and object. In effect Schneemann continues her project of promoting the power of presence, this time establishing a sense that absence is the absence of presence; and that, cannily, is her way of putting presence up front in our concerns even when unredeemably absent. This is how she continues the comment on the photograph:

> To confront the paradox that we deal with created images—painted, sculpted, performed—as "reality." As if paint, plaster, celluloid, stone, paper, exist to convince us of a life force as vital as our own flesh and blood . . . and *subject to our social moralities!* This . . . shelters an unconscious, debased primitivism—surrounding, endowing inanimate objects with projections of our repressed vitality. (192)

What Schneemann is after here is precisely parallel to the sense of a momentary deity that Ernst Cassirer's *Language and Myth* made part of the permanent currency of the discourse of presence.[4] She argues that we debase that sense when we take inanimate texts to intimate vital immediacy, when we impute power and therefore threat to the secondary's way of unfolding the presence of absence. How this complicates any reading of *Fuses* should be clear enough. What it does to the fusion of act and allegory in *Interior Scroll* complicates that performance into one of Schneemann's exemplary moments of late modernist discourse.

She presented *Interior Scroll* twice, first at a gathering of women artists on Long Island in 1975, then at a film festival in Colorado two years later. The performance seems simple enough. After an initial preparation (in the first performance reading from her earlier writing, in the second reading a statement of protest about male misunderstanding of female eroticism) she unrolled a long, very narrow scroll from her vagina and read the text inscribed on it, which came from her film *Kitch's Last Meal*. The text tells of her meeting with "a happy man / a structuralist filmmaker" who is far less self-aware, less self-ironic, than the London psychiatrist:

> he said we are fond of you
> you are charming
> but don't ask us
> to look at your films
> we cannot
> there are certain films
> we cannot look at
> the personal clutter
> the persistence of feelings
> the hand-touch sensibility
> the diaristic indulgence
> the painterly mess
> the dense gestalt
> the primitive techniques
> (*More than Meat Joy*, 238)

and the parody continues with an exchange of insults, Schneemann's ear for absurdities stressing his capping condescension:

4. *Language and Myth*, trans. Suzanne Langer (New York: Dover, 1946).

he said we can be friends
equally tho we are not artists
equally I said we cannot
be friends equally and we
cannot be artists equally

he told me he had lived with
a "sculptress" I asked does
that make me a "film-makeress"?

Oh No he said we think of you
as a dancer

(239)

Still, Schneemann thinks of *Interior Scroll* as more than a mockery of structuralist distaste for immediacy. Going back to her earlier work on "vulvic space" and myths of a Mother Earth Goddess, she plays with readings of space that turn absence into the mirror of presence, in effect mocking readings of the female as lack/lacuna by treating the primitive serpent/phallus as nothing more than the reverse of the shape of the primal space:

> I thought of the vagina in many ways—physically, conceptually: as a sculptural form, an architectural referent, the source of sacred knowledge, ecstacy, birth passage, transformation. I saw the vagina as a translucent chamber of which the serpent was an outward model: enlivened by its passage from the visible to the invisible, a spiraled coil ringed with the shape of desire and generative mysteries, attributes of both female and male sexual powers. (234)

Male because of its mirror-image shape, female because it is the outward model of this elemental chamber, the serpent finds its home in vulvic space; and yet there is no question of the primacy of that space and of its place in conceiving the world in every possible mode: "The experience and complexity of [the cosmic Mother's] personal body was the source of conceptualizing, of inter-acting with materials, of imaging the world and composing its images" (235). With primitivism like this, bathos is just around the corner, and sometimes Schneemann cannot avoid its touch: see, for example, another version of the serpent/vagina play in a poem called "For the

Black Tarantula."[5] Yet in *Interior Scroll* she counters that potential with an irony that saves her from primal sentimentality. The long and narrow scroll that she unrolls from her vagina has the serpent's shape and placement as well as the serpent's way of uncoiling and stretching out. But the analogies work both ways: the serpent, so understood, takes on the scroll's characteristics. Identified with the place on which the secondary is inscribed, this ultimate symbol of maleness comes, for still another reason, to be one step less than primary, whatever it thinks of itself. The secondary, in its role as an uncoiling serpent, is finally no more than the voice of a pipsqueak phallocentrism that slithers out of its snugness in the place of primal space to argue, brassily, for the primacy of the secondary. In every sense of the phrase Schneemann puts the secondary in its place. It is precisely such ironies that link the late modernist Schneemann with figures like the post-modernist Jo Spence, who begins her autobiography with a photograph of herself sitting on a chamber pot, melodramatically shocked to see that she has "an imaginary lack."[6]

II

Recall, again, the paper cover of *More than Meat Joy*, the buttocks, the multifoliate figure, the water, the suffusing blue-green. Consider, then, the cover of Steve McCaffery's *North of Intention*, which has on its face the photograph of an object called *Mask*, made by Mira Schor in 1977.[7] The mask is heart-shaped, nearly flat, the holes for eyes and mouth all approxi-

    5. *Cezanne She was a Great Painter: The Second Book, January 1975* (New Paltz, N.Y.: Documentext, 1975), 8.

    6. For other readings of *Interior Scroll*, see Jeanie Forte, "Women's Performance Art: Feminism and Postmodernism," *Theatre Journal* 40 (1988): 221–22 and 226 (speaking of how Schneemann identifies the personal and the political), and Henry Sayre, *The Object of Performance: The American Avant-Garde since 1970* (Chicago: University of Chicago Press, 1989), 90–92 (on the same subject as Forte). Forte has several useful comments about Schneemann and contemporary feminist performance. Sayre's other comments on Schneemann, particularly 166–73, place her work convincingly in terms of the significance of performance in contemporary art. Forte and Sayre list several other studies of Schneemann.

    7. Steve McCaffery, *North of Intention: Critical Writings, 1973–1986* (New York: Roof Books, 1986). For another reading of *North of Intention*, see Marjorie Perloff's *Poetic License: Essays on Modernist and Post-modernist Lyric* (Evanston, Ill.: Northwestern University Press, 1990). For other comments on McCaffery's work, see George Hartley, *Textual Politics and the Language Poets* (Bloomington: Indiana University Press, 1989).

mately the same size, their contours torn and jagged. The mask is covered with writing, not printed but script, some of the phonemes decipherable but few adding up to words that make sense in the language systems within which McCaffery works (Fig. 2).[8]

Schor's mask never pretends to be anything other than itself; yet is it, in fact, fully a mask? It is in the nature and meaning of a mask to be a cover for something, to hide or disguise what is underneath it. A mask is a Peircean index that, as all indexes do, points to something with which it is connected but not identified. Insofar as a mask is an index it is also a metonym, implying a context, layers, strata, a relation of surface and depth, figment and substance. That is, it implies a setting with a three-dimensional geography because we look through and beyond the mask to that which it covers and indicates.

All of which makes this instance a curious mask indeed. If on the surface that we see, there is an illegible writing (illegible at least to us, in the condition in which it reaches us), behind the mask as it appears on the cover of *North of Intention* (that is, the image of the mask as it is designed to "introduce" *North of Intention*) there is, finally, only the whiteness of the context on which the image is printed. Nothing is pointed to, nothing shows behind or through which would make the mask an index. Further, if this mask is a metonym we have no idea of the context in which the metonym takes part because there is only the metonym to be seen (not "read" because the writing is innocent of any sense, which is not to say that it is, in any radical sense, innocent). It would be wrong to think of that whiteness as figuring potential, announcing a space to be inscribed: the writing on the mask, readable only phonemically, is worn, smudged, much of it the subject of erasure, the residue of a writing that had been. So, too, is the mask, itself ragged and torn, a remnant or a relic, something that had been. What the writing might have said is no longer available, which means that the writing and the mask can point to nothing beyond

8. As McCaffery told me in a letter, the mask is, in fact, hinged as a book and opens out with the writing we see on the cover inscribed on the back side of the mask. In another letter McCaffery pointed out that he never saw the mask but that the cover image was chosen with his final approval. At the least this indicates a more-than-subliminal sense of the relationship of the mask to the content of his book, not only on his part but on that of the makers of the book. McCaffery sees the assertion of that relationship as a "diacritical intervention" into the question of authorial intention. He also sees it as an agitation of a crucial question: "Where does a text commence? What's the relationship and relative status of the dust jacket (printed and carrying a visual datum) to the blank stiff boards?" Of course the same issues emerge in my reading of the cover of Schneemann's *More than Meat Joy.*

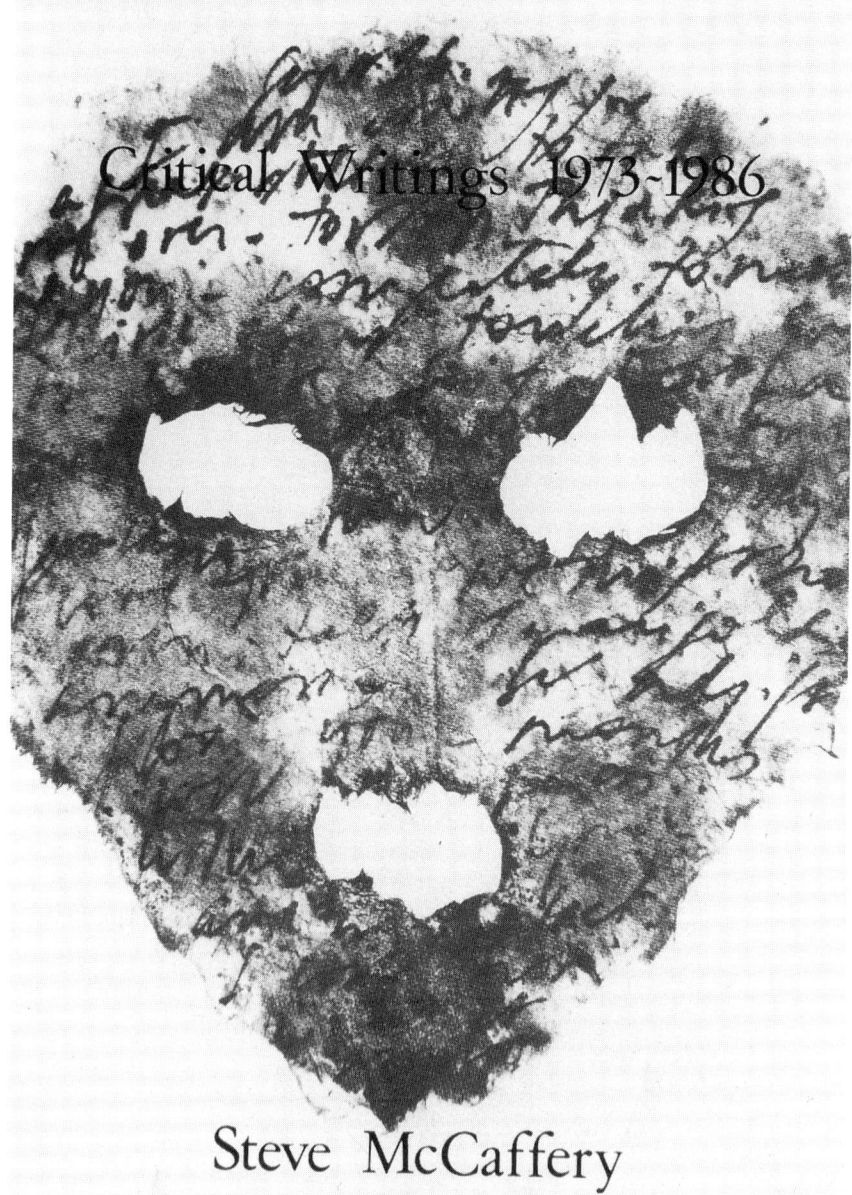

NORTH OF INTENTION

Critical Writings 1973-1986

Steve McCaffery

Fig. 2. Mira Schor, cover from *North of Intention*

themselves. Most precisely, they point to the nothing beyond themselves, that whiteness which in Stevens's "Snow Man" is "the nothing that is." The whiteness is therefore the space of an immediate absence, the site of that which might well have been (given these conditions we shall never know just what or when it was). It is certainly not the site of that which has not yet come, not the site of a potential (the site where a certain potency could work, the place to exercise a certain erotics).

That the mask's erotics are certain as well as of a certain kind comes clear not only from the relations of erotics and writing but from the status of the mask as a site of writing. It is a scene of writing that, oddly but effectively, suggests the onetime being of the maker of the writing, the scribbler of the script. It can so suggest precisely because the writing is script and not print, the work of a hand and not of a press. Thus the writing and the mask, whatever their status as indicators of absence, act also as indicators of the presence of the writer, as lacunae through which consistency can slip away, as Blakean Contraries which need each other to exist, but not as Blakean Negations which seek to undo each other. Still, it is important to distinguish among the conditions the indexes point to: the smudges not only indicate an earlier stage of the writing but carry the writing on to that later, beclouded state we can perceive and touch; but the presence of the scribbler whom the smudges indicate has no carried-over state that can be immediately met. The scribbler is even more absent than his scribblings because it is through this continuity that we follow the fingerings of his former presence. In fact it is tempting to identify the absence the masks reveals with that of the scribbler, among us only in his negative revelation, "the nothing that is."

This pastness whose presence is emphatic recalls Carolee Schneemann's comments on the photograph in which a nude holds a sign across her body; the photograph is Schneemann's way of reminding us of presence by dwelling emphatically on its absence, but the mask on the face of *North of Intention* stands in mischievous contradiction to any such reminders because the point of McCaffery's cover is to stress the up-frontness of absence, the blank where once was presence. That is, Schneemann and McCaffery offer different intentionalities, make countervailing claims about what is to be found and where: behind the young woman's sign are all the erotics of a body, masked; behind the tattered mask is, precisely, nothing, and whatever sort of erotics nothing can make happen. Schneemann's extension of presence into every stratum and rift (Keats had said of Shelley that he should load every rift with ore) finds its contrary in McCaffery's suggestions of the presence only of absence, whatever the available rift. Writing, he suggests, is only the mask of what-had-been. Were we to develop the conceit that the mask and its scribblings are worn and old we could argue that any writing is already dated by the time we get around to it. It takes its life from its antecedents, has in effect already been written before we write it down. Whenever we get to it, thus, that life has largely passed. This means that even the scribbling on the wall that the nude, ecstatic Schneemann had performed in *Up to and Including Her Limits* can be no more than past (passed) as soon as it is presented. It moves at once into the status of the films and videos that were showing simultaneously while Schneemann swung around; and in fact Schneemann makes precisely that point: "self-body is consumed in the action ('used up'), finally leaves the space. Film and video continue" (*More than Meat Joy*, 231). Film and video, she argues, have the consistency of the secondary, whereas the primary, though always present to itself, enters and exits the scene, its presence emphatic but occasional. (Compare Rothenberg on the slippage into "mere history," Antin on the shift to the talk-poem's stages of recording.) Once again Schneemann's work seems difficult to neatly categorize; Steve McCaffery's will prove equally so. Each is careful to offer the opposition a place, establishing at least the possibility of ambiguity: McCaffery, after all, chooses for his cover the image of a mask with traces of script. Of course in both cases this offering is the work of a rhetoric designed to confirm what each argues to be the Only Credible Way. In each case the shadings are finally tiny, something more than tokens but something less than fully convincing about the efficacy of the Other Way.

What we have seen so far deals with a limited spatial time that seems largely to be past, though we need contemporary absence to make that seeming happen. Of the future there is no regard. Something of the full effect of the cover of *North of Intention* comes from our shifting from temporal space to geographical space. What we see of the mask helps us to begin that move: the small amount of modeling that shows in the cover image— around the inner contours of the eyes, a slight and possibly illusory rise where the nose would be—cannot undo the impression of commanding two-dimensionality, just what we would expect from a page. In fact there is a precise parallel between those slight suggestions of modeling and the occasional "word" that appears to come through in what remains of the text: for example, what seems a "with" at the lower left of the mask. Despite those tentative suggestions of something beyond the surface, the flatness of the mask and the a-referentiality of the language mirror each other precisely, working as metaphors of each other and also, we suspect, as metonyms of some larger field. Just as the mask has a patent nothing behind it, failing in its need to be indexical because there is (only) nothing to index, so too does the language fail to do what we expect it to do, refer. It is as two-dimensional as the mask itself. The cover, thus, images the mask of language.

Consider another puzzling relationship, another possibility of metaphor. The two-dimensional surfaces of the mask and of language define a kind of presence that exists, largely, in order to denote absence. So too does the present moment, defining a kind of presence that is largely indexical. We can speak, then of the metaphorical relations between the spatial and temporal geographies that inhabit the cover of the book. In so speaking, however, we get even more geographical, telling of surfaces (what else is there to tell of?) and what happens on them.

What the mask of language helps us begin to understand about the geographies involved is continued by the title. *North of Intention* implies another sort of geography, one in which intention has a place if only as the sort of place from which deviation is possible, from which we ought to divert. Yet whatever the possibilities in figuring intention as a place, it is finally a mode of desire, a going-out or going-forth in search of connection, and it is therefore a condition within the erotics of the text. It is part of the text's actions, part of that which moves within the geography that possesses the text (considering the intensity of what goes on within that geography, we cannot comfortably say that the text possesses it). Still, if the work of language is ultimately two-dimensional, desire is limited in the direction it can go, however intense the intention, the intentionality. That leaves McCaffery's reading of others' texts a limited space to work on ("on" rather than "in"; the prepositions reveal the dimensions).

The space is limited because writing has no place to go except the two-dimensional surface on which its functions are confined. We can profit once again from the obsessive geography that informs McCaffery's work, that trope which leads him to emphasize what he calls the "post-semiotic poem."[9] The poem beyond semiosis is finally beyond reference, beyond conditions

---

9. See bp Nichol, "The Annotated, Anecdoted, Beginnings of a Critical Checklist of the Published Works of Steve McCaffery," *Open Letter*, 6th ser., 9 (Fall 1987): 86. (The entire issue is devoted to McCaffery's work.) The checklist runs across the top of the page; running below it and along with it is an interview of McCaffery by bp Nichol. What this setup has to say about questions of text, voice, and presence makes this piece one of the most complex in which McCaffery participates (whatever "participation" might mean in such a context, among such ironies).

that make the usual meaning of "meaning" possible. It is the poetry of the Language Poets and all the attendant figures that get in under that tent. What post-semiotics intends appears at various points in *North of Intention*, in many of McCaffery's poems and in his performances and videos. That intention appears succinctly in the essay that begins *North of Intention*, particularly in passages like those in which he speaks of reading and "the opaque condition of writing" (19). The art of reading (seeing, scanning) shows syntax to be "the movement of a textual surface without a pre-determined destination." Syntax has (is) energy, finds itself thrusting through spaces in which it performs as a mode of libido. Our prejudiced reading habits lead us to insist on "a verbal presence that would offer itself for consumption," that is, a condition in which we read for, give and consume, reference. But writing that stresses what McCaffery argues to be the nature of writing affirms "the incidentality of the signifier rather than the transcendality of the referent." In so affirming it rejects our habitual "pursuit of words along certain referential vectors to a corresponding world outside the text." It rejects, that is, a three-dimensional geography, all that is not the mask. Instead, such writing emphasizes "a first order experience of graphemes," their materiality, substantiality. The result is "non-commodital productivities," which take place in "the communal space of a human engagement" (20).

North of Intention is an exposition of certain modes of contemporary poetics, Language Poetry particularly. McCaffery shows himself to be a first-rate critic, especially in his essay on Michael Palmer. As McCaffery puts it, Palmer "offers a sustained challenge to the reader's habitual and conditioned pursuit of depth" (44). That challenge is impelled by the quest for "a language of objective surface, holding attention at the level of an opaque, syntactic system that argues against the word's deictic functions and obstructs the passage through a text towards a referential destination." The act of passage is that libidinal thrust which seems more and more to be the central McCafferyan energy, one that he finds in his cohorts particularly. Palmer's ultimate project is to "settle textual experience within the materiality of writing as a spatio-temporal phenomenon," to satisfy his "concern for surface and material relations" and show their place in playing out "a developed proliferation of indeterminacies."

How, then, does one position oneself within such a geography? What is it that positions itself? What does it mean to shift from "oneself" to "itself" in describing such phenomena, as these sentences have done (as I have done with these sentences)? Is "positions" as transitive a verb as "reads," "writes," "loves"? And just how transitive are they? What does libido have to do with such positioning or being positioned? If the process is as passive as "being positioned" suggests, is the libido that works through McCafferyan geographies that which does the positioning? If so, who or what wields the libido? Or is it only wielded without a specifiable "who" or "what"? Does putting such pronouns within quotation marks give them a substance, hypostasize them (a surreptitious imputing of being and its attendant presence)? Who or what is so sly? Society? Culture? Can such abstractions have such feelings/attitudes as slyness and the intention thereof?

One moves from Schneemann to McCaffery and hears McCaffery muttering in a voice that speaks the strains (in all senses) of Schneemann's irritable subtext. One can imagine McCaffery muttering that the "one" who moves from Schneemann to McCaffery is no essential one: it is not sole, whole, or the source of creativity (the pun on vagina as "hole" in terms of whole and sole/soul, already enunciated by Yeats's Crazy Jane, seems implicit in Schneemann). Nor, in fact, McCaffery would mutter, is it a "who" that moves but a "which." McCaffery works certain postmodernist stances on the subject's positioning into his libidinal geographies, informing not only his poems but his remarkable performances—part of whose purpose is to show just how performative theory can be. Precisely like Barbara Kruger, and in as work-defining a way, McCaffery draws on contemporary readings of the nature of the shifter (in his case coming, he says, from Otto Jespersen) to speak of the subject's location and intentionality (if a ghost that inhabits syntax can have intentionality). In his interview of McCaffery printed in *North of Intention* Andrew Payne cites Zukofsky's *Bottom on Shakespeare*, which is concerned with identity and the Other. McCaffery responds by rejecting what he sees as

> an ideological confusion between pronoun and identity which graphemically shows itself in the "hieroglyphic" status of the "I" on the page. I doubt that Zukofsky and Olson every really tackled the pronoun as a shifter, ever explored it as a complex topography of enunciator and enunciated with its fundamental status as a geographical marker and not an identity; a "here" rather than a "self." (120)

The subject as shifter moves within a geography, marks that geography's spaces; in effect takes part in cartographical acts. We now know a good deal more about the topography of McCaffery's two-dimensional landscape, his land of radical unlikeness figured on the cover of *North of Intention* as the mask of language. (It is a land of unlikeness because likeness implies identity and therefore the efficacy of metaphor. That the mask is itself a metaphor complicates the question of referentiality in ways that de Man and Derrida, among others, have acknowledged.) McCaffery puts the point even more precisely in the interview with bp Nichol in *Open Letter*. His earlier book, *Shifters*, had, he says, been important "in coming to terms with lyricism, and the place of the self within a writing." Given the shifter as "a word that changes its meaning according to the situation of the speaker," he grew convinced of "the essentially geographical or spatial nature of 'identity' in writing; that an 'I' and a 'you' mark less an identity than a position" (*Open Letter*, 87). McCaffery now appears as a cartographer of the subject, arguing for the need for a spatiality within which the subject moves to the tune of its radical shiftiness, that music which, he would argue, is the only consistency to be found.[10]

Such finding, of course, makes McCaffery uneasy not only with those who find other consistencies but with the relations of the other consistencies to "lyricism, and the place of the self within writing." McCaffery's remarks on Olson within the context of Zukofsky echo his other remarks on Olson, whom he reads as an exponent of no postmodernism but of a late modernist lyricism centering on an ongoing, consistently present self. In the interview by Andrew Payne, McCaffery characterizes Olson's packaging of ear, syllable, heart, and breath as "the privileging of all anteriority as a positive value." In that context origin and cause go together with breath, presence, and "immediate-being-as-truth." Opposed to them is writing, which takes in posteriority, imprint, and "corpse-as-death" (*North of Intention*, 127–28). Olson's attitude implies "communication as still being exchangist in nature," and that shows him to be "oblivious to writing as a fundamental trace structure in which each 'syllabic instant' must always be a breached presence . . . that announces an irreducible absence within the very system of the sign." Here, McCaffery argues, is "the crux of representation," and it was encountered not only by Olson but (McCaffery's logic is exact, none of the emperors are wearing clothes) Pound as well: the problem is found not only in the theories but even in "the intense and revolutionary polyphony of *The Maximus Poems* or *The Cantos*." In his essay "Language-Writing: From

---

10. Compare the following, from his comments on Michael Palmer: "Inscribed throughout Palmer's work, as its syntactic motion, are the protean, nomadic locales of the subject's disappearance, provisional topographies." *North of Intention*, 53.

Productive to Libidinal Economy" McCaffery uncovers Olson's not-quite-covert ideology in the suggestion that breath, "by providing 'solidity,' 'thing-ness,'" comes close to presence and is therefore (in a spatiality he shares with most postmodern theorists) "anterior to writing" (*North of Intention*, 147).

The cover of *North of Intention* argues that Olson is wrong, that we cannot come close to presence, for although we can actually touch the mask and hear the sounds of language being made, those actions do not resolve the difficulties of presence. Instead those actions bring to the surface other complications. One can take the mask and its inscribings as indexes of what had been. Yet one might prefer to say "has been" rather than "had been": past definites are simply too pat, too flat-out assertive about the irrevocabil-ity of absence, whereas indexes are supposed to establish some sort of link, to point somewhere. The index can be taken as a sign without a referent because what it points to *is* not here; yet it can also, at the same time, be taken as a sign with a referent because it points insistently to what *was* here.[11] It is the latter attitude that substantiates (another foxy verb) the indexical reading of photography in texts such as Barthes's *La Chambre Claire*. Yet Barthes manages to combine both attitudes at once by reading any photograph as arguing, simultaneously, for what we have spoken of as "has been" (the speech of the index) and "had been" (the speech of pure absence).

McCaffery is not so openly ambiguous as Barthes (no one is, no one enjoys ambiguity and ambivalence more, no one so clearly shows how they effect *jouissance*). Instead, McCaffery seeks to play out a tricky, delicate balance that goes far toward characterizing the conditions of his work. In one aspect of it he stresses immediacy as much as late modernist perform-ance artists like Carolee Schneemann or late modernist performance poets like Jerome Rothenberg do, stressing it specifically in terms of materiality: the feel of the mask, the sound and texture of language as they exist on the surface of the text in the moment of the text's utterance. Rothernberg shares McCaffery's emphasis on the materiality of language, shares it in his own sound poems and in those he collects in his anthologies. Yet McCaffery does not have the corollary that appears in Schneemann and Rothenberg

---

11. At a number of points in his comments on the index Peirce talks about its "real connection with the object" or some related issue; for example, "a genuine Index and its Object must be existent individuals." *Philosophical Writings of Peirce*, ed. Justus Buchler (New York: Dover, 1955), 108. In any temporal reading of the index this means that the object existed at one time, whatever it is doing now.

and throughout late modernism, that sense of the fullness of presence of a centered and coherent self, ebullient in the immediate moment no matter what happens to it once the moment has gone by. It is precisely that distinction that McCaffery seeks to hold onto to differentiate his own concern with the materiality of language from that of late modernism.[12] For McCaffery the self that appears in the immediate moment has no more presence than a text. More precisely, one should say that it has no more presence than any other text, for he argues at several points that the self is itself a text.[13] Still, the self does not have what every verbal text has, the materiality of language, its look and sound. Since it is only in the look and sound that the text has materiality and presence, that means that the self has no presence at all.

What then do the text and the self-as-text have? Insofar as the text has materiality it is surely present to us; but if it has no self at the center, no "essence" of the sort Carolee Schneemann espouses and performs, then it cannot have "presence" in the fullest and most meaningful sense, whatever up-frontness it has. McCaffery, it should now be clear, would not equate presence and up-frontness in the way that Schneemann and Rothenberg and Antin do. Neither text nor self-as-text, however up-front in the moment, can have the Benjaminian aura that, despite the arguments for its disappearance in modernism, is one of modernism's defining principles. (There is no modernism without at least some *hope* of the auratic.) What McCaffery seeks to define is, thus, a presentness without presence, possessing all the up-frontness materiality has to have in order to be itself, possessing none of the "unicities" on which essentialism depends and therefore none of the subjectivity emergent from essentialism (see *North of Intention*, 209–10). McCaffery's videos and performances seek to flesh out (another uncomfortable figure for this context) precisely that reading of presentness.[14]

12. He is fastidious in making that point: see, for example, in the Payne interview, his denial of "the appeal to 'a semi-aphonic corporality' or any kind of nostalgic return to a pre-sociosymbolic matrix." See also the comments that follow in "that variant strain of sound poetry that anchors itself in performance, supports the relegated status of the written text," and anchors its ideologies in "a certain strain of 19th century vitalism that persisted through Dadaism and Futurism. *North of Intention*," 124. McCaffery is speaking particularly of his own early work but his comments relate to a number of other figures as well.

13. See especially *North of Intention*, 119 and 129–30, the latter specifically Lacanian.

14. McCaffery's videos, which I shall be writing on in a sequel to this study, offer some of his finest performances. The collection of short pieces called *V Beyond the Ideo* (McCaffery pronounces the "V" as "Five") contains incisive work on language and the slippage of meaning, and on writing as such. The longest piece in it, "Paradise Improved," is already a classic of postmodern perform-

That is not the reading of presentness that appears in some other arguments that speak of themselves as postmodern; for example, Michel Benamou's introduction to *Performance in Postmodern Culture*, which can stand as a model.[15] The shift from structure to act, object to process, now generally accepted as one of the grounding movements in contemporary art, leads some, like Benamou, to see performance as the defining genre of our art.[16] As Benamou put it, performance is "the unifying mode of the postmodern" (*Performance in Postmodern Culture*, 3), and that is so not only because pages and museum walls offer an unacceptable fixity but because performance as now understood rejects "the binary opposition between play and seriousness which is characteristic of Western thought" (5). I doubt that opposition was ever as binary as Benamou claims: what to do with, to point only to the beginning of modern times, Rabelais, Cervantes, and Shakespeare, as well as all that Bakhtin has shown about carnival and heteroglossia? Benamou, however, sees different problems: there is "the presence active in presentation and re-presentation" (3), inherent within them whatever the rejection of assertion about pages and objects and presence. How to handle this insistence on *a kind of* remaining presence while at the same time supporting the Derridean argument that one ought, in such situations, to affirm free play? Benamou quotes Derrida on how we hover between an insistence on the absence of a center and the point we seem to be working toward, the affirmation of play (5). And yet, as Derrida points out, even were we to get there "a desire for centrality is a function of play itself" (5), which may explain why we cannot let the subject of presence rest. There is, it seems, at least that passion for centrality, whatever the modes and styles through which our texts do their work. That aspect of the textual erotic (Benamou does not put it in those terms but they seem eminently accurate) is not the sole property of any single wing of theory. A conservative thrust pervades every wing, a universal nostalgia from which none is exempt. Given this patent pervasiveness, Benamou has to conclude that there is "an undecidable argument between presentation and re-

───────────────

ance. Putting a performance into video puts an art that, to some, is the quintessence of immediacy, into an art that, to some, is grounded in irrevocable absence. What that means for McCaffery's concern with issues of presence takes his ironies into some of their furthest reaches. See my comments in the next chapter on performing photographs.

15. Michel Benamou and Charles Caramello, eds., *Performance in Postmodern Culture* (Madison: University of Wisconsin–Milwaukee, Center for Twentieth Century Studies, 1977).

16. Much the same position on the prevalence of performance appears in Henry Sayre's *The Object of Performance*. As the blurb to Sayre's book puts it, a number of artists have in common "a view of art as primarily performative."

presentation, Being and absence, presence and play" (3). As he phrases it elsewhere, "between these two propositions, performance as presence, performance as play, we cannot, perhaps must not, decide" (5).

In his essay "On Styles of Postmodern Writing" that concludes the anthology Charles Caramello rephrases Benamou, speaking of "the infinite hesitation between presence and playfulness" (222). He specifies some of the terms of that hovering in the undecidability between "speech/writing, intentionality/code restraint, intersubjectivity/intertextuality" (224), and goes on to quote Barthes on the writerly text, which offers a "perpetual present" and links up with "the infinite play of the world" (225).

What is there a presence of in the Benamou/Caramello remarks about the infinite, undecidable play between presence and performance? What is it that positions itself within such presence? And where does it position itself: where is this what located? Some of these questions appeared in a performance called *The Library of Cruelty* that McCaffery gave in Binghamton on 16 April 1988, where he came out on the stage dressed in a kimono and carrying a ventriloquist's dummy. With a quasi-silly smile that never left his face (though who or what owned that face was sometimes dubitable—"his" is only a single possibility), McCaffery tipped a half-moon shaped disk onto the top of his head, transforming himself into a "Chinese ventriloquist," manipulator of the Anglo-Saxon dummy. After asking that the audience seat itself in alphabetical order (echoes of the structure of Barthes's autobiography, its dictionary order as reasonable as any order into which we put the stories of our lives), he explained that Chinese ventriloquism involves recording one's voice on an audio cassette and creating the simultaneous illusion that one is not speaking and that the sounds are coming from one's voice. He then turned on an audio tape and mouthed the recorded sounds of his own voice, that voice speaking in a patently fake Chinese accent.[17] The stage was dark, the robed figure dimly lit. The glow of the tape recorder was the most conspicuous element in the scene. That auratic glow competed for the audience's attention with the dimmer figure of the Chinese ventriloquist, who worked at the facial gestures that were faking the forming of his words. Some of the complexities of aura in a Benjaminian context emerged in McCaffery's performance, which established and commented on (commented on its establishing of) precisely

17. This performance with a tape recorder implies, as I have suggested, all manner of relations between McCaffery's work and that of David Antin, with which McCaffery is quite familiar. The patent connection of tape recorders to photographs opens up a number of complex relations among McCaffery, Antin, and radical elements of visual postmodernism.

that context. Echoes of Benjamin's reading of the auratic in a context of mechanical reproduction played throughout the performance as simultaneous commentary and ironic subtext (the halo-like disk on the head of the Chinese ventriloquist carried still other extensions of aura as subtle emanation, here from an aureole); and of all the ironies at play perhaps the most potent was the fact that the point of aura was the light emerging from the locus of mechanical reproduction.[18]

The mission of the ventriloquist, the voice tells its audience, is "always to please, never to irritate." He must, that is, give pleasure, not vexation. Most precisely, he must afford Barthesian pleasure and not Barthesian *jouissance*, which can irritate and vex to the point of excess. Further, this ventriloquist must affirm as well as delight, since pleasure, as opposed to *jouissance*, confirms cultural categories: the text of pleasure, we recall Barthes saying, "comes from culture and does not break with it." This means that the Chinese ventriloquist will instruct as well as delight, a task that makes him historically Horatian and makes this performance a trip through topoi of the history of theory, a travelogue as well as a traveling show. And yet the title of the ventriloquist's lecture also takes its travels, the speaker announcing changes in his title as the lecture takes different tacks. That index which is the title keeps shifting its aim; what it points to is just as stable and locatable as the who or what at the center from which the voice emerges. And we can guess, even at this point, just how stable and locatable the who or what is and therefore just how cultured and unvexatious the voice from (of?) the machine really is. The smile on the ventriloquist's face is at once silly and sly. McCaffery plays his ironies off the poles of that oxymoron.

18. At this point McCaffery's performance touches on what contemporary performance figures like Laurie Anderson have seen, the ironic possibilities in the simultaneous interplay of aura and mechanical reproduction enacted in rock concerts. It is routine now to see tiny figures on a stage, their voices massively projected through electronic media, their figures projected onto giant video screens. The proportioning of "live" and "represented" plays out a sardonic allegory that takes Benjamin into the theory of rock (re)presentation. Anderson complicates this issue considerably in *Home of the Brave*, at once a tribute to and satire of the self-constituting possibilities of electronic media: the masks the figures occasionally wear play off against the projected figures, some massive, some not, some "live," some not. Work as different as Anderson's and McCaffery's makes clear that the question of self-constituting is as basic to contemporary performance as to other postmodern arts. For suggestions on the interplay of "live" and "represented" in the work of Bruce Springsteen, see Steven Connor, *Postmodernist Culture: An Introduction to Theories of the Contemporary* (Oxford: Basil Blackwell, 1989), 149–51. See also Sayre, *The Object of Performance*, 191, for other comments on the undermining of stage presence in Laurie Anderson's work.

Still, whatever the shifty title, those ironies take the activities within the performance one step further, playing off against that shiftiness a stern and stable theme: the subject of the lecture throughout is the making of "the book" and especially the book as "bachelor machine," with all the attendant echoes of Duchampian erotics. Taking as part of his task the combating of "a virulent strain of linguistic sphincterism," the ventriloquist outlines the logical model of the Western-type book, that piece of "sado-erotic machinery" which is improbable, useless, incomprehensible, delirious. As confirmer of cultural categories he worries about questions that none of the subjects of his echoes would worry about: is the opening convincing? does the ending have logical justification? And he worries them so far that they exit culture's discourse into an ultimate recognition of the power and prevalence of writing: the book as bachelor machine is "a mechanical metaphor for metaphor itself," what the Chinese call, he tells us, a "meta-five." As part of its pleasure-giving the ventriloquist's talk is a repertoire of bad jokes, with hints of their linguistic makeup. (McCaffery has told me that his own humor is involved with putting logical structures and metaphors at risk, an effort that makes him an heir to Dada as well as to Groucho Marx.)

He ends with a look at the nature of the audience and with an inevitable extension of the identification of self and text. Language, the voice says, "needs both speaker and listener to make a single dummy." Since "to speak is really to control," the "audience who listens is [the] audience who is spoken through." "We are all," the voice says, "the victim of somebody else's speaking . . . dummies in the form of bodies already written and already spoken."

This means that the voice the audience hears is always-already-recorded, always "was" as well as "is." The center from which the voice emerges can be cited but not sited. The site of the performed lecture, on the other hand, is the location of belatedness, that which has been elsewhere and is now imposed on the audience in the audience's status as "victim." McCaffery's performance is clearly an allegory of reading; but since there is no real difference between reading and writing (they are both subject to "difference") his performance is ultimately an allegory of writing as well. His performance, then, figures reading/writing, which are not simply simultaneous but the same act seen from differing perspectives. Framed in terms of other concerns, they are present to each other, though with every discontent that presence is heir to. This means that McCaffery's performance is also about the history of performance, which is to say the history of the readings of performance (just as this pleasure-giving "alien" ventriloquist effects a mocking history of the duties of Western literary theory).

It is also about theory and its relation to performance, not simply the theorizing of performance that every performance accomplishes but the performance of theory, its enactment in play. One of McCaffery's major contributions to contemporary performance comes from his understanding of the play element in theory, that capacity within theory which makes it possible for theory to be taken as performative. That such a capacity may well be inherent in every discourse is a likelihood subtextually suggested in McCaffery's work, suggested, in fact, by nearly every McCafferyan performance. Much of this has to do with his fascination with metaphor, which is not only the prevalent figure through which his performances work (metaphor extending to its narrative extension in allegory) but one of the regular subjects of his performances, one of the themes enacted as metaphor enacts its own capacities. Given that meeting of means and theme as well as McCaffery's recognition that theory can be *played* (not simply played with), his reading of the question of play in performance comes out to be commentary on the nature of theory as such.[19]

Consider once again, then, the Benamou/Caramello reading of contemporary performance, poised somewhere between presence and play and fighting or giving in to what Derrida calls that "desire for centrality," which no one seems able to avoid. What McCaffery's audience experienced was a slippage between the figure of McCaffery, who claimed to disappear into his impersonation but never did so completely (that claim was among the wilier of his ironic moves), and the figure of the Chinese ventriloquist, who shared many of the concerns we have seen elsewhere in McCaffery but was never fully him or any other. If we want to call the figure in the kimono "Steve McCaffery," we also have to acknowledge that he was at once speaker and instrument, ventriloquist (however disguised, it was his own voice coming out of the machine—whatever "his" and "own" might mean in this context) and dummy. He mouthed as all dummies are made to mouth, so that what he was holding was a wooden image of himself, a metaphor that is also synecdoche for all such empty voicers.

And yet how empty after all, how wooden after all? None of the audience went up on the stage and kicked the figure standing there but none of us

19. Sometimes McCaffery's performances play out specific theoretical issues, in part, surely, because of their celebrity status and therefore their status as public performance. One of his best performances along these lines is *Of Grammatology*. It is in two parts: in the first, called "The Reading," he climbs a short ladder and spills out onto the floor, from a large paper bag, a number

had any doubt that he was a flesh-and-blood figure going under the name of Steve McCaffery, standing there live and costumed in front of the audience, holding a conventional ventriloquist's dummy who was, from this point of view, the only blockhead around.

Is that what Benamou and Caramello mean by "presence" in their argument for the undecidability between presence and play? It would seem so, and that leaves room for the late modernist arguments of Schneemann, Rothenberg, and Antin about the potency of up-frontness in any performance. Yet (and we return to a distinction we saw before) the centrality they assume to be part of every performance cannot be "sited" in McCaffery's performance, any more than it can in the mask on the cover of *North of Intention.* For McCaffery this has to mean, again, presentness without presence; and that means that the comments about the undecidability between play and presence have no ultimate point because the only play around is the play of difference, an infinite play inhabited by absence. Given McCaffery's passion for geographies we can see it another way: difference is ultimately spatial, which means ultimately cartographical (in a highly specialized sense that involves elaborate tracings); but the maps it makes show little but those broad dark holes that mark the unsitable.

What kind of erotics is possible in these holes which deny all but their own illimitable absence? What kind of Eros do we find when only difference can be found? The Chinese ventriloquist promised culture-confirming pleasure but ended with an excess of absence that spilled over in the sort of *jouissance* that responds to black holes. Is the ventriloquist, then, the subject of Eros or is he Eros himself, the one who pushes and prods until the erotics works itself out? The excess that he ended with happens as much to him as it does to his audience, just as the speaking-through he is speaking of happens as much to him as to his audience: he too is one of those "dummies in the form of bodies already written and already spoken." Where, then, is the source of authority, the position of that which does the ultimate speaking? We can only inhabit the spaces that its indexes inhabit, a pointing that never ceases and never gets anywhere, however much one moves in the direction indicated. Taking these issues in terms of absolute authority, of the ultimate Eros, the narratives implicit in the McCafferyan mode sound more and more (at this late point in postmodernism, when perspective

---

of pieces of cereal, Post's "Alpha-Bits." Taking off his shoes and socks, he spreads himself on the pieces of cereal and crushes them, grunting and making barking noises. In the second part, "The Writing," he puts more Alpha-Bits in a cereal bowl, pours in milk and begins to eat them with a spoon, all the while talking in sounds that only occasionally emerge as words.

becomes possible) like the narratives explicit in Kafka, in texts like *Before the Law* and, particularly, *The Castle*. The extraordinary McCafferyan wit seems more and more infused with the sort of chill we have felt (it is inseparable from Kafka's erotics) in some of the greatest of the high moderns, where presentness without presence is not simply a possible mode but the underlying one, that which speaks and through which all the rest is spoken.

One of the attendant ironies lies in what this does to irony. Classical irony is duplicitous, twofold in all sorts of sense. In order for such irony to work, something has to be visible through the ironic mask, something peering upward through the cracks to announce the "true" meaning, what is "really" intended. What happens when there is, behind the mask, only the bleakest of whiteness or, alternatively, the possibility that something is there and the impossibility of knowing whether and how we shall encounter it, whether all that we shall encounter is those who claim to see more? Kafka offers the possibility of incompletion, McCaffery its certainty, and whatever their considerable difference (it is one of the radical differences between modernism and postmodernism), the effect on classical irony is essentially the same. In either case such irony can never consummate; it must remain hanging, suspended, unresolved. If McCafferyan Eros eventuates in its appropriate *jouissance*, that absence of which it is the excess can only continue to confirm itself, continue, therefore, to keep classical irony perpetually impending, never finally fulfilled. In fact, much of the effect of McCaffery's proper irony lies in what his work does to classical irony. If his Eros completes itself, the Eros of this version of classical irony does not; it is forever without *jouissance*. McCaffery's ironies are accomplished in conditions different from those that classical irony expects. His ironies abut Kafka's in that they emerge from the discrepancy between expectation and actuality. That discrepancy creates distinction and therefore difference and makes a book a piece of "sado-erotic machinery," the erotics of the book based partly on the materiality of its surface, partly on the outcome of difference. In direct contrast to the conditions of classical irony, McCaffery's finds its climax in the completest incompletion. That unresolvable interplay of ecstasy and lacunae defines the tenor of McCaffery's work and sets its sounds, its conditions, the contours of its bliss.

5

Presence and Its Discontents, 2: Performing Photographs

In 1980 Steve McCaffery published a series of ten short pieces called *Scenarios*, printed offset onto a card folded twice.[1] Here is the final piece:

> *The Dark Bar Scenario* (based on Exodus 33:20–23)
>
> a man backs into a dark bar with a brown paper bag on his head. the rest of his body is naked.
>
> in the centre of the floor is a large stone over which the man trips.
>
> the stone, too, is inside a brown paper bag.

At the back of the pamphlet McCaffery argues that these pieces "are best considered as short movie scripts or intermedia texts falling between the

---

1. *Scenarios* (Toronto: League of Canadian Poets, 1980).

categories of motion picture and poem." In this context "intermedia" means something more than "hybrid," just as "text" means something more than "script" or "poem" separately.

Taking this piece as a poem, one can read it to an audience, as I have heard McCaffery do to considerable effect. Obviously intensely readerly it behaves like a poem, lending itself to understanding in all sorts of modes, centripetal inspections of the materiality of its surface, more formalist explorations of its paradoxes and ironies. Scenarios, on the other hand, do not ordinarily get written or read as language poems or new critical poems, Michael Palmer's or Robert Lowell's. Scenarios are ordinarily outlines of intent, blueprints for action, suggestions about a series of moves to be made. The scenario emphasizes the gestures to come, not the description of those gestures, prospective actions, not immediate textures. Yet these comments are clearly too categorical and binary to contain *The Dark Bar Scenario*: the mode and the text resist such narrowing-in. The vulnerability of the figure—unseeing, naked—the darkness of the bar, the large stone that threatens (but how can stones threaten?) and is as unseeing as the man (but how could stones be seeing?) combine into a mode at once minimalist and conceptual, dada and haiku, stressing haiku's capacity to set off limitless reverberations out of the brief and elemental, stressing performance's capacity to realize the palpable suggestions of darkness, the feel of the blinded stone. This text is not just situated *between* poem and scenario but is simultaneously each, and it is not just a pairing of genres that partake of aspects of each but something that arises when each speaks to the other, educates the other, becomes the other. Not poem or scenario, then, but (here we need three-dimensional inscribing) poem-as-scenario, scenario-as-poem, circling like a Möbius strip.

And that only begins to outline the complexity of this text. Given that this is a piece by Steve McCaffery one can expect it to deal with temporal questions and specifically with obsessions about presentness and presence. Language, for McCaffery and others, is always in part (perhaps largely) retrospective. Yet scripts, as outlines of intent, point always to gestures whose presentness we shall be coming into and not leaving behind. For some artists—Carolee Schneemann up-front in unequivocal being, Jerome Rothenberg at the point of chanting his poem, David Antin at the stage of improvisatory performance—such gestures epitomize the full immediacy of the moment and its participants, extolling the indissolubility of presentness and presence. McCaffery's scenarios, on the other hand, not only inhabit absence but foresee a presentness to come, acknowledging the

inexorability of difference while embracing all differences. Given such ironies we can understand how *The Dark Bar Scenario* suggests that poems and
scenarios are alike in their need for enactment, that each is a kind of script
in that each needs an enactor to realize its potential (or at least one possibility within its potential). That the same could be true of texts generically
may well be part of what emerges from the McCafferyan scenario.[2]

Alternatively, we can take this as a reading of one kind of poem, David
Antin's for example. Antin has spoken of the written versions of his talk-
poems as "notations or scores of oral poems," which appears to put those
pieces in line with McCaffery's scenarios.[3] Scores and scenarios are each a
kind of script, the metaphor of "score" widely accepted, the umbrella of
"performance" covering all realizations; and yet there are needling subtexts
that ought to undo some of this comfort, certainly any associated with the
equation of Antin and McCaffery. Of course the texts of each are, at once,
poem and score, Möbius strips that refuse such distinctions and keep the
kinds incessantly circling. But that is to take the comparison of Antin and
McCaffery at its most general level. Once we get beyond that stage they
diverge rapidly, together sketching a map that illuminates much of the
geography of presence and its discontents. Those differences have to do
with more than matters of length or even the look of the page, Antin's
explorations of space. The pieces in Antin's *tuning* and *talking at the boundaries* are records of what was said. McCaffery's *Scenarios* are indications of
what could be done and, concomitantly, said. We are never invited to act
out an Antin piece as we are a McCaffery. As McCaffery puts it at the end
of his commentary on *Scenarios*: "The artistic deal is this: as author i'll
provide the film if you promise to provide your own camera. Alternatively
we can both perform them separately." Antin's pieces were never invita-
tions; and if there is an important sense in which we are expected to
participate in an Antin performance, our place within it is firmly specta-
torial, our own positioning fixed *and* requisite as we observe his working-
out of certain possibilities within the conditions that prevail. We are among
those conditions. The McCafferyan scenario has a good deal in common

2. At this point McCaffery and others link up to theorists with whom they would seem to
have little in common. Wolfgang Iser, for example, argues for texts as scripts that need to be
finished by the individual reader, the openness of the text's potential apparent from the uniqueness
of each separate reading. See "The Reading Process: A Phenomenological Approach," in *New
Directions in Literary History*, ed. Ralph Cohen (Baltimore: Johns Hopkins University Press, 1974),
125–45. Of course this is what we hear from Barthes throughout.

3. *talking at the boundaries* (New York: New Directions, 1976), v.

with what Antin has said to be the extent of his preparation: Antin says that he comes to his performances with nothing more in mind than the sort of outline with which one enters upon a Mozart cadenza. This means that the Antin texts we finally come to read are, in general, records of past events, transcriptions of an activity (I say "in general" because he sometimes redoes the words of his performance). Further, they are, as records, necessarily incomplete. They can only suggest what happened, much of which escapes even the taped version of the talk. Antin's "scores" act, then, like the photograph of a performance, incomplete, imperfect, but history all the same, working as an index that points to what can never be reproduced. If Antin speaks of the score as a "notation," it is so in the sense that transcriptions of a Louis Armstrong solo are notations, memoranda after the fact and for history. "Score," then, means for Antin the equivalent of the photograph as record, whereas "scenario" means for McCaffery suggestions of possibility.

Some of the slipperiness of these issues emerges in the work of Allan Kaprow, Antin's colleague in San Diego, inventor of Happenings and constant commentator on the meanings of those and related modes. In several early remarks Kaprow, sounding much like Antin, said that performances are unrepeatable. "Happenings," Kaprow argues, "should be performed only once," in part because so much in them is due to chance; in part because so much of their material—newspapers, food—is perishable; in part, finally and most important, because to repeat them is to compromise the concept of Change.[4] To violate that concept is, in effect, a metaphysical error. As Kaprow puts it earlier in the same essay, reality is to be understood as "constant metamorphosis," the universe radically "non-fixed, organic" (169). What this means for the Happening as representation should be clear enough: not only is the Happening microcosmic but its nature argues unequivocally that representation is entirely possible, that its gestures and events can mimic the nature of things. Behind this assertion one hears the early romantic notion of the artist as God's imitator, the surrogate maker of the model cosmos. He fashions fabrications that show him central, single, and potent in a way that comes down through all modernisms. (Antin finds this notion so discomfiting that working out his uneasiness becomes central to his art.)

4. *Assemblage, Environments and Happenings*, ed. Allan Kaprow (New York: Harry N. Abrams, 1965), 192–94.

And yet, just after his categorical statement about the uniqueness of each Happening, Kaprow (perhaps concerned with the implications of his metaphysics) seems willing to forgo the idea that all Happenings can happen only once. He sees a compromise in which there is both repetition and difference, difference that is, at once, inexorable and controlled: "Nevertheless, there is a special instance of where more than one performance is entirely justified. This is the score or scenario which is designed to make every performance significantly different from the previous one" (194). Here and elsewhere in *Assemblage* Kaprow quotes instances of such texts from the Fluxus artist George Brecht. In the early and mid-seventies Kaprow did a series of his own that he called "Activities."[5]

Take, for example, *Routine,* one of the Activities published in chapbooks in the early and mid-seventies.[6] *Routine* consists of an introductory comment and five sections, each with a script that is framed, top and bottom, by illustrative photographs, "how-to" images designed to complement/supplement the written text (Fig. 3). Note the photographs above and below this text.

The upper photograph is of two figures, a black man and a white woman, standing on a sidewalk perhaps five yards apart; she is holding the long mirror in which he sees himself reflected. The perspective is intense, the man's shadow lengthy and slightly diagonal to the thrust of the sidewalk. The lower photograph is shot straight down the sidewalk; the figures are now much further apart, no one is casting a shadow, the reflection of the man is no longer visible in the long mirror. Questions of symmetry, visual and generic, questions of representation and therefore of presence, play around these images even more subtly and dramatically, than they do around the text, which appears to bear the influence of George Brecht's Fluxus scripts. Kaprow's commentary, printed at the front of the chapbooks, details the realization of the idea of *Routine,* "the first of three related Activities with the same title," each alluding to "the deadpan stylizations of vaudeville routines, and to routinized behavior in everyday life." Its sixties-ish combination of didacticism and group self-help ("Several couples actually thought

5. For an overview of the Activities, see Jonathan Crary, "Allan Kaprow's 'Activities,'" *Arts Magazine* 51 (September 1976): 78–81.

6. Kaprow published *Routine* himself in 1975. It was sponsored by the Portland Center for the Visual Arts in Oregon. A photocopy of the chapbook, along with photocopies of other Kaprow Activities, appears in *Performance Anthology: Sourcebook for a Decade of California Performance Art,* ed. Carl E. Loeffler and Darlene Tong (San Francisco: Contemporary Arts Press, 1980), 159–64. The anthology contains important material on Kaprow, including a substantial bibliography of his writings.

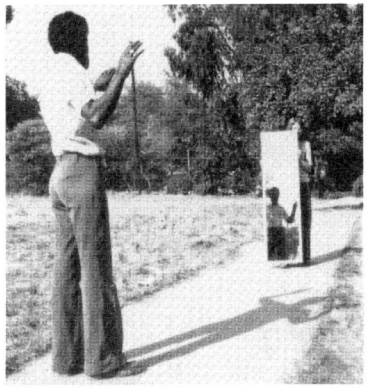

1

standing somewhere
facing a friend holding a large mirror

trying to catch one's reflection

signalling to tilt the mirror variously
until the reflection is caught

both moving apart a few steps
repeating process

moving apart again and again
repeating process
until it's no longer possible
to see oneself

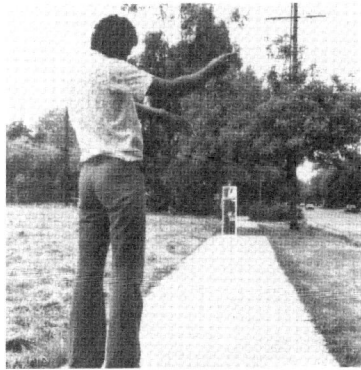

Fig. 3. Allan Kaprow, from *Routine*. Photographs
by Alvin Comiter

they got to know each other better. A few rediscovered an ancient way to flirt") dates the performance in ways that flesh out the temporal ironies shot all through *Routine*. Suggestions of other aspects of those ironies appear in the prefatory comment on the photographs. The photographs here do not document *Routine*. They were made and assembled to illustrate a framework of moves on which an action or set of actions could be based. They function somewhere between the artifice of a Hollywood movie and an instruction manual. The pictures explain the words as the words explain the pictures. Thus the conversion of an event into an exhibit or magazine article becomes a species of mythology.

Kaprow's comment about the function of the photographs recalls McCaffery's comment that his *Scenarios* "are best considered as short movie scripts or intermedia texts falling between the categories of motion picture and poem." If the lines between Antin and McCaffery appear, in part, in their linking of related modes, those between Kaprow and McCaffery not only establish other links but suggest some complicated relations between late modernist explorations of the conditions of presence and those drawn out by the purest postmodernism.

Kaprow's "mythology" seems to mean that these photographs illustrate something that, in pure Aristotelian fashion, could possibly happen. They are, that is, scenarios, scripts of credible events. Yet they inhabit more than potential because these photographs, like every other, are indexes to history, suggestions of old gestures that can never again occur. And that makes the function of any photograph within a Kaprow Activity a more complicated affair than any simple reading of modernism, early or late, can comfortably handle. If these photographs, like all others, are records of irrecoverable events, they are also examples of how the acts the text suggests can be worked out in performance. That is, they are, at once, notations of the onetime and suggestions for the future, images of the past definite (this happened in this way, whatever the limitations of any photograph's credibility) but also images of the conditional (these are circumstances in which one could do these things; these things are models of their kind). Nothing in Antin or McCaffery works exactly this way, yet given McCaffery's reading of language as already spoken, there is much that could be aligned between his packaging of the pre-uttered and the potential and Kaprow's own packaging of that same curious syntax, a patterning of language which combines moods and tenses in ways that ought to make us more uneasy than they do.

To put it another way: these photographs function not only as records but as elements in what Kaprow calls "an instruction manual." He speaks of *Routine* as having "the artifice of a Hollywood movie," meaning, most likely, that it is "staged," made up for the manual. Yet in order to stage these images the participants had to act out what the text suggests, a condition which sometimes makes it difficult to tell whether the photographs in a Kaprow Activity are intended as images of what actually took place or as performed suggestions of a way it could come about (of course if they are the latter they are the former as well). Some of the published Activities, *Satisfaction*, for example, contain patently staged photographs of suggested group activities.[7] *Echo-logy*, on the other hand, offers not only the text of a performance involving a group passing mouthfuls of water and silently mouthed words down a stream but also what is patently a photographic record of that Activity being performed.[8] In an Activity like *Testimonials*, which asks partners to "scrape, press, daub and print their marks on the environment" and on each other, the photographs show them doing precisely that, leading to what I have just described as "performed suggestions," which do what they tell us to do in showing us what to do.[9] In every one of these cases some version of the events has to occur in order for the photograph to show how they could occur (a condition which ironically recalls the necessity for something to be there so that a photograph can happen). In a Kaprow Activity enactment is inescapable. Past, present, and future are linked in uncommon ways that this particular package of text, photograph, and potential performance seems especially designed to bring off.[10]

And yet "especially designed" may not put the point properly, for such a package could get in the way of all sorts of other questions that an art like Kaprow's is seeking to work out. Consider his understanding of the nature of the Happening. In a statement printed in Michael Kirby's *Happenings*, a seminal collection of comments and scripts, Kaprow speaks of his own work as conceived on four levels: "one is the direct 'suchness' of every action, whether with others, or by themselves, with no more meaning than the sheer immediacy of what is going on. This physical, sensible, tangible being is to me very important."[11] The other levels include, second, their being "performed fantasies"; third, their being "an organized structure of events";

7. Kaprow published *Satisfaction* himself in 1976.

8. *Echo-logy* (New York: D'Arc Press, 1975).

9. In Loeffler and Tong, *Performance Anthology*, 215–18.

10. "Fiction" is a hard term in these contexts, and enactment is inescapable; yet Kaprow is fully aware of the photograph's capacity to deceive, as he shows in *Take-Off*. See Crary, "Allan Kaprow's Activities," 79. For a quasi-Michalsian comment on the photograph as dream, see Kaprow, *Assemblage, Environments and Happenings*, 21.

11. *Happenings: An Illustrated Anthology*, ed. Michael Kirby (New York: E. P. Dutton, 1965), 49.

and fourth, their having a "symbolic or suggestive sense." This sounds very much like Dante's four levels of meaning or Blake's fourfold vision. In Kaprow's case the hierarchy rests on an immediacy of the sort we have seen in Carolee Schneemann and can see in performers as different in "smoothness" as William Wegman and Spalding Gray. It is the unequivocal up-frontness endemic to every late modernist understanding of the nature of performance, the radical stratum on which such performance rests and from which it develops. Kaprow elaborates on his reading of that stratum elsewhere in his work and at several points in an interview with Richard Kostelanetz.[12] He spoke to Kostelanetz of his attendance at a class run by John Cage, which he went to in order to "find out how to use tape machines"; but he "found taped noise too abstract and needlessly detached from action" (105; consider that comment in terms of the work of Antin, not to speak of McCaffery). Later he says of his shift from abstract expressionist work to three-dimensional assemblage: "I wanted more tangible reality than it was possible to suggest through painting alone. I wanted above all to be literally part of the work" (107). Still later, in a remark that Clement Greenberg, otherwise very different, would understand in his own way, Kaprow says that he rejected "too simple a ritual base" because "rather than have a presence that is blinding, it betrayed its source. You may later analyze and appreciate all the sources of this or that; but while it is going on and being conceived, it must seem overwhelmingly present—be itself, not *about* something else" (129). The Happening, like the formalist work of art, must, it seems, have a self-presence that awes. It must be about itself and therefore without reference, autonomous and centripetal, ultimately autotelic. This is Kaprow's clearest statement about the radicality of presence, its placement at the point of origin as that point's sovereign trait.

What, then, to do with a piece like *Poses,* a set of seven cards, each with two or three photographs and dated March 22? They come in a standard plain manila business envelope. On both the envelope and the first card is a text describing the events of the performance:

Carrying Chairs Through the City

Sitting Down Here and There
Photographed
Pix Left on Spot
Going On

12. Richard Kostelanetz, *The Theatre of Mixed Means: An Introduction to Happenings, Kinetic Environments, and Other Mixed-Means Performances* (New York: Dial Press, 1968).

The text on the cover concludes with "Note: occurred in and around Berkeley, California, March 22, 23, 1969." In each of the photographs someone sits on a chair that appears, among other places, on a pedestal, in the fork of a tree, in a parking lot, on a boxcar. The photographs on the cards are clearly records of the performance; nothing about them suggests that they are, like the photographs in *Routine*, representations of mere possibility. Some of the photographs are marked "photo: Allan Kaprow," whereas Kaprow appears in others as a photographed performer. His role, then, would seem to be alternately active and passive according to his relation to the lens or, from another perspective, active in two ways, in one of which he works only as historian.

And yet in this pre-Activity (it is "pre-" because the photographs are not designed to show "how-to") Kaprow divulges some of the complexities he was to encounter in the Activities. It is not the photographs of the performance that open the complexities up but others that appear within those photographs. Recall the line of the text that says "pix left on the spot." A number of these photographic records include among their contents a photograph pasted down somewhere within the recorded scene, the side of a pedestal, the railing of a wharf, a railroad track. In most cases the word "photo" is written on the surface of the recording photograph. An arrow inscribed on the surface points to the recorded photograph, that which is pasted down within the photographed scene. One of the photographs of a scene shows Kaprow's Lee Friedlander-like shadow spread out on a plaster of concrete surface. An arrow drawn on the photograph with the words "my shadow" attached points to the image of Kaprow's shadow, while another arrow with the words "photo where chair was" points to the image of a pasted-down photograph. A shadow within the scene takes a photograph of a photograph, the whole a parody of Platonic caves and all that other play about the distance among beds and their images and models. Kaprow changes the furniture and drops the matter of transcendent models but the play remains the same. As photographer of the performance he records a moment of presence that has pastness pasted within it. Yet the pastness imaged by the photographs within the photographs is not at all neutral: the content of the pasted-down images shows them to contain records of a previous stage of the performance, one that we know about only through what those minuscule images show. Consider, then, what it means when we use the photographs in the chapbooks as indexes to recover the various stages of the performance. The indexing begins with the photographs on the cards we are holding, those which make up *Pose*, and continues with the photographed photographs to which the arrows point. We are set on a *mise en abyme* that has as much chance of concluding as the Möbius strip that figures the workings of a McCafferyan scenario. And yet there *is* a kind of arrest, for in an important sense the plunge into deeper degrees of difference and absence is temporarily checked when the photograph pasted on the boxcar or wharf rail is seen to be part of the performance recorded in the photograph on the card; seen to be, that is, part of the up-front presentness that Kaprow has always argued to be the essence of performance. The pasted-down image of an absent gesture was as much a part of those actions around Berkeley as the chair on which the performer sat or, indeed, his act of sitting. Yet to be most precise we have to say that the image was part of the second stage of the performance: what it records is that first stage, which we can get to only through this image within an image, this history become history.

It should be clear that Kaprow is arguing a scheme quite similar to that which Antin develops in the move from talk to tape to text. And like any version of this situation in Antin, *Pose* opens up a discourse that finds it necessary to counter the claims of immediacy with that which figures its contrary; but it is obvious that the discourse in *Pose* also finds it necessary to counter the potential smugness of the locus of absence by making it take part in the purest sort of immediacy. Carolee Schneemann managed to make a place for the claims of the secondary without permitting it to become (or pretend to have become) the primary. Kaprow was less refractory because he grew fascinated with the claims of the photograph and sensed something of what those claims could do to his own bedrock positions. At the least they reveal the dark holes that threaten the comfort of late modernist up-frontness, especially its comforting feeling that it has closed within itself, only itself.

Pose, then, represents the transition from Happenings to Activities. If it has little of the Activities' openness to possibility (the whole is clearly rendered in a past definite, the photographs of the performance claiming to be nothing more than a record), it complicates the claims of presence in a way that defies much of what Happenings mean. *Pose* and the resultant Activities historicized the Happening, which is not to say that they put it out of business but that they put it into a context of other possibilities and went on to explore that context.

At the same time *Pose* complicates the question of the photograph, opening up its potential for a *mise en abyme*. Any such breaking-down of boundaries sits ironically with an art form that begins in a tightly enclosed box and ends on paper that is usually sharply framed. Kaprow seems to have sensed that paradox, much as Duane Michals did early on in his work, and though Kaprow did not explore the paradox's potential to the degree that Michals continues to do, he saw where it could go within the framework of what he had done, how that framework could be undone by the photographic frame. And indeed that Michals turned these issues into photographed performances shows his own understanding of what Kaprow was working out. The performative elements in the photographs of Jo Spence and John Coplans take these issues in directions different from those pursued by Michals and Kaprow, though every one of these figures has some essential relation to every one of the others.

Kaprow does not do in *Pose* what some of these others do in their work, turn the question of performance and photography into a question of "performing photographs"—taking "performing" with all its grammatical ambiguities (adjective? gerund? these and probably more?) and therefore with all the uncertainties in the stance of the subject. In *Pose* he brings out with unmistakable clarity a binary claim essential to any modernism: performance as read in modernism emphasizes the pure immediacy of the moment, whereas photography as read from the days of the daguerrotype emphasizes the irrevocable pastness of the content of the image. Put in such neat packages these issues fashion a shapely oxymoron that continues as long as the modernist argument for the coherent subject at work in the immediate moment continues its dominance. The shapeliness further continues as long as there is a distinction between, say, Kaprow as recorder and Kaprow as subject of the record; that is, between the same person as historian and as performer. Of course there is an important sense in which the images in the Activities are performative photographs (photographs which are, at once, performed and pre-performative, exemplifying "how-to"); but that is not the same as the far more difficult question of the photographer as performer, a question that defines much of the photographic work that inhabits the murky area between modernist explorations and that of artists like Steve McCaffery. Lucas Samaras, for one, has undone the precision of the distinctions between the photographer and the performer, whereas Sophie Calle redoes the implications of late modernist work in ways that take it in directions only its subtexts have envisioned. The tightness of the oxymoron starts, then, to give way, fissures appearing not only in its facade but in its base as well; and yet such suggestions of statuary are much too monolithic, too rounded and monumental, to pin down Calle's ironies or even the experiments in performing photography of figures like Duane Michals. In fact, some of the best of Michals's performances ironize monumental issues.

II

Michals is one of his own most frequent subjects, undisguisedly his contemporary self, whatever the purported condition of the persons he depicts. Indeed, one of his projects is to make certain that we notice him playing a role—which (to complicate the issues in ways that must delight him) is sometimes himself at a stage of his life he has not yet lived through. Whether he or some other is the subject of his impersonation, part of the point of the self-projection is for us to see the Other through and because of his image. In *Duane Duck,* for example, he uses his own head and hands, up-front in the photograph, to shape the image of a duck projected against a wall by light coming from off camera.[13] Not only shaper but shadow, he is outside and within the image he shapes, seed and subject, autobiographical in a way no single category can control. The image is as much a refusal of pigeonholes as an assertion of possibility. It continues that refusal in a sly, sardonic play of self-reflexive irony, extending our understanding of the meaning of "self-projection" by showing a literal example of himself projecting himself. Making a pun performative, he turns the metaphor of self-projection into an *act* of self-projection, reifying a figure that informs much of his work.

His actions in *Duane Duck* have further subversions in mind. Part of their ultimate intent is to free the image from those multiple "boxings" that dog every photograph. We know that modern performance, at least since Hugo Ball, takes much of its impetus from a disgust with the concept of the artwork as object, static, aloof. Forever as it was at its inception, this object offers itself as, at once, origin and end in a way that Ball would see as stultifying desire. Complementing those objects is the museum, itself an object as well as an institution, a nest of chinese boxes which encloses all such instruments in an isolated, quasi-sacral space. Consider, then, the photograph as a "museum quality" object of art: the open shutter not only gathers light within the box of the camera but ultimately gets that light

13. The photograph is reproduced on the cover of Michals's *Photographs/Sequences/Texts* (Oxford: Museum of Modern Art, 1984).

onto the surface of the square or rectangular photographic image. Insofar as the image earns the label "museum quality" it ends within an enclosing frame placed on the wall of the museum, the last in a set of boxings that is also a chain of metonyms.

Any such succession of boxings counters that radical combination of up-frontness and anti-stasis seen all through modernist claims for performance, what Ball and his legatees saw as the only track for desire. Michals continues the succession of boxings but with his own distinct qualifications, the compulsion to satisfy a special set of desires. Aware of the claims of modernist performance yet partial to the frame in its classic implications (he builds on those implications to define much of his art), Michals seeks to play on several sides at once. He does so in *Duane Duck* by performing a frolic of self-projection within the frame of the photographic image. By multiplying self-projection Michals calls into question not only the contours of self-projection but its origins and ends. Consider, for example, that the maker of the photograph is undefined: Michals might be taking his own picture with an extension bulb *or* someone else might be taking it for him. If he is taking the picture, the meaning of "maker" has to take in that aspect as well. If he is not, the meaning shifts to take in a different multiplicity, a plethora of makers. If he is taking the picture, he is outside and within, seed and subject, just as he is with the image of the duck he projects. What he does, in that case, is create a doubling of himself as maker (and we know how "doubling" relates to "duplicity"). And if he is taking the picture that too results in a plethora of makers. At no time, in fact, can we call any one image, unseen or not, *the* image of the maker, sole claimant to that stance. Consider, too, the puzzle of what it is that is projected, more specifically the puzzle of what of Michals is projected: his head and hands, for certain, but at what point does he stop acting as Duane Michals and become Duane Duck? Or is the concept of stopping too abrupt, too diametrical and boxed, the sameness of the given name suggesting a continuation? Such quizzicalities result in a mocking inability to fix the finality of the act, to keep its contours from dissolving. Desire, it seems, never ceases to be active; it stays open to possibility as long as walls do not cut it off. *Duane Duck* is a play of boxes, explicit and implicit, frangible or firm; indeed, *Duane Duck* is a play *about* boxes, a performance of all manner of relations to enclosings.

Other projective issues appear in *Myself with Feminine Beard*, where Michals's face is superimposed on the image of a woman's crotch, the triangle of pubic hair becoming a beard around his mouth. Whatever the likeness of mode, *Myself with Feminine Beard* emerges as the sardonic contrary to

Duane Duck. Here there are no shadows of Michals transformed into the image of an Other but qualities from the Other transferred to himself. To be more precise, to be more difficult, this move involves a projection from the Other upon an *image* of himself, a turning of the projecting table which turns the image of the would-be *auteur* into a recipient of the results of his own acts. In an important sense Michals is the subject of his own desire: the multiple sexualities in the image extend to the profoundest narcissism, which is no less potent because ironically self-aware. Early on in our reading this image gives up all confining contours and divisions, celebrating, simultaneously, radical similarities of function and polymorphous *jouissance.*

The imagery is Magritte's, the new conception Michals's own.[14] *Myself with Feminine Beard* is a reverent parody of Magritte's *Le Viol*, which, in its various versions, images the head of a woman with breasts for eyes and a crotch for a mouth. In the 1945 version the crotch is hairless. In the 1934 version the crotch has hair, that version clearly the source of Michals's intertextual play.[15] What Michals is after in *Myself with Feminine Beard* is a staging of sexual metaphor, a doubling that figures identity in a coming together of difference. Yet Michals's image is more immediate and personal than Magritte's. There is nothing of the performative anywhere in Magritte, even in the occasional figure with the bowler hat (Magrittean ironies lean heavily on the distancing monumentality of those quasi-self-images). Michals makes the Magrittean model performative, self-conscious, and self-directed, and specifically concerned with the prefix of any terms that begin with "self" and end with some sort of act. Where Magritte's shape is solid, the fusion firm and irrevocable, Michals's is diaphanous and dwells on an interplay of texture and transparency. Michals's image is more playful and more tentative, less sure of itself than Magritte's, more open, more gestural, defining itself as act as much as it defines itself as image. More precisely, it defines this image as a kind of act, sharing none of the Magrittean monumentality, taking in everything that is unstable. (Magritte's awareness of the instability of images takes a very different form.) One clear indication of such assumption of instability is the fact that Michals's title begins with

14. The influence of Magritte goes deep into many areas of Michals's work. For his photographs of the artist and his milieu, see *A Visit with Magritte* (Providence: Matrix Publications, 1981).

15. A variant of the earlier version appeared on the cover of the 1934 edition of Breton's *Qu'est-ce que le Surréalisme:* see Richard Calvocoressi, *Magritte* (Oxford: Phaidon, 1984), 6. Though *Le Viol* has to do with hegemonic readings of the female body, her face turned into her torso, her personality into her person, Michals chooses to ignore that point in his reworking of the image toward polymorphous sexuality. The not-so-subliminal overtones of rape in Magritte's image seem to have escaped, or been ignored by, the Surrealists as well.

a shifter, "myself," one of those words that will couple with anyone who happens to be standing in its place. Michals is up-front but transient, immediate but unfixed, more personal but at the same time querying the stability of that which is personal—a query that begins with questions of gender and has no end because there is no end where shifters are concerned. And yet as the querying goes on, it goes along with, emphasizes, the immediacy of the figure to which the shifter points. Michals once again has it both ways at once. Here, further, he shows that the late modernist self-centering informing so much of his work has sometimes to share the scene with a decentering of the self and its undoing into a subject, his work much more anomalous than it is usually taken to be.

In photographs like *Duane Duck* and *Myself with Feminine Beard* Michals works out on himself what it feels like to be not only the duck but the maker of the shadow that is the duck's substance, not only "myself" as Duane Michals playing with double exposures but what it ought to feel like to have polymorphous sexuality stamped on one's face. But despite the doubling of "Duane" he never entirely fuses himself with the duck: the projection is so arranged to keep them carefully apart. Nor despite the double exposure, does he fuse himself fully with the woman with whom he shares *Myself with Feminine Beard.* After a short exposure to the photograph our eyes and minds adjust to seeing Michals and the woman as distinct and separate images, the adjustment impelled in part by the "logic" we bring into play. That adjustment is accompanied by an open sense of relief as the images of Michals and the woman move apart before us, a relief that his irony knew how to predict and control. Our "undoing" of the linkage is as much a cause of the instability of the image as its diaphanous shapes. In fact our "undoing" shows that instability to be ideological as well as phenomenological. Any argument that Michals works largely in transcendental desire has to cope with the ironies of images like this, which show in their workings the shaky contours of our own most comforting desires, the compulsions of ideology as well as of that which compels ideology.

In 1978 Michals published the photographic record of a commissioned journey to Egypt.[16] The journey's purpose was, openly, to test Egypt on himself, seeking out (largely performative) ways to make contact with the ancients. One of the self-performance photographs, *Self-Portrait Asleep in the Tomb of Merekura at Sakkara,* appears on the cover of *Merveilles d'Egypte* as well as inside. Slumped on the stairs before a portal that appears to

16. *Merveilles d'Egypte* (Paris: Denoël-Filippachi, 1978).

contain a statue, deep in an interior chamber whose sources of light are as mysterious as the inscriptions that surround him, Michals opens himself to a contact that he is likely never to have, putting himself in a position where the dreams within those chambers could work their way into him. As he puts it in his note to the image: "I asked myself what sort of strange dreams one could have in an Egyptian tomb. Perhaps on awaking I would see that five hundred years had flowed by."[17] But no unusual flowing of time appears here or anywhere else, only that seeking to touch and be touched by ancientness that comes out in his comments on the dreams and impels all his performances in this place of the wholly Other. Still, he seeks linking by means of the nature of the acts he performs, seeks ancientness by performing acts as ancient as any. The urge to touch and be touched takes the form of a mode of sympathetic magic: deep in the place of death Michals goes to sleep, playing on the association of sleep and death, becoming like those entombed around him in order, in that fictive becoming, to entice the dreams to appear to him.

In Michals's Egyptian images performance touches on magic, Michals becoming a shaman working his wiles on the local gods. The photograph of Michals asleep in the tomb records a necromantic rite, its subject an attempt to tap *illud tempore*, that time where all time is present; and yet that attempt at absolute presentness is figured in a mode of art that is, by its nature, inimical to presence. Lingering in the background of this and other Michals images is a version of the old feeling that photography is a mode of necromancy, a species of magic that seeks to contact the dead. That dallying with necromancy turns up at a number of points in *Merveilles*, for example in one of the final sequences, *Ritual Fire at Luxor*. At Luxor as at Sakkara Michals seeks to touch an absence whose indexical remains are forcefully, massively present. Trying once again to conjure up the old gods through sympathetic magic, he enters the mise-en-scène as all that its other elements are not, alive and immediate, the outsider holding a newspaper whose language is not his own; and it is through this assertion of difference, especially his presence in this scene that speaks otherwise mainly of absence, that he seeks to bring his difference to meet the difference of the wholly Other. Difference is everywhere in these images, as are all manner of puzzles about its relation to immediacy. Putting a newspaper into this scene puts into this place of the lost Other as crass an instance of the temporary and immediate as the postdynastic world can offer; that putting, of course, is

17. Ibid., 100.

ironized by the foreignness of the language, foreign not only to Michals but to the spooks that surely inhabit this place (difference and absence are so multiple in this scene that they threaten a *mise en abyme*). All that putting of persons and papers turns this scene into the stage of an oxymoron, its components on the one hand the temporary/temporal figures of Michals and the newspaper, on the other the massive indexical fragments of old origin, shards that finger the finality of absence.

And as though to make room in the scene for the return of that absence Michals withdraws his own immediacy after the second image, leaving space in the remaining four for the newspaper to burn itself down and, in the final photograph, for all traces of his and the newspaper's presence (impossibly, there is no ash) to have taken themselves away. Michals's performance continues in his absence, is continued *by* his absence, that lacuna as much a part of his performance as the placement and lighting of the fire. Michals makes absence performative; he makes it appear in his postures and their disappearance, in the call that never gets answered, in the photograph that is more than a record because its making is, itself, always a performance of absence.

When Michals performs for his photographs (his presence within them as unquestioned as Carolee Schneemann's in any of her photographs; no McCafferyan ventriloquism here), what he makes performative is a network of what he is not. The resultant multiplicity emerges from a play of radical conditions and not just perspectives on those conditions. That means that we have to take such photographs with something more fundamental than a shift in point of view, subtler and wilier than cocktail-party expectations based on the deceptively fey surface of Michals's work. The "logic" we spoke of in terms of *Myself with Feminine Beard* (the ideological compulsion that causes our minds to separate the images of Michals and the woman) finds an apparent moment of triumph in that prying-apart, the games Michals plays allowing us to win to show us how we have lost. With the Egyptian photographs a species of illogic seems to Michals the only mode to make the point of performing photographs. He goes far beyond the contemporary conventions of mixed media to show that the assumptions of those conventions are largely unexamined, the fullest meaning of mixing seen clearly, cogently, only when mixing is seen as the progeny of illogic. One of its tenets seems to be that no mixing of media can avoid sentimentality unless it knows the essential conditions (conditions in the sense of demands as well as the way things are) of what it brings together; conditions that might result in squawks more raucous than anything that comes out of Laurie

Anderson's violin. The unconsidered result may well be cozy connivings of media that hear nothing of subtextual muttering, or else hear nothing in it. Robert Wilson's *Stations* is, at once, comfy and deaf, comfy because deaf, however much it plays with all manner of frames (windows and especially doors, but also more subtle suggestions of silent films) within the frame of the televised image. Though Wilson never faces the problem of framing up-frontness, or the relations of framing to the Chinese box of frames implicit in a work like *Stations*, it is just such issues that Michals incessantly explores/performs, particularly in the Egyptian photographs where the indexical is the condition from which all exploration begins. What he seeks out is absurdity, yet absurdity is not only that which he discovers but also his mode of exploration. Again he works his way through archetypal business, here that kind which identifies the way and the goal.

Take, for example, *I Build a Pyramid*, a sequence which continues the shamanic-ritual aura (Figs. 4a–4f). Its mise-en-scène is ostentatiously stagy, ancient pyramids as the backdrop, Michals alone up front laboriously building a model of that which stands behind him. That his positioning also recalls friezes of the sort that appear on such remains pulls in conventional intertextual touches, art-historical links; but there are other links as well, for his repeating of those old images is still another version of shamanic reenactment for the sake of making things happen. Stooped over the local stones he performs an abbreviated version of the laborious making that made the monuments behind him, his own immediacy standing in for the ancient presence, his own presence at the scene emphasized by his exertions and, near the end, his departure patently spent. By building as the ancients built, Michals makes his gestures both metaphoric and metonymic, part of their purpose the making of a likeness of the structures behind him, part also the making of a version of the gestures that made those massive indices. Every level of his performance figures attempts at sequence and repetition, not only the sequences *within* the separate acts of building but the sequence *between* origin and echo (the latter also one of the varieties of repetition at work within the scene). The sequences within the acts are different from those between the acts: those within are continuous and effectual and result in the making of the object; those between suffer from all those fractures of history that have compelled this reenactment. That difference establishes and shapes some of the radical ironies that resonate in this scene.

Such moves are shrewdly self-serving. By playing with the possibilities of multiple figuration, by reenacting action and object, by establishing sequence on so many levels of the scene, Michals weaves a web of sympathetic

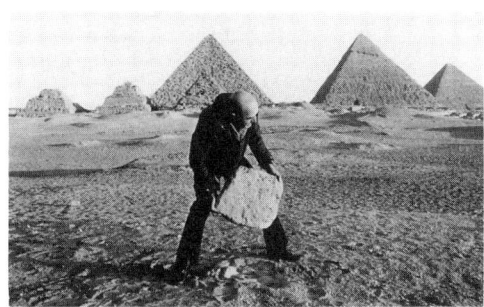

Fig. 4a.   Duane Michals, *I Build a Pyramid 1*

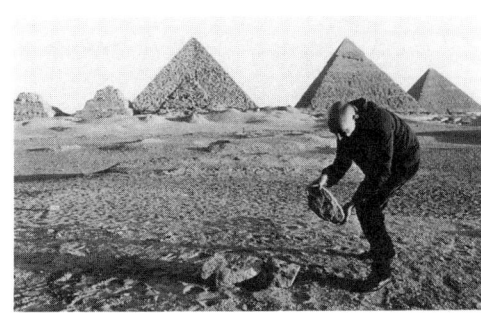

Fig. 4b.   *I Build a Pyramid 2*

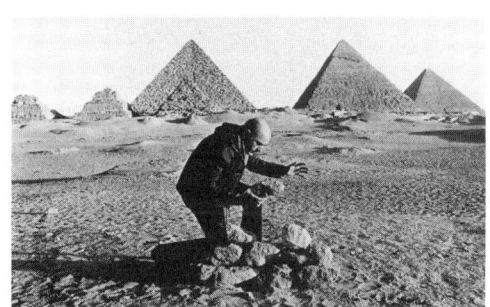

Fig. 4c.   *I Build a Pyramid 3*

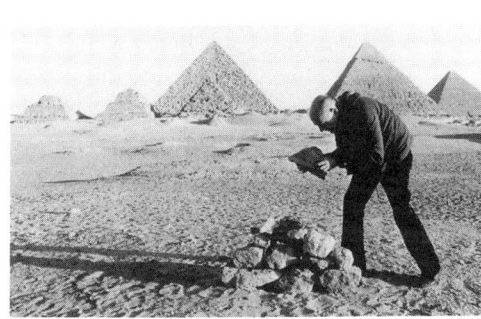

Fig. 4d.   *I Build a Pyramid 4*

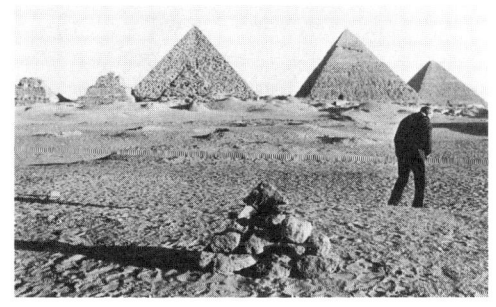

Fig. 4e.   *I Build a Pyramid 5*

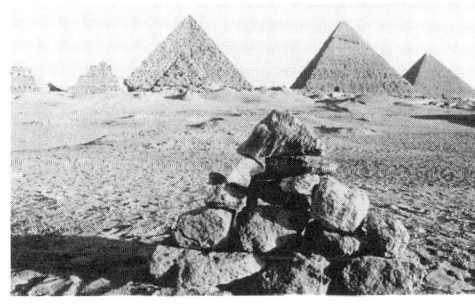

Fig. 4f.   *I Build a Pyramid 6*

magic that seeks to fill in the lacunae between origin and what now passes
for an end. The reenactment does what the ancients did on the soil where
they did it; but it stands for more than those particular acts because it stands
as synecdoche for every similar act, especially but not exclusively the ones
done here at those times. Insofar as he does such things Michals represents
a group; insofar as he represents the group he is necessarily a member. By
performing this ancient making Michals coolly asserts his links to ancient
origins. If the web makes multiple meanings, it also produces multiple effects, not least his canniest attempt to establish the contact he seeks in
such places. His mode of partaking is a version of the continuities Jerome
Rothenberg works on in his ethnopoetic performances.

But *I Build a Pyramid* is more than a mock-up of ancient making. Like
every photograph it is a record that makes history (causes history to be
made) as well as mirrors it. As a mirror of history it seeks to assert that
bridging of the lacunae between his foregrounding acts and the stern eternal
triangles that stud the bare background. As a maker of history it determines
forever how we shall see that seeking. Yet there are other actions involved,
for the sequence also shows Michals as a Minimalist sculptor of the sort (the
early Jackie Winsor, for example) who turns found materials into radical
geometries. He makes things with museum potential that will go away only
when we kick them away. Michals on the sands of Egypt is a Conceptualist
performer who works through a sequence and goes off when the sequence
does; but he is also a manipulator of objects who leaves behind a construction that stands for very much that performance cannot. Still, though there
is a sense in which these very different modes meet in the person of Duane
Michals, they meet as kinds so different that his withdrawal from the scene
splits them irrevocably apart. The final image shows Michals to have disap-
peared but with the object still stolidly there, as stubborn about its status
as the larger and more polished but essentially similar shapes that line the
horizon behind it. Only things remain. Keatsian questions reoccur (the urn
as index and remainder, reminder of old sacrifice) as they do elsewhere
in contemporary performance; and those questions bring us back to the
distinctions Michals suggests among event and object and historicizing image. *I Build a Pyramid* uncovers all manner of aporias in the spaces between
old actions and Michals's reenactments, among the old and new pyramids
and the hustle that made them happen.

Which brings us back to the various claims of the photograph. Given all
the aporias among the acts, among the acts and the objects, among the
objects themselves, the photograph would seem to suggest a reconciling

gesture. It offers a comprehensive feigning, representations that cannot escape representation's dubieties but have at least the virtue of putting all the modes they mimic on precisely the same plane, the plane of visual fictions. Whatever we cannot get—the feel of the performance or its result-ant thing—we can get a set of semblances whose differences have been consumed by the capacity of the photograph to turn everything into itself. The performance and its object finally come together on this neutral black-and-white ground, come together through its voraciousness.

Yet all this benign adjudication falls completely apart when we see *I Build a Pyramid* on the wall of a gallery or even on successive pages of *Merveilles d'Egypte,* within, that is, some version of the framed world. The sequence is then seen as, irrevocably, a set of objects, just as much as the grubby pyramid Michals built onto the scene or the larger, sleeker versions behind it. All the claims of the photograph to reconcile the modes fall away before its status as one more boxed object, its unavoidable difference from any mode of performance, its unavoidable likeness to the things that sit at the scene. That likeness skews the attempt permanently and reinstalls the lacu-nae to the forefront of our seeing. It points out once again that in this context of so much difference there is an ironic affinity that will never go away.

III

The framed world is a boxed world; its boxes are all in a row, and the sequence of its elements illustrate ideology. The photographic version begins with a radical metaphor (*chambre* does the point precisely) and can end in, as we have seen, the frame of a museum image or, another possibility, the rectangular shape of a surveillance file. The connection of those boxings is at least as interesting as any obvious dissimilarity; consider, for example, Mapplethorpe and Cincinatti, as well as the various surveillances we shall see enacted in Vito Acconci and Sophie Calle. If the ends of each possibility are ultimately ideological, so too are their paths to those ends, each emerg-ing from different acts of the same power structure, working at different aspects of its need for self-esteem as well as self-continuation. No user of the camera can shun ideological statements—convictions, compulsions, commitments about ideas and power relations—however private the intent, whatever the motivating desires. Jo Spence has written well on the power elements in the standard mother-child images taken by commercial photographers, while informal family photographs work out the ideologies of the snapshot, often with extraordinary subtlety.[18] Each of these genres of image has ultimately to do with belief and power structures and their enactment in our lives, especially our relations with others—those elements, taken together, which lay the ground for any generic reading of ideology.

Given those elements as determinative, it is clear that the late modernists we have been looking at have been working out versions of classic modernist ideology. Whatever their differences, they continue modernism's emphasis on up-frontness and coherent presence, with all that those conditions entail of the powers of immediacy and of the individual within the moment. (That those powers have extraordinary sociopolitical ramifications—one can do much with the ideologies of "aura"—is relevant to all we have seen, though it will not directly concern us here.) Such powers are enacted within the practices of Stern as collective, Rothenberg as shaman, Antin as spontaneous talker, Schneemann as player-out of the erotics of the primary, and Kaprow as framer of acts of prefigured spontaneity. There are several patent senses in which these aspects of modernist ideology conflict with elements of the photograph's perennial ideology, especially its power to "fix" and therefore its power in regard to the history. (That the latter power is partial and therefore only indexical makes it no less powerful, no less ideological.) Still, those conflicts are by no means diametric or binary: nothing in the relations of modernism and photography can be called either of those. Further, the matter of "fixing" is as much a part of history, an act that occurs in history and that also makes history, as any chant by a Rothenberg or Happening by a Kaprow, even the sayings of the McCafferyan ventriloquist who knows that he (not to speak of his speech) has always-already-happened. If the photograph is "fixed" during the acts in the darkroom, there is no other sense in which that metaphor works as well in any of the other acts connected with photographs.

It is clear that any questions having to do with ideology will also have to do with the audience of ideology, the viewer of the photograph or the performance, the reader of the text. That these questions also have much to do with the situation of the photographer, who is always, at once, both audience and participant, is a matter also worth considering. Such questions finally involve the photographer's stance in relation to reality, history, ideology (and those only begin the sequence of nouns that could follow), as well

18. I discuss Jo Spence at greater length in Chapter 6.

as the photographer's relation to the photographable scene, a point which takes in, in part, what the photograph is supposed to be doing (which is not always the same as what it inevitably does). Take, for example, Kaprow's role in those photographs in *Pose* under which he is noted as their photographer, photographs in which he is not a performer within the scene but a recorder of the scene. In that stance Kaprow appears as documentarian, maker of an image of an ephemeral gesture whose only remaining life is in what the photographer-as-archivist offers. Similar conditions appear throughout Kaprow's work because many of his group performances have only the participants as audience. The photographs of such performances are therefore archival by design, they too approach the character of a transcription of a Louis Armstrong solo (but only approach it because an actual transcription puts the notes in a more or less complete sequence, whereas only a moving picture could record the gestures in a Kaprow performance with a similar narrativity). But the photographs *within* the photographs that make up Kaprow's *Pose* are more than simply parts of the record of that performance around Berkeley on 22 and 23 March 1969. In their opening of a *mise en abyme* they undo the fixity of the fixing of the scene of the performance. They also undo the stability of the stance of the photographer-as-archivist, who ordinarily works in complicity with history to overcome history. That instability undoes all claims for the photographer's unqualified externality to the scene, a modernist myth (think of Weston and Strand) that works in concert with myths of the artist's autonomy and the visual equivalent of what used to be called "la poésie pure." The undoing of that myth makes clear the nature and extraordinary degree of the photographer's involvement. If there is a sense in which that nature and degree shift according to intention (the photograph as record of a family outing, of a mother-daughter scene, of Nijinsky's choreography of *The Firebird,* of Duane Michals's making of a pyramid, of Yves Klein's "leaping" into a street that sometimes has a bicyclist in it, sometimes not), there are other senses in which the photographer's positioning is always the same, though not always recognized as such.

These questions of history and immediacy and the ideologies in which they work (as well as questions similar to those in Kaprow's *Activities* and McCaffery's *Scenarios* about the relation of the work as performed to our perception of its performance) have emerged in the productions of a number of contemporary photographers. They emerge with particular urgency in staged photographs.[19] Such stagings are by no means a postmodern inven-

19. For a number of instances of such work, see Anne H. Hoy, *Fabrications: Staged, Altered, and Appropriated Photographs* (New York: Abbeville Press, 1987).

tion: the staged photograph, with its grounding in performance, has a history nearly coterminous with that of photography as an art. Hippolyte Bayard's 1840 image of himself as self-drawn victim begins what has never ended, Bayard's mode never changing in kind whatever the changes in medium and surface on which the image is recorded.[20]

The relation of performance to contemporary versions of such photographs was acknowledged in an exhibition held at the Photographer's Gallery in London in 1986.[21] Designed to illuminate "the legacy of conceptual and performance art in the context of the directed photograph," the show suggested several of the implications in performance images "specifically constructed for the camera" (7). Artwork, that is, might be found at several stages of the experience, different kinds at different stages. More, then, than a document-making machine, the camera aimed at a performance can make that which is document and artwork at once (7, 11). Though at one point the organizers suggest that the camera is "witness or audience" (11), they argue more persuasively elsewhere that the camera is only a stage in the entire experience, that "we as viewers complete the situation as audience after the fact" (7). Such photographs intend a complicated relationship that asks of the audience a multiple attentiveness. The audience should respond not only to all it will ever know of how the performance went; it should also respond to the image of the performance, which becomes its own breed of artwork in recording the work of another art. This is more than the conventional mixing of media: this is an *encounter* of media that gives rise to a relationship in which mixing will always be tentative, suspicious as well as cooperative, the elements within the mix as likely to come apart as together. It also suggests more complex temporal relations among the audience and the art materials than any single temporal dimension can comfortably hold.

In one of its aspects this distancing parodies modernist readings of performance in terms of up-front immediacies; but it pulls in for parodic inspection other aspects of modernist ideology, especially the romantic-modernist reading of the isolated artist, alone with his work, radically self-sufficient, writing for an audience that can continue into the crowds of those not yet born, who may be more numerous and perhaps even happier. The staged photograph shows a kind of continuation but it also shows the artist's dis-

20. See the beginning of Chapter 7 for more on this photograph and Bayard's considerable relevance.

21. *Photography as Performance: Message Through Object and Picture* (London: Photographer's Gallery, 1986).

tance from his audience to be very different from that envisioned by, say, Rilke in the tower at Muzot. Postmodern performance for the camera draws on the camera's stance as our surrogate, that centering I-Eye built on Renaissance ideas of perspective and therefore on humanist, person-centered positions; but it draws on this anachronistic phenomenology for the sake of a very different positioning/reading that sees every artwork as always-already-happened, untouchable by our immediacies. Laid out in radical definition by Hippolyte Bayard and others that followed him (we shall look at other versions in the Victorian O. G. Rejlander), performing photographs of the sort that Duane Michals makes are so supple that they can take all kinds of ideology into parodic account, leaving none unscathed. That is as good a sign of health as any genre could ask.

Such signs appear nowhere more clearly than in the classic late modernist photograph by Yves Klein that shows him leaping into the air over a Paris suburb street. In the single-issue newspaper *Dimanche*, which Klein published for 27 November 1960, the image is headed "Un homme dans l'espace," underneath it the caption "Le peintre de l'espace se jette dans le vide."[22] In fact this image (surely the best-known performance photograph) appears in two forms. The one in the newspaper shows a train in the background and a bicyclist pedaling away from the scene, unaware of the leap behind him, a patent play on Icarus that Klein surely relished. Another version, less well known, shows no train and no bicyclist, no audience, however unaware, anywhere in sight. (The versions are printed side by side in *Retrospective*, 204.) The intertextual package brought in by the unknowing bicyclist is sufficient to link that photograph to antique ironies and therefore establish the image's claim to be part of a long-standing history. But the bicyclist's disappearance transposes one set of ironies into another. All of the relevant ironies inherent in the difference between the inadvertent tumble of an Icarus and the willful leap of a Klein work subtextually through a sequence in which Icarian arrogance is only part of a far-reaching system. In the image without the bicyclist the Icarian elements shift into the Baudelairian type of romantic-modernist artist practicing his dangerous craft within the confines of a world unaware that he is there. As the subtext's thematic changes so does its incessant rumbling; and yet it is clear that these different readings are not at all incompatible, that the figure who is

22. The front page of *Dimanche* appears in several studies of Klein's work: see *Yves Klein, 1928–1962: A Retrospective* (Houston: Institute for the Arts, Rice University, 1982), 192.

at once Icarus and Shelley as well as undeniably Klein can hold all the facets together in fluent solution.

Those differing textualities confirm what now seems to be the accepted reading of this image, that it is a fabrication, a staged photograph, a montage, and not a "whole" image of an unlikely leap. Yet we know little of Klein if we think such a leap entirely unlikely, though the conditions of its occurrence are surely not what the photograph claims. In elaborate analyses as close to definitive as we are likely to get, Thomas McEvilley and Nan Rosenthal argue for the leap as *partial* fabrication, Klein leaping into a tarpaulin held by students from a judo academy across the street.[23] The ultimate image was put together by two photographers who shot the scene; and in fact there are additional photographs of Klein leaping out into space (not, as he suggested, *up* into space). In an important variation recorded by McEvilley one of Klein's cohorts argue that Klein did in fact make a leap of the sort imaged in the photographs, his intended witness too late to see it (Klein limped for some time after the claimed event), and that he saw no reason to risk his life again, having proven his point (*Retrospective*, 64). The result was a decision to make photographs of a scene that, whatever else happened, never happened in the way the image claims. (Here Klein prefigures Kaprow's Aristotelian imaging of what could have happened.)

All of which makes the image deliberately difficult to fix, a difficulty Klein encouraged by telling conflicting stories about what really happened. In fact, it can be argued that Klein's conflicting stories continue the performance in another mode, his telling of those stories designed to question every self-positioning involved in the making of such art. That questioning has to include the photographers of the scene: since the photographers are arguably actors within the performance, they can be said to be complicit not only in the making of the images but in the furtherance of the performance.[24] Where, then, are the edges of the performance, the places beyond

23. See McEvilley, "Yves Klein: Conquistador of the Void," in *Retrospective*, 19–87, and Rosenthal, "Assisted Levitation: The Art of Yves Klein," in *Retrospective*, 89–135. The business about judo may not be merely tangential: Klein had a fourth-degree black belt in judo, and it has been argued that any judoka at such an advanced level of skill ought to be able to make such a leap safely without a net; see McEvilley, "Yves Klein," 64.

24. A related point about the photographs of Klein's leap has been made by Andy Grundberg: "The photograph is at once the enduring document of an ephemeral artistic event and a collusive element in its execution." See "Conceptual Art and the Photography of Ideas," in *Photography and Art: Interactions Since 1946*, ed. Andy Grundberg and Kathleen McCarthy Gauss (New York: Abbeville Press, 1987), 135. Since Grundberg speaks of a single photograph I take him to be

which it can be said to be *not* happening? Once we enter the world of Klein's leap that question gets difficult to answer; all circumstances are askew. Further, since the positionings include those of the viewers of the image, the point of the performance's ending gets to be equally difficult: does, it, for example, end anew with each viewer? Klein's obfuscations question not only the stability of the performer's positioning (his airborne image puns sardonically on that status) but the stance of the audience as well. They question the audience's stance not only in relation to the performance(s) but to their own subsequent viewing of the photographic record (which one? Icarian? modernist?) of the performance that probably happened. They also question the performer's equivalent of the scene of writing: where did this event happen—given that, as imaged, it never happened that way at all? One could argue that it happened in the dark-room, beyond any audience, when the negatives were cut and spliced. Alternatively, one could argue the possibility I just broached, that the performance concludes only when a viewer contemplates the photograph. After all, the imaged event occurs only in the photograph and every per-formed photograph exists to be seen and the conditions of Klein's leap are reimagined each time the photograph is seen. Klein's suspension images no irresolution (even his claims for levitation imply a conclusion) but, instead, a condition of openness that takes in the stances of everyone involved from the various originating makers of the photograph (each with a different point of origin) to the various viewers, who include everyone who ever contemplated the photograph of Klein's leap. The latter point brings us back to conclusions without conclusiveness. Take any viewer of Klein's photograph at the show of performance photographs at the Photographer's Gallery in London in 1986: each viewer's closure at the gallery was extraor-dinarily delayed; the event was completed by the London viewers some twenty-six years after it "happened." Yet given that Klein's performance had already been concluded at previous contemplations, it is clear that this performance is continually being finished and never will be finished until it is shown for the last time, until the bottom of the *abyme* is reached. Questions of origin and end open lacunas that permit the seeing of nothing but their spaces. Klein puts aporias at every possible outlet of the performing photograph, forward and backward, then, now, and later, involving every participant in every aspect of each art.

---

referring to the image with the bicyclist. The question gets even more complicated with the variants side by side.

No reading of the framed world that seeks to honor its frames can survive a sustained reading of Klein's work on the leap. No honoring of Klein's passion for levitation can survive the ironies that emerge from the result— which, to further those ironies, cannot be thought of as a single, autonomous image but as a package propping a facade that shows, among other things, how much of a facade any claims for wholeness can be. Much of Klein's undoing of such claims comes from the wholeness-breaking ambivalence that pervades his reading of the leap: he confirms *and* parodies all manner of modernist ideologies about power and autonomy and the artist's isolation within the pureness of his product. That he also undoes any audience claims for confirmable, conclusive readings puts into question not only the stances of audience and photographer but the uses of any such image for those aspects of ideology that sustain and further power. Can we effectively use such images to these or any ends when it is difficult to "fix" (the verb seems inescapable) the ending through which one attains such ends? If, as seems likely, all claims for objectivity have long been put by, what sort of motives emerge in performing photographs? How to describe those motives, given not only what we have seen of the varieties of complicity but the ramifications of the personal that obsess artists as radically different as Gerald Stern and Steve McCaffery, Carolee Schneemann and Cindy Sherman? In what sense can we speak of the ideologies of the personal in terms of acts that involve art forms as different as performance and photography, especially when both are brought to work together?

Such questions come into open play in a remarkable pair of performances, nearly eleven years apart, the second an elaborate answer to the implications of the first. In his *Following Piece,* performed on the streets of New York on 7 October 1969, Vito Acconci stood on a street corner until he spotted an interesting person, then shadowed that person for three hours until, perhaps in desperation, the shadowee entered a private place where Acconci could not go.[25] A photographer followed Acconci following his victim (no other noun seems more appropriate), the result a series of images, some from the front, some from the back, of Acconci in close pursuit. A month later, after a three-week series of such outings, Acconci sent out a set of typewritten reports to a small group in the city, the language of the reports a parody of *Dragnet*-style police melodrama:

> At 7:28, he entered the Italian Kitchen, 124 East 14th Street. . . .
> At 8:10, he entered the Academy of Music movie theatre, 126 East

25. For a description and some photographs, see *The Art of Performance: A Critical Anthology,* ed. Gregory Battcock and Robert Nickas (New York: E. P. Dutton, 1984), 183–85.

14th Street. . . . At 10:05, [he] left the theatre, after seeing only parts of both movies; he walked east on 14th Street. . . . At 10:23, he entered a building, 534 East 14th Street, between Avenue A and Avenue B. (183, 185)

Acconci's followee is not in quite the same position as the unknowing bicyclist who turns Klein into Icarus, though there is much of the aleatory in his meeting with his pursuer. He is not entirely the object of an accident at the scene since he did catch Acconci's interest, completing some unexplained expectation on Acconci's part that the passerby's appearance fulfilled. Of course that mocks any claim for the objectivity of the pursuit, since the source of the passerby's pursuable qualities is the pursuer's opinion concerning what identifies this particular passerby as an object to be pursued. And that only begins the mockery, setting the conditions through which we will read every element to follow, especially the ominous tonalities that emerge from the *Dragnet* parody. (Of course those tonalities extend to the photographs intended to confirm the reports and therefore to the maker of the photographs, her shutter-work as complicit as Acconci's pursuit.) Those tonalities enfold a blend of ominousness and irony that is openly Kafkaesque, though more the Kafka of *The Trial* than *The Castle*. There is nothing in Acconci of the cold sublime of *The Castle*, much more of that intensification of the everyday that characterizes the body art of 1969, the ominousness emerging in part through the implicit suggestion that this *is* every day. That suggestion, its ironies, and all the attendant tonalities also extend to the participants. David Bourdon reports that his copy of the report (the one quoted in the text) was entitled "Private Piece for David Bourdon," the "private" here echoing Bourdon's description of how the pieces end when the followee "enter[s] a private place" (185). The irony of the echoes multiplies at many levels: the "private" associated with the person who is guilty because followed (that particular guilt is one of Kafka's essential points) echoes in the privacy of the report sent to the recipients, their alliance figured precisely in Bourdon's quite possibly unconscious use of "private" for both parties. This complicity extends to other aspects of the recipient's role: that the report is private suggests a confidential link between the pursuer and the recipients; and that the pursuer emits prejudice as well as his own paranoia (why pick *this* person rather than another?) taints every aspect of the recipient's participation, since the recipient is clearly considered the pursuer's *semblable* and *frère*.

Of course this is another situation in which a performance is not completed until the participant works out his part; yet what is completed here has as much to do with guilt and the irrational as with the playing out of roles. This piece offers no boxes in which to separate out guilt, no places where it is and places where it is not. Acconci undoes boxings differently from how Klein undoes them; Acconci is more political, more accusatory, more ideological in a way that makes all ideologies as suspect—and probably for better reasons—as the man who walked by the corner where Vito Acconci happened to be standing that day. At that point the boxes of the filing cabinet and the rectangles that go in it echo the boxes of the camera and its own resultant rectangles, that echo arguing for complicities no framing can leave out of the world it seeks to contain.

It is precisely such undoings that begin to take Acconci's performance out of its immersion in Sixties modalities, further than Kaprow was able to go with his photographs within photographs and even the openness of his scenarios. Still, Acconci's *Following Piece* shows no more than a beginning. If he is rooted in the immediacies of Sixties body art, he is rooted even more dramatically in a central and centralizing consciousness, its concord and clout confirmed by its ability to be, indivisibly, pursuer and reporter. But Acconci's refusal of boxings takes its toll on such confidence, putting an inevitable strain on any claims for a single, integral potency that grounds the work. The discourse of *Following Piece,* a primary example of late modernist up-frontness in its body-art phase, actually has within itself a set of conflicting tensions that turn the piece into an exemplary instance of transitional work. It suggests what was to follow in the performance photography of figures like Sophie Calle, the contours of whose art are just beginning to emerge and to define possibilities that take the issues of *Following Piece* into very different modes of enactment.

Born in 1953, Calle has two major printed collections as well as several other sets of images. Despite the comments on the back cover of *L'Hôtel* that she seeks "expériences curieuses, hors du quotidien," it is precisely in the dailiness of the actions she observes that so much of her irony lies (compare Acconci and contrast Schneemann).[26] Note that the dailiness is in the actions she *observes,* not entirely in her own actions. If the dailiness of those actions figures the surveillance that routinely affects our lives, the camera its perpetual tool, her actions depart the diurnal in the intricacy of their positioning. Those actions are, at once, profoundly connected to what

26. Sophie Calle, *L'Hôtel* (Paris: Editions de l'Etoile, 1984).

she observes (whatever the observee happens to know of them), yet distanced in a way that never makes the claims for objectivity of a Lartigue or an Evans. No such claims can characterize a stance and attendant tonality grounded in an observation that seeks to enact surveillance and yet manage intimacy.

In "Les Dormeurs,"performed in April 1979, Calle invited twenty-eight people to sleep, in relays, in her bed for an entire week, while she photographed them at all hours. Because they are sleeping in her bed the observees are always in some relation to her, mirroring, partaking, the relations sometimes implicitly sexual. Her voyeurism is therefore always to some degree narcissistic, always, to some degree, of herself in every scene, echoing the capacity of the photograph to show ourselves as others see us. Yet it is herself twenty-eight times, in twenty-eight different relations, part of the point to question her consistency throughout such conditions. Though she is consistently the voyeur her relations to her object inevitably change as the object changes, her presence and absence never finally demarcatable or separable from each other.[27] Some of the same issues emerge in a 1981 piece called, in its American display, "The Detective," where she has an accomplice arrange for a detective agency to have her followed for a day, with photographs as a record.[28] Calle herself supplies the report, which has little in it of the *Dragnet* tonalities Acconci favored. The notations of the time are followed not only by details of her movements but by her description of places to which she led her pursuer, places that spoke of her life and would help her pursuer to get to know her better. The piece also plays out other, related desires, especially her pleasure at becoming part of his life, at structuring his day. At the end of the report she wonders if he liked her, if he will think of her tomorrow. All of these are ultimately acts of self-confirmation, self-substantiation. They seek to establish her self-coherence, all that the detective's photographs (included in the show) claim of her veracity as a person. If this piece continues the questioning of her self-consistency seen in "Les Dormeurs," it also continues that work's erotics, its quest for intimacy. Here too she is complicitous, though here she performs as

27. Beds and intimacies appear in a different form in a photograph by Calle reproduced in *Perspektief* 30 (November 1987): 71. It is shot from above, showing a bed in a courtyard, the inscription (in English) as follows: "It was my bed. The one in which I slept until I was seventeen. Then my mother put it in a room she rented. On the 7th of October 1979, the tenant lay down on it and set himself afire. He died. The firemen threw the bed out the window. It was there, in the courtyard of the building, for nine days."

28. For text and some photographs, see 13–16 of *Culture Medium* (New York: International Center of Photography, 1989), the catalogue of an exhibition that year.

the fully aware subject/victim who brings the surveillance about (shades of Kafka's comments on the guilt of the pursued).

In *L'Hôtel*, one of her two books, Calle records a performance begun on 16 February 1981, where she has herself engaged as a chambermaid in a Venetian hotel. She sneaks her Instamatic in with her cleaning tools, photographing the bed, the closets, the mess the occupants leave for the maid to straighten up. Here Calle openly plays detective, rummaging through wastebaskets, reading letters (including fragments she pieces together), recording images of rumpled clothes, packages of cigarettes and sanitary napkins, bedside reading, the places where slippers are kept. Seeking to work out lives from intimate detritus she explores indices and their possibilities as fragments for interpretation (at one level *L'Hôtel* is an exploration of deductive method). Her attachments to these people are more subtle and insidious than those in her other performances. She pockets some minor items, uses some perfume, finishes a piece of a croissant left behind—the latter a parody of communion that makes her point plain. She overhears a loud conversation, then listens to the couple noisily making love; but she always deliberately avoids seeing any of the occupants (once she runs into one of "her" people and tries to forget what he looks like). The closest she wants to get is what she finds in a pillow: "l'empreinte arrondie d'une présence" (24) [the rounded imprint of a presence]. *L'Hôtel* offers masterly postmodern play on aura and absence, indices and complicities, the camera and its modes of possible/inevitable participation, the fragmentation of selves and the same sort of self-reconstruction she wanted for herself in "The Detective."

During January 1980 Calle kept up a practice she had been performing for several months, following strangers in the street simply for the pleasure of doing so. She tracked them, noted their movements, photographed them, then abandoned and forgot them. At the end of January she was introduced to a man whom she had followed earlier that day, and he told her that he was leaving for Venice the following day. On the following day so did she. The result was Calle's other book, *Suite vénitienne*, a suite of photographs of her pursuit (*poursuite*; the puns reverberate from the cover on) through the streets of Venice of the man she identifies only as Henri B. (Fig. 5). The photographs are accompanied by a journal that is partly a report, partly a diary in which her italicized comments on her pursuit alternate with her statements about the facts of the situation.[29] Whatever Calle knew of

<hr>

29. *Suite vénitienne* (Paris: Editions de l'Etoile, 1983). It has a concluding commentary by Jean Baudrillard with the English title "Please follow me." The book has been translated by Dany Barash

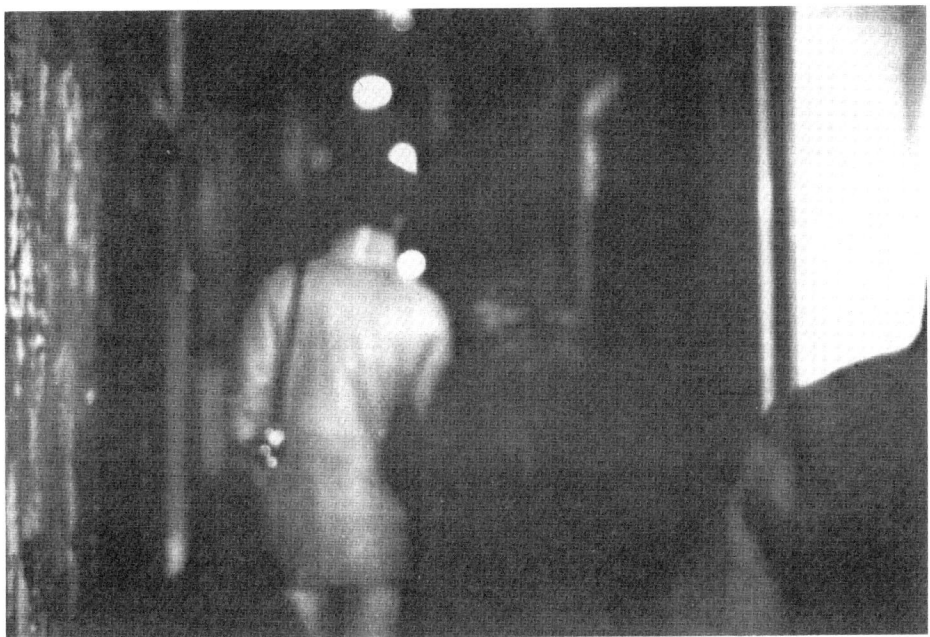

Fig. 5.   Sophie Calle, from *Suite vénitienne*

Acconci's *Following Piece* does not finally matter, however near (it is very near) the resemblance between their work. *Suite vénitienne* continues and comments on Sixties modes of street art and performance photography, enacting a metamorphosis into other modes that honor and reject the pursuits of a dozen years before.

Calle's introductory comments on her tracking of others for the pleasures of the moment describe an act that needs nothing beyond itself; yet it is not at all like a play of Greenbergian pure form since its point is in the pleasure, the gist of the auto-telos being a mode of autoeroticism that comes and vanishes with the act. In fact she explicitly singles out the pleasure and rejects any other attractions: she followed people around Paris "pour le plaisir de les suivre et non parce qu'ils m'intéressaient" ((8) [for the pleasure of following them and not because they interested me]. Calle is equally clear about the self-centering impetus of her desires: the pursuit of others

and Danny Hatfield (Seattle: Bay Press, 1988). For a brief commentary on the work, see Catherine Liu, "La Suite Vénitienne," *Stroll* 4/5 (1987): 42–44.

is the mode through which she solicits present, immediate, fleeting gratification, nothing whatever within it of a regret for the fleetingness. The
masturbatory strain is more than subliminal, the passions more than subtextual. What she does with the notations of the followee's actions or the
photographs she takes is never made explicit, but the photograph opposite
her initial comments, the first in the book, though never identified, is
clearly one of those images. Offered alone, without the attendant report,
it images nighttime floating figures in a dreamscape where light bounces
from the nape of a neck or the side of a building, no element attached to
any other or to any sort of ground. Nothing so surreal, so openly internalized
for satisfaction's sake, will appear in the rest of the book. The book will
shift from autotelic immediacies that echo late modernist up-frontness to
other intentionalities not so easily brought to closure. The ironies that have
her pursuit begin and end at a train terminal (the Gare de Lyon) frame her
acts in a textual box whose contours will always be under threat. The cover
of the French edition prints a counterpart box of *en face* pages, putting
within that box the box of a photographic image. This prefatory gesture
prefigures the framing the text will attempt with its placement of the termi-
nals, but without any suggestions that the attempt might go askew. What
will happen to the text will happen to her passions as well, their autotelism
unsettled along with most other closures.[30]

In fact, Calle's Venetian pursuit differs not only from Acconci's piece but
from her own earlier work in the way she wants to relate to her desire. If
there is a sense in which Acconci's performance concludes when its distanced audience receives a report of what happened, if there is a sense in
which Calle's Parisian pursuits conclude when her feelings predictably fizzle
(their emptiness an expected relief), Calle's earliest reading of her Venetian
passion wants nothing like such endings. Hers was a different sort of passion,
whose pleasure is partly in its own self-sustaining continuation; and that
pleasure exists largely because of the *absence* of that which she especially
fears: "Mon enquête se déroulait sans lui. Sa découverte risque de tout
bouleverser, précipe l'échéance" (22) [My inquiry was going on without
him. Finding him would risk undoing everything, precipitating a conclu-
sion]. For the first time one of her pursuits rides on absence (echoes of old

30. The cover of the American edition does not print part of her Venetian pursuit, but instead,
the introductory surreal image offered as part of her earlier, Parisian practice. This substitution not
only misleads but nullifies all the complexities fostered by the cover of the French edition.

romances and their grails). For the first time fear becomes an element in Calle's erotics, masochism a constitutive strain.

Other absences, fractures, go along with other patterns of feeling to prove the Venetian experience different in kind from similar events. Calle finds out quite quickly where Henri B. is staying and waits in the street, disguised, for him to appear (26). Impatient, going for a walk, she recalls a phrase from Proust about loving someone one is not pleased with, then turns that matter to herself:

> Je ne dois pas oublier que je n'éprouve aucun sentiment amoureux pour Henri B. Ces symptômes, l'impatience avec laquelle j'attends sa venue, la peur de cette rencontre, ne m'appartiennent pas en propre. (26)

> [I must not forget that I have no amorous feelings for Henri B. These symptoms, the impatience with which I await his arrival, the fear of the encounter, do not properly belong to me.]

What the pursuer feels is not a part of her; *she* is elsewhere, the character who feels amorous presumably played by her from a distance, much as Cindy Sherman says she plays out her various enactments. Those feelings, Calle argues, are not hers *en propre*, not properly her own, her property. If we saw her at the beginning cherishing the absence of an ending, we now hear of another cherished absence, that of her who does not love, fear, or feel impatient. The lacunas increase, and do so even more as new feelings emerge. Sitting several hours later on a bench at the Piazza San Marco she watches a boy with a fierce-looking dagger chasing pigeons: "Je me dis que j'aimerais qu'il en tue un" (26) [I say to myself that I would like him to kill one]. The eruptive echo of the feared, rejected *aimer* and its sudden link with violence solve none of these mysteries of personality and add to the store of passions unfolding through the performance. It is these pages (26–27) that Calle puts into a box on the cover of *Suite vénitienne*. Those pages record a crisis in her pursuit, and by putting them on the cover she images at the outset the difficult relations of passion and fracture, subject and genre, that her book embodies.

Those relations are connected with matters of stance, matters that take in all that Calle is and does in this performance. (All that she is and does includes the one who loves, the one who says she doesn't, the one who performs and the one who photographs Henri B.; there are surely more.)

Those connections come clear in a pair of passages that suggest a subtextual narrative. When she arrived at Venice, she saw herself "aux portes d'un labyrinthe, prête à me perdre dans la ville et dans cette histoire. Soumise" (12) [at the gates of a labyrinth, ready to lose myself in the city and in this story. Submissive]. She is giving herself to that which is, at once, labyrinth, city, and text, herself openly passive, textual to the degree that city and labyrinth are text. Calle is a textual being (whatever the difficulties in that oxymoron), which is one way of putting what she tries to express later by denying that *she* feels the love that "she" has declared. That was on Tuesday, February 12. In the elaborate entry for Tuesday, February 19, where Henri B. finally realizes that she has been following him, she stands there nearly speechless, eventually accepting his suggestion that they go for a ride: "je suis à sa disposition" (56) [I am at his disposal]. Her narrative has taken her from being submissive to a city/text to being submissive to the object of her pursuit.

This means that the question of who is now (and has been) subject, who is object, who is at which syntactical position in that sentence which is this performance, is the ultimate puzzle of *Suite vénitienne.* Which—to put it differently—is Other, and to whom? We saw in Acconci and Kafka that such pursuits are finally matters of surveillance, and that the one who is under surveillance is always in some sense a victim (of course this amalgamates the Other and the victim, another way of clarifying the politics involved). It has to be important to us to identify the pursuer, the Object, the victim: we have to be able to read the performance's syntax. Yet Calle's position as the photographer conducting the surveillance only complicates these issues, largely because of how she works photography's radical stances. One of the more problematical paradoxes about photography is how it functions both as an instrument of possession *and* as an instrument of Othering, at once and in equal proportions. That Calle has been using her camera as such an instrument in all of her pursuits, Parisian and Venetian, is clear enough. The pursuit of Henri B. gets especially complicated because she wants to possess from a distance, without her object knowing of it, without that reciprocity she fears because it would end the open-endedness her endless passion prefers. The camera is clearly the appropriate tool for that stance: no other mode of artmaking could make him hers in quite so circumscribed a way, the frame as possessive enclosure. None could make him so fully the object, herself so fully the subject. In fact she is so much the subject that we never see Calle in her images, whatever her presence at the scene, her participation in its actions, but always look out at him just as she sees him, from the back and from varying distances, the way that the subject of the sentence looks out at the predicate object. Calle turns performance photography into a study of intentionalities that reveals all sorts of connections between the subject and the object, the latter often (but not always) at the subject's disposal.

Henri B. is as subtle as she, as quick to sense the implications of the camera and their roles in the syntax that these performers (the subject has turned plural) enact throughout this performance. When they finally meet, an event she openly fosters—"Je suis peut-être lasse de jouer seule" (56) [I am, perhaps, tired of playing alone]—he makes some remarks about her eyes that indicate his recognition, then steps back to photograph her. This is an instantaneous, probably instinctive, move that shifts to him the role of the possessor, the Other-maker. The syntax of their relationship is shown to be made up of shifters in which the subject/photographer/I had no fixed and unwavering, quasi-Cartesian, content but only that which is given it by the participant's current moves. Though those moves use modes of possessing, the possession is claimed by entities as unstable as any pronoun. Such readings make plain how the act of making photographs is a gesture of syntax. That gesture throws open once again the question of who, precisely, is the victim in this melodrama of ownership and pursuit, surveillance and submission, intentionalities as complex as the stances they inform.

After Calle sees Henri B. photographing her she recognizes these points at once, just as he had and surely because he had. During their walk she spells out her recognition of that struggle for power which is also a struggle for a place within syntax:

> J'aime [now she can use this verb in a context that includes him] la maladresse avec laquelle il cache sa surprise, son désir d'être maître de la situation. Et si, en fait, j'avais été la victime inconsciente de son jeu, de ses trajets, de ses horaires. (56)

> [I love the awkwardness with which he hides his surprise, his desire to be master of the situation. And if, in fact, I had been the unconscious victim of his play, his movements, his schedules.]

Now we can see the full import of her statement, just after this, that she is "à sa disposition."

Baudrillard uses English—"Please follow me"—for the title of his essay on *Suite vénitienne*, perhaps because the language is other to her French and figures the requisite Otherness of the one who is pursued. The clause has to be spoken by the one who is followed, showing him/her to be desirous in the way of witting counterparts, such as Sophie herself in "The Detective." But it could not have been spoken by Henri B. in Venice before he recognized her eyes and possessed them with his film; and it could never have been spoken by any of the unwitting others in Calle's Parisian pursuits. In fact, what Baudrillard would do with the likely uneasiness of an Acconci pursuer is not entirely clear. He wants unscary intentionalities that are pleasingly symmetrical, identical in their passions and their awareness of those passions, different only in their position within the syntax. Yet Baudrillard's argument falls before at least one pedestrian fact: Henri B. did not know that Calle was following him. That argument makes sense only after he recognizes her, only after her one-time object has taken her onto film. Baudrillard elsewhere asserts that the pursuer in some ways seduces the pursued as well as herself (82–83). Baudrillard is wonderfully astute on the way the pursuer seduces herself into the life of another; but that concurrent seduction can occur only within the awareness of the pursuer, not the unwitting pursuee that Henri B. was before he recognized her eyes. That too makes her passion masturbatory, and refuses the pleasing symmetry (the critic's pleasure is at stake here) Baudrillard wants to design. Though Calle can suggest that she has, all along, been his unconscious victim, subservient to his movements, that has less to do with seduction than a mutual victimhood that each can recognize only when both become aware. Once Henri B. takes her picture he can say "please follow me" in full understanding of how the syntax of that request fits in with the syntax of their performance photography.

In fact, though, he does not say it. Once he becomes aware of her the pursuit is over, the subject shift not quite irrevocable but never to be as distinct as it was before his recognition. (In terms of the movement of narrative his recognition plays out the role of a classic Aristotelian *anagnorisis*.) She thinks of photographing him from an apartment near his hotel but that fizzles because of her fear that she might be annoying him. She thinks of leaving Venice but also thinks of staying on after he leaves, taking his room and sleeping in his bed. Whatever that says about her passions, such an act would stress succession, not simultaneity, absence, and not shared presence; and that would be consistent with the rest of this piece and the rest of her work. Temporality is, for Calle, a continuous making of absence, a fashioning of traces that owe their existence to absence. One sees that in *L'Hôtel* and, less patently but as persuasively, in *Suite vénitienne*.

That she does not take his room and his bed and embrace his absence has finally to do with her need to complete the performance with the semblance of a narrative conclusion, the matching of termini. That is why the final image has him going through a gate in the Gare de Lyon marked "Sortie." Calle knows that such a matching puts a symmetrical presence into spaces that also speak absence. It is that simultaneous speaking of absence and presence, the subtextual chorus that sounds through all her work, that puts the theatrical finish into the appropriate perspective. The classical columns on either side of the "Sortie" mockingly suggest the framing of a proscenium stage. She ends in the sort of ironies her medium can generate.

Similar ironies had been apparent from the beginning, generated by a pervasive play of absence and presence, her own in particular. Sophie is always at the scene but not perceptible within her images. She comes to be perceptible only at the end, within the image of another Other-maker: a street photographer takes her picture in the square, her blonde wig covered by a cloth, a pigeon just leaving her hand. This is Sophie as others have seen her, Sophie who is made the Other by the camera because Henri B. has taken her picture. She might as well confirm that new condition by showing herself within the scene, this once at the end, acknowledging the change in her status to that of pure Otherness. In fact what had characterized Calle's stance in *Suite vénitienne* up to the point when she was photographed in the square is her refusal of visible Otherness, the kind of Otherness that being photographed bestows, the kind Acconci had to accept when he was recorded going through his own pursuit. There are three figures involved in Acconci's *Following Piece*, the anonymous pursuee, Acconci the pursuer, and the photographer Betsy Jackson, who is never seen in the picture and has no immediate part in the performance, there only as historian/recorder. In *Suite vénitienne* Calle is simultaneously photographer and performer, acting on the periphery where the photographer works but also wandering about as one of the performance's centers. She acts out multiple roles that usually are argued to be radically separate, necessarily so if the work is to have "integrity," if it is to be taken as integral, as a whole. By so acting Calle argues for the performative aspect of any such photograph-making, the absurdity of any claim for documentary. She also argues for the concomitant absurdity of claims for "integrity" in the usual sense, that kind of wholeness that comes out of accepted compartments: if her photographs fashion a version of history, they are also openly, blatantly, part of her performance, the most tangible result that her actions offer.

She is complicit in several ways, none of them completely separate from the others.

To preserve the completest possible roster of participants and thus the fullest integrity Calle would have needed another photographer at the periphery of the scene, picturing her following Henri B. and taking photographs of him—including those scenes in which he is taking photographs of others. The roster would then have involved three different photographers, one the subject of two, two the subject of one. The "outside" photographer would be the most commanding subject in the syntax of photograph-making, though each would have been the subject at certain points in the action, all taking turns acting out the business of shifters. (Only Sophie and Henri B. would have been subject in the sense of subject *to,* enacting that extraordinary pun which shows how syntax, positioning, and power inform every aspect of photograph-making.) But in *Suite vénitienne* there is no "outside" photographer, therefore no ultimate completeness to the scene. In fact, Sophie's stance as the unperceived pursuer/photographer adds to that incompleteness. She is placed within the action but not within the scene we see. This means that the scene is always incomplete, marked as much by the absence of what we know is beyond the frame as by any perceptible presence. Sophie is Absent but not Other, invisibly performative, essential to the fullness of the performance but, because of her stance, blocking that fullness forever.[31]

Whatever Calle might owe to Acconci's *Following Piece* or similar late modernist work is hardly irrelevant, however tiny the debt now appears. Her work is one of the most searching explorations we have of the genre of performance photography, and as such it necessarily comments on previous modes of performance as well as previous exemplifications of the relations of photography and performance. The echo of Acconci's or similar work defines her own work with precision. It acts largely through the contrast of Acconci's aggressive centrality to Calle's parodies of pure centrality, her insistence on the presence of a multiplicity of centralities, here, there and elsewhere, their circumference nowhere discernible. Sophie is herself a legion of centers, the unseen photographer, the aloof one who says that those statements of love do not apply to her, the tongue-tied pursuer who is now subject-to and now finally aware of mutual victimhood. None of

31. There is a clumsy version of a similar positioning in Robert Montgomery's 1946 film noir *Lady in the Lake:* the camera eye is also Philip Marlowe's eye, the detective himself visible only twice, when he passes by mirrors. The film, which calls its gimmickry blatantly into notice, has none of the ironic readings of positioning that inform and sustain Calle's work.

these roles is primary. Each is always in some sense subject to all the others, each a subject only for one strain of the syntax through which it acts out its role. Calle is herself a plethora but she could never be a collective in the way that Gerald Stern can. The move from Acconci to Calle spells out the stances and contours of very different modes of being in the world.

6

The Photographic Self-Portrait: Fissures and Ideologies

Historians of photography tend to treat Oscar Gustave Rejlander as a minor purveyor of Victorian high camp. Best known in his time for photographs like *The Two Ways of Life*, with its multiple images, moralism, and controversial nudity, Rejlander is now most interesting for images like *Hard Times*, one of its versions still significant for its proto-Surrealist play with the solid and the ghostly.[1] Though he was usually attuned to what the times seemed to call for, Rejlander was also aware of what was going on in the photography of his time, as recent critics have shown.[2] And if suggestions, however valid, that Rejlander should be seen as a father of art photography sidestep

1. Reproduced in Naomi Rosenblum, *A World History of Photography* (New York: Abbeville Press, 1984), 227, and also in Beaumont Newhall, *The History of Photography* (New York: Museum of Modern Art, 1982), 75. One ought also to examine the Dada-like play in "Woman Holding a Pair of Feet."

2. See Edgar Yoxall Jones, *Father of Art Photography: O. G. Rejlander, 1813–1875* (Newton Abbott: David & Charles, 1973), and Stephanie Spencer, *O. G. Rejlander: Photography as Art* (Ann Arbor: University of Michigan Research Press, 1985).

too gingerly his pervasive sentimentality, several of his images tackle questions that photography has always faced, questions that have been kept intense by contemporary theories about the promises photography makes. Though he can be seen as an early progenitor of the directorial mode, he also uncovers conundrums that call into question the efficacy of that mode.[3]

Among Rejlander's images are a series of self-portraits in which he plays at dress-up, pretending to be a Democritus or a Garibaldi or some kind of soldier. Playing at dress-up has always fascinated photographers, and this seems particularly true of the photographers of the middle of the nineteenth century. Collections of photographic self-portraits show quasi-classical poses but also Near Eastern images, such as Nadar in Western fringes, derived from Delacroix and popular Orientalism; and if some had a tinge of the intentionally comic, few had the solemn self-importance of F. Holland Day's series of himself as the dying and entombed Christ.[4] Rejlander's own self-images take an entirely different tack. Less garish and more playful than most, they sometimes flaunt what Holland's self-portraits never had, multiple ironies that emerge from a sardonic, incisive probing, the shape of which is only now beginning to come clear.

These ironies are especially evident in the multiple-exposure photograph of 1871 in which Rejlander appears as both artist and military volunteer (Fig. 6). In a copy addressed to Henry Peach Robinson, Rejlander inscribed its title as "O.G.R. introduces himself as a volunteer to H.P.R."[5] None of these stances is fictional in the way of Nadar or the pseudo-Orientalists: Rejlander was actually a volunteer in an "Artist's Company," and recent work has shown that he continued as a painter, although primarily a photographer, for much of his professional life.[6] Still, the painter's easel in the photograph holds not a painting but a copy of Rejlander's most popular and profitable photographic print, a shot of a squalling child done for Darwin's *Expression of the Emotions in Man and Animals*. Originally titled *Mental*

---

3. A. D. Coleman argues that Rejlander and Henry Peach Robinson are responsible for "the advent of directorial photography as an active mode." See "The Directorial Mode: Notes Toward a Definition," in *Photography in Print: Writings from 1816 to the Present*, ed. Vicki Goldberg (Albuquerque: University of New Mexico Press, 1981), 487.

4. Among the best of such collections are *Self-Portrait in the Age of Photography: Photographers Reflecting Their Own Image*, ed. Erika Billeter (Bern: Benteli Verlag, 1985), and *Staging the Self: Self-Portrait Photography 1840s–1980s*, ed. James Lingwood (London: Butler & Tanner, 1986). The prevalent orientalism seen in so many images of the time should be studied in terms of the image of the Oriental as Other described in Edward Said's *Orientalism* (New York: Random House, 1979).

5. Jones, *Father of Art Photography*, 38.

6. Spencer, *O. G. Rejlander*, 13.

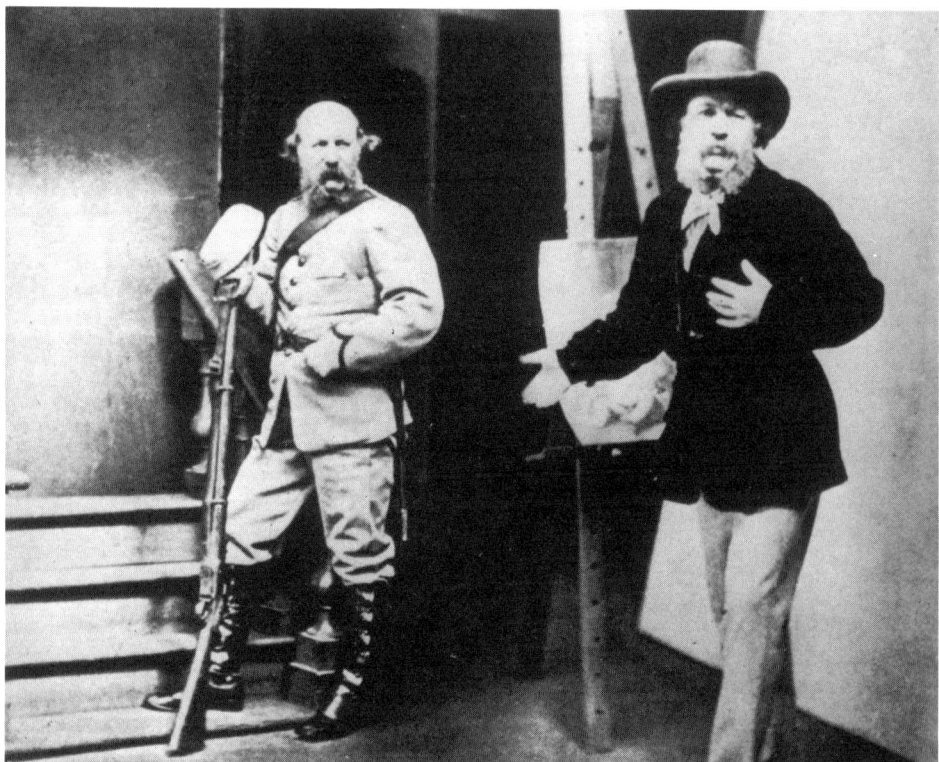

Fig. 6.   Oskar Gustav Rejlander, "O.G.R. the Artist Introduces O.G.R. the Volunteer. The Royal Photographic Society, Bath"

Distress, it came to be known as *Ginx's Baby,* after a character in a popular novel. Given this context, then, the figure at the right can be read as a concatenation of Rejlander's visual interests, the entire image a documentary of his varied activities; and yet the business of diversity does not end at that point, for a thrust among the planes of the image leads to more complicated places in a more encompassing context, one that fills out the social milieu suggested in Rejlander's well-known street and genre scenes. A line of gazing within the image moves out from Rejlander the Volunteer, staring sternly, suspiciously, at Rejlander the Artist, then leads the Artist, in his turn, to stare into the camera eye that is our surrogate at the scene. The title inscribed to Robinson clarifies this larger context. In so presenting an aspect of himself to a friend and fellow photographer (though in fact to everyone for whom the camera's eye stands in), Rejlander's photograph establishes a context of social discourse, the bourgeois ceremony of introduction coded in the Artist's stance, the slight bow, the gestures. And the image within the image, the photograph on the easel, adds still another element to Rejlander as bourgeois, for it is a palpable symbol of his success in commercial photography and thus a further self-definition, an additional placement of himself within the Victorian social order. That point is confirmed in the image of 1872, *Ginx's Baby and Co.*, the photograph of the squalling baby once again on an easel, Rejlander sitting to the right of the easel with an enormously fetching look on his face that mimics the look of the child but also suggests a gloat and a smirk. This sardonic match of expressions, at once echoing and conflicting, plays out a plethora of tones and ironies, the ironies emerging in part because of the popularity of the photograph of the bawling baby. Artist and volunteer, Rejlander is above all bourgeois, flaunting the symbol of his success just as a capitalist flaunts a logo. In a sense, then, the image of Artist and Volunteer becomes a kind of *carte de visite*, Rejlander presenting his selves and their status to the world within which he wants to be read, to Henry Peach Robinson, to us.

That the system inscribed in this photograph contains multitudes of acts, as well as the selves appropriate to each, comes clear not only from the line of the gaze and the suggestions on the easel but from the relationships implicit among the various figures involved. Take, once again, the inscription for Robinson: "O.G.R. introduces himself as a volunteer to H.P.R." What that inscribes into the scene involves not only social codes and their attendant class relationships but a syntax that extends to the visual structures as well as the verbal ones. Rejlander's title reads Rejlander into the image as at once active and passive, simultaneously subject and object of the verb. We, the wielders of the eye for which the lens is an agent, stand outside the scene because we are outside the image, but stand as part of the total order because we (not just H.P.R., who is finally our surrogate in this intricate social discourse) are the verb's indirect objects, elements in the syntax that orders the whole. But the degrees of subordination at work in the syntax extend to still other relations among the figures in the order. This is patently a studio scene, not just a scene that takes place within a studio but, specifically, a scene of a studio; and as all such scenes it comes finally to be a scene of the artist as maker—here, most precisely, the artist as maker of himself. Part of this has to do with the stance of the Volunteer, who stands with one foot on a set of stairs used as a prop in a number of Rejlander's studio scenes. He is, as the stairs suggest, about to become the subject of an image. Another part has to do with the positioning of the

Artist and the easel, the latter almost in place and about to be put to use. Rejlander is therefore not only subject and object of the verb but subject to his own actions as artist, participant in a play of power, participant most of all in a play of self-creation. Beyond all the social discourse lie suggestions of the artist as fabricator of himself, maker of himself insofar as he is maker of his self-portrait. And since what this image holds is a multiple self-portrait—for the Artist as maker of himself is himself part of the scene—the selves exhibited in the image are both, then, fabrications, acting together as wielders of the verb as well as objects of its actions. Probing essential questions about the photographic self-portrait, Rejlander sets a subtext in motion that will undo the complacent suggestions of the open and courteous surface whose discourse insists on the coherence of the scene.

Such coherence comes ultimately from a figure implicit in the context but never properly introduced, Rejlander carefully excluding him from the courtesies of the scene. That figure is the Fabricator (the capitalization seems inevitable), who takes charge of the operation that gets out this photograph, who is responsible for everything except the lifting of the lens cap during the recording of each of the elements. What comes through is a world of multiple selves, each sufficient for a particular role, the Fabricator being the only one that takes in all the others and gives them a place in coherence. That coherence is consistent with the social coherence suggested in official versions of Victorian public discourse and supported in the corpus of Rejlander's images, although the Fabricator himself comes out of the late romantic tradition, which emphasizes the potency of a central creative figure. Yet by introducing the Fabricator only through the image of his fabricated surrogate, Rejlander not only accedes to that coherence and that tradition but, sotto-voce and subtextually, suggests their undoing as well. If the Artist within is also the echo and surrogate of the Fabricator without, acting out the latter's role inside the contours of the scene, the image cannot restrain the suggestion (it is never more than that) that the Fabricator himself might also be a fabrication, thereby keeping perfect consistency with all that he has made: after all, if that is the Fabricator's image in there, and if that image is a fabrication, what is there to keep the Fabricator from being a fabrication? Nothing in Rejlander's photograph suggests a special mode of being for the capitalized Fabricator, but everything within the syntax suggests at least the possibility that the whole, inside and out, is one vast text, a universal weaving. (Of course perfect consistency requires that we, too, be part of the weave, for we are the indirect objects in the syntax of introduction as well as the direct objects of the Artist's gaze.) And if that seems an ironic, destabilizing version of the coherence for which the public discourse argues, there is no guarantee that the coherence itself is anything more than a fabrication, itself part of the texture of this ultimate weave.

The logic of compelling suggestions is one thing; acceptance of that logic is another. In fact it is questionable whether Rejlander would openly go that far, whatever the inherent logic, whatever his status as a progenitor of art photography. Given his position in the waning years of the romantic tradition, given his obvious, hard-won place as an exponent of the age's discourse, he was working within limitations dictated by desire. If Rejlander is convincingly seen as an early proponent of art photography, his images also make clear how much he supported the popular, cleaner readings of his age, whatever the distresses depicted in photographs like *Hard Times* and *Poor Jo*, whatever his admiration for the Victorian *auteur*.[7] That is why Rejlander makes no obvious place for the Fabricator himself: to make room for the Fabricator might destroy the accepted reading of the central creative figure. Better for the Fabricator to be assumed rather than examined. Further, there are suggestions that Rejlander is not entirely pleased with the thought of absolute fracture between Fabricator and image, whatever the implications in his multiple self-portrait. These, too, he tries to control, to absorb into the whole. By simultaneously playing both ends of the scale Rejlander seeks to have it all ways at once, what we may choose to see as an example of willing acquiescence, what we certainly have to see as the broad range of a knowingness that saw more than it said, that causes the knowing mimicry in *Ginx's Baby and Co.* In seeking to balance his act in this way Rejlander did as Hippolyte Bayard had done a generation earlier, probing at issues that have taken their intensest, most open form in the queries of our own time.

Rejlander's syntax of subordination suggests several of those issues, particularly matters about positioning that are inherent in the self-portrait. Take, for example, the fact that the photographer, like every subject, has to get in front of the lens in order to have his picture taken. However

7. It is clear that Rejlander took on the social establishment in images of this sort, just as he took on the art establishment with his composite images. Yet one need only compare his crossing sweeps with similar figures in William Blake and Lewis Hines to see how establishmentarian so many of his figures are. Naomi Rosenblum's comment in her otherwise excellent remarks on Rejlander unwittingly makes that point abundantly clear: Rejlander's "portraits of chimney sweeps reveal an individualized grace that does not depend on social class." *World History of Photography*, 351.

elementary an issue, it complicates his job immensely, for he cannot both look through the lens and be that object which disturbs the flow of light and registers on the emulsion. Of course one can set up a timer or hold an extension cord and trip the shutter from a distance (options not available to Rejlander) but one is still not on both sides of the lens at once. Photographers have routinely solved this problem by aiming the camera into a mirror, the most direct way to turn oneself into the object of one's own gaze; yet what one sees in the mirror is itself a representation, a cousin and prefiguration of the representation that is to come in the photographic image. Not only does one remain on one side of the lens but the photographic image becomes a mirroring of the mirror, a double representation, a fiction of a figment. With double (duplicitous) irony it defeats the impossible desire to stand in both places at once; and yet the history of the photographic self-portrait shows no rebellion against this condition but a willing acquiescence to the nature of the machinery, surely because of the possibilities it brings forth. What begins as a technical matter of the medium gets very quickly involved with questions about genre (the self-portrait) and the positioning of the self, finally and most unsettlingly with questions about subjectivity.

We are dealing with two radically related issues, matters of representation and matters of fracture. To turn oneself into the subject of a photographic self-portrait is to make oneself subject to oneself, working with different roles which one can make "simultaneous" only by making the wielder of one of the roles a representation of the maker, a figmental surrogate. But of course what we have made is a *fiction* of simultaneity, a representation of what it would be like were it able to be at all. With or without the mirror there is an essential (basic and requisite) split between oneself as maker of the image and the image of oneself in the photograph one makes, a division not only of tasks but of qualities of being. To put it another way, the fracture appears to be not only in the continuity of the tasks but in that which performs the continuity, the subjectivity that seems otherwise to underlie the whole and hold the whole together. Rejlander acknowledged this possibility of a fissure and sought to overcome it when he set up the syntax of his image to suggest a continuity, that line of sight going from the Volunteer to the Artist to whoever is outside the image. If we stand at the end of the line in the throes of an introduction, Rejlander the photographer stands at precisely the same point, dressing himself in various suits, placing the props, arranging the camera. But once all that is done, Rejlander has to fracture the sequence of tasks by turning the camera over to someone else and getting in front of the lens in order, finally, to become a representation of himself. Representation and fracture, then, seem inevitably to go together, their relations working not only for the photographic self-portrait but for any form of the genre in any mode of art, indeed for any kind of autobiography, visual or verbal.

It is because of just such issues that metaphors such as the "staging of the self" (also the title of an excellent anthology of photographic self-portraits edited by James Lingwood) have all sorts of built-in problems, quandaries that seem, finally, to undo the metaphor's claims and show it as ultimately unworkable. "Staging" necessarily involves multiple positioning, at least of actor and audience, most likely others as well who make (not just make up) the matter of the mise-en-scène. Of course this implies a simultaneity of positioning, the actors perform while the audience watches. And yet it is clear that what is involved in the photographic self-portrait is not the simultaneity implied in the metaphor of staging but something very different, something involved in difference, much like that Derridean *différance* which takes in, at once, both distinction and deferral.[8]

And it is precisely in this condition, this lack of simultaneity that the characteristic elements of the photographic self-portrait come fully into play. In fact, the lack is unusually intense in photographic self-portraits because certain kindred elements in photography and autobiography come together at that point and supplement one another, intensifying one another in a way specific to that mixture. Contemporary theorists of autobiography speak frequently of the autobiographical subject as not only fictive but always Other. To take the comments of one reader, Marc Eli Blanchard speaks of "the *fiction of self-writing*[,] the idea that the other produced . . . is the same person as the 'I' who was writing."[9] Blanchard also argues that the autobiographer necessarily takes a metonymical relation to his own life (109), a point I take to imply that autobiography is made out of metonymically related Others whose relation to one another always involves that sort of distinction which also includes a deferral. That same series of events happens in every photograph, whether of person, place, or thing, of the photographer or another. The taking of a photograph begins what is, in effect, a process of Othering; most accurately, the making of an Other that never existed before the emulsion was exposed and will remain Other at least in part because the figure will always look as it looked at the moment

---

8. Derrida deals somewhat summarily with questions of autobiography in *The Ear of the Other: Otobiography, Transference, Translation*, trans. Peggy Kamuf, ed. Christie McDonald (Lincoln: University of Nebraska Press, 1988).

9. "The Critique of Autobiography," *Comparative Literature* 34 (1982): 101.

of becoming Other. Of course what this means for the photographic self-portrait is that the Othering involved in the making of any photograph and the Othering involved in the making of any autobiography come together to produce an Otherness that draws upon the potency of several modes of art. When the photographer steps around to the other side of the lens, when he points his camera into a mirror, he establishes a taut, intractable distinction between himself as maker and subject that can never be entirely bridged, whatever the identity of name between himself and his image. In fact, insofar as he is subject to himself he is always-already-other, inevitably fractured, inevitably distanced and distinct, differing in placement and function (for his is the function of a fabrication) once he steps inside the scene that will become the place in the frame.[10]

That is one of several reasons why *The Portrait of Dorian Gray* stands as a crucial text in our understanding of the relations between positioning and fabrication. Wilde's text posits an Otherness that grows out of an assumed identification between the image and its original. It builds most of its ironies on what is perceived as a link between Otherness and Origin, a link that persists even as the fractures grow wider. We have already seen the suggestion of such a link (though "hope" may be more accurate than "suggestion") in Rejlander's multiple self-portrait. Between Rejlander and his image there is an irreparable fissure, yet the syntax of the gaze coming out of the image toward us suggests—pleads for—a connection as well, a tie between self and portrait. And it is in precisely such a plea that we hear still other suggestions for photography implicit in Wilde's text, especially what that plea implies about the qualities of longing, one of the primary emotions in the complex that surrounds the photographic self-portrait.

As the question of Otherness turns up in photography, it seems often to be involved with a deep-reaching nostalgia that in one way or another, has affected many of our ideas about what photography can do. The Barthes of *Camera Lucida* offers a viable short-cut to several conclusions:

> The Photograph is the advent of myself as other: a cunning dissociation of consciousness from identity. Even odder: it was *before* Photography that men had the most to say about the vision of the double.

10. There is a sense in which the Othering accomplished in the photograph mimics that seeing of ourselves as Other accomplished by everyone else. We thus take part in the group definition of selfhood, which for some, is all that there is. In any case that representation of the seeing of ourselves as Other is still another aspect of the complex of positionings involved in the photographic self-portrait.

Heautoscopy was compared with an hallucinosis; for centuries this was a great mythic theme. But today it is as if we repressed the profound madness of Photography: it reminds us of its mythic heritage only by that faint uneasiness which seizes me when I look at "myself" on a piece of paper.[11]

Much of the nostalgia inherent in the photographer's self-positioning comes out in such fabulous undercurrents, for if, as Barthes suggests, there are myths of the double involved, there are also related myths like the Aristophanic story that Socrates reports in the *Symposium*. That tale fixes the lust for an overcoming of disjunction in a craving for an ancient oneness, a condition in which terms like "spatial" and "temporal" cease to have any meaning because oneself and one's Other occupy the same space and, always, the same time. No shuffles of positioning seem able to recover that ancient oneness. The result is an extraordinary ambivalence that characterizes our relations to photography, an attitude we have already seen in Barthes's reading of photography.

That attitude draws much of its tone from the difficult relationships between photographs and time. Whatever one's attitude toward nostalgia and its often (always?) attendant indexicality, the question reveals, in its own way, the requisite temporal grounding of every self-portrait, visual or verbal. That grounding is particularly intense and problematic in the photographic self-portrait, largely from the nature of the medium and several prevalent attitudes toward it. No matter what we title a photograph its subtextual subtitle is always "once upon a time." Whatever the extent of the preparation involved, the photograph freezes a moment that is immediately and forever absent, and grows in degrees of absence as the moment of taking recedes. But the past is past only in relation to the present. The present is that punctual scene which defines and gives meaning to the past, gives it, in effect, its pastness, which means that the moment of the taking of the photographic image is the reference point through which one always reviews the image.[12] That there are different ways to understand this point,

11. *Camera Lucida: Reflections on Photography*, trans. Richard Howard (New York: Hill & Wang, 1981), 12–13.

12. Paul John Eakin puts a related point about verbal autobiography as follows: "The past that any autobiographical narrative records is first and foremost the period of the autobiographical act itself." See his *Fictions in Autobiography: Studies in the Art of Self-Invention* (Princeton: Princeton University Press, 1985), 22. For more general discussion, see Burton Pike's "Time in Autobiography," *Comparative Literature* 28 (1976): 326–42.

different emotions to be aroused by it, can be gathered from a reading of any collection of photographic criticism. In one sense it can be argued that the photograph takes us out of history in that the frozen moment seems immune to history. This is, of course, the Dorian Gray business again; and it is precisely that attitude (which may well include aspects of the Wildean chill) that effects the nostalgia, the enactment of Aristophanic longing. And yet the photographic image seems also to call for precisely the opposite attitude, an argument for the *immersion* of the photograph in history, its profound and defining involvement (defining in the sense of speculating what the photograph *is*) in every dimension of temporality. Of course this is by no means the only possible basis for arguing such immersion: any reading that makes a case for the photograph as social discourse, as instrument of temporal power, necessarily takes such a stand, as we shall see in Jo Spence's comments on her profession. But there is more than power involved. To speak of the image in the photograph as somehow taken out of history is to argue, ultimately, for its immutable, eternal presence, as well as to argue further for the photograph as index. Given the instant bathing of the image in irrevocable absence, that argument becomes seriously problematical, difficult to sustain when taken in so pure a form and without ironic qualification. And yet, whatever the difficulties in holding such contrary ideas, versions of such holding turn up so often in our thinking about photography that they offer one more reason why our attitude toward photographs sustains what seems an ineradicable ambivalence.

Still, whatever the nature of the absence that begins when the photograph is taken, whatever the gap between the photographer as maker and the photographer as subject, one is tempted to make an exception for that crucial moment in the photographic process, that moment whose temporality seems unique in its kind, in which one presses the shutter release while another stands in the role of subject. It would seem that that moment collapses the spatial and the temporal into a single dimension, so that one may be tempted to speak not only of the spatializing of time but the temporalizing of space. Yet that moment, too, is deceptive, for what seems to be a fusion is in fact another gap, in some ways the most ironic of all. The photographic self-portrait contains an implicit narrative with a relatively unified series of acts, the main action of the narrative the preparations leading to the moment when the lens opens up. That the narrative may also include a subsequent manipulation of the image complicates but does not change the narrative's relation to history. The narrative is part of the history that informs every photographic act, and it culminates in the moment of the taking of the image, the point at which one is realized as a subject. Yet at that instant one performs the gesture that has complicated every theory of photography from Bayard's time to our own. One turns the actual making of the image over to a mechanism, ironizing the question of distance because a machine comes between oneself as maker and as subject and does that for which all one's previous activity had been the preparation. The elaborate dance of positionings involved in putting together the photographic self-portrait reaches its ultimate spatiotemporal refinement at precisely this point, yet subject and maker are still irrevocably distant, their fusion forever deferred. A machine, that is, with subtextual implications as well as functional ones, comes in to undercut the last possible claim for any kind of fusion between the maker and the maker as subject and exposes the fallacy that argues for perfect union between the photographer and the photographed. This climactic moment offers no more than a figment of union, a fiction of satisfied desire, a delusion that casts aspersions on the nostalgia that might well follow.[13]

In fact it can be argued that as the image shatters any possibility of a link between photographer and subject, it forges a substitute link between the image in the photograph and the moment in which it is taken. The image of Rejlander that sits next to and mimics the image of Ginx's baby is a record of instantaneities, and one of those is the instant at which the image came into being and, in so doing, became wholly Other. The photographic self-portrait records a metamorphosis that is only of that moment and lasts no longer than that moment. This means that the self within the image—Rejlander as Artist as well as Rejlander as Volunteer, Rejlander as only begetter of the image of Ginx's baby—is itself no more than momentary, no more than the self of that moment.[14]

Putting the point another way, the self within the image is the self *for* that moment, fitting that image for *only* that moment, but fitting it more

13. The culmination of the narrative in the moment of taking the image is not only the narrative's climax but its conclusion as well, still another indication of the relation of photography and desire. Though the climactic moment may offer no more than a fiction of satisfied desire, all manner of other aspects of the entire enterprise rest on various analogues of the making of photographs and love, occasions for *jouissance*. Yet to limit the emotions involved to analogues of sexual passion would be to limit the range of photography's encounter with desire, for that particular passion is no more than a metonym for the variations of desire that drive the photographic image.

14. It is obvious that Rejlander's combination images, such as the Artist/Volunteer and the notorious *Two Ways of Life*, complicate this question considerably. Whatever the times of taking the images—and they are necessarily different in combination photographs—they combine into a single image that offers its own instantaneities, its own moment of the instantly Other, even though

precisely than any other selfhood could. If the image is a figment, it is the fiction that belongs to that moment, the point at which Rejlander sat next to the image of the squalling brat and became an image of the maker of the image. The act of taking the photograph creates the self for that moment, for that context, for that occasion.

Yet Rejlander is not content with just a single circumscription, for in each of these photographs there are several occasions at play. In fact we can even speak of a play of occasions, a multifaceted version of occasionality. If the figure of Rejlander in each of these self-portraits is an image of the maker of the photograph we are seeing, he also images the maker of the photograph within the photograph, the shot of the squalling brat, which means that the image of Ginx's baby that appears in each of these photographs implies a maker who was appropriate for the moment of *its* taking. Thus does Rejlander break open any possible circumscription, suggesting in its stead a set of mirroring fictions that seem to refuse conclusiveness. It is clear that they seem also to refuse continuity, for they are contained in, created by, their occasionality. Whatever Rejlander's technical clumsiness in producing his images, this father of art photography had a sense of where he could go, where his images were taking us. We are getting to see even more of the impetus for that look in *Ginx's Baby & Co.*, more of its dense and complex content.

But perhaps the look holds suggestions that it would rather not bring to the surface. If these images hold all manner of instantaneities, we are entitled once again to question the status of the maker of these images. If the figure within the image is a record of Rejlander as artist, does this mean that the maker of the image is himself no more than a succession of such instants, himself the scene of a series of instantaneities that change as the moment changes and are never twice the same? Since several different occasions when Rejlander was maker are implicit in each of these scenes, and since the self of each occasion has its peculiar appropriateness, we can guess at the answer though we know we shall never hear it from him. We know that Rejlander ducks precisely such questions, but we know also that those questions emerge from his self-portraits just as surely as they show his sardonic self-congratulation or all those comforting facets of Victorian social discourse. If Rejlander's knowingness causes the look in *Ginx's Baby & Co.*, it also causes the equally knowing uneasiness the images cannot suppress.

---

the images of which the single image of the combination photograph is composed were taken at different times and became instantly Other at different occasions.

What Rejlander suggests, whether he wills it or not, is that the making of a self-portrait is also, simultaneously, the making of a self, that making a text and making a self are finally the same act seen from different points of view. If we choose to speak of the self in the moment of composition, we probably have to say that the self *is* that moment, that it *is* that composition, that the moment holds a gesture of self-composition. If that ultimate suggestion cannot comfortably cohere with any of the discourses that Rejlander openly cherished, it is there all the same, remaining, in several ways, the most disturbing suggestion of all. Given the conflicts between his insights and his desires, Rejlander's look had to depend on what it could not say, trusting to the swarming energies of its subtextual life.

And yet we can carry these conundrums to still another stage, one that indicates once more the fertility of Rejlander's speculations on his specular positioning. However one may wish to argue for the Fabricator as himself yet one more fabrication among the figments of self that surround us, all of those selves-for-the-occasion at work in Rejlander's self-portraits are the result of a capacity for self-positioning; more precisely, a capacity for self-constituting that has to remain consistent *and consistently itself* whatever the shifts of the occasions and the selves that are made for them. To argue for breaks in that consistency would be to assert that during such breaks there is no longer any capacity to fashion changes of selves appropriate for changing occasions; and yet it is precisely the continuity of those changes of selves, the persistence of the changes, their dependability, that we use to argue against the unchanging, irreducible center that is the classical humanist "self." Still, it is not just a question of the constancy of change (an acceptable paradox) but the necessary constancy of the capacity for making changes that spells the dilemma out. The constant activities of one part of our being make possible the inconsistencies of another part of our being— for the latter are the same inconsistencies that may lead us to suspect that we are inconsistent throughout. No argument that insists on pure occasionality can handle such conundrums; nor can such an argument be entirely at ease with the spectral Fabricator. It may be tempting to personalize the capacity for self-constituting in the person of the Fabricator, as we did in discussing Rejlander, where it seemed an appropriate figure for issues that turn up in his work. Yet to do so continues the question of self-constituting in and for the occasion—the Fabricator, the appropriate figure, *recognized as a figure,* for this point and scene. That, as we have seen, gives us all sorts of trouble.

We seem to be reviving an ancient flirtation with essence. These and similar quandaries may seem to suggest in the strongest terms that in certain of our assumptions we continue to work within the terms of a "centering" discourse, grounded, however unwillingly (unwittingly), in humanist hypotheses. Though that may well be true for some of the figures we shall be reading—their ideologies haunted by their private *Unheimliche*, Banquo and Jacob Marley in Cartesian disguise—it is not, I think, universally the case. But it is certainly the case that all sorts of related conundrums worry the work of most of those figures, most often subtextually. One can observe these stubborn issues not only in Rejlander's suggestions but in the activities of contemporary figures as different as David Antin, Cindy Sherman, and Barbara Kruger, not to speak of Jo Spence and John Coplans. Such complexities account for much of the density of texture of that which we call postmodern.

II

The questions Rejlander raised about the relations of self and text in the photographic self-portrait have never been resolved, although they have shifted in tone. Those issues turn combative, grim, in the work of Jo Spence, whose autobiography rephrases the history of modern photography in terms of the relationships of bodies and power.[15] Spence's awareness of the authority of the tradition of photography as a fine art, Rejlander's tradition, emerges in her comments on the difficulties she would face in getting her work known in "the 'art' arena" (106). It "would be subjected to entirely different criteria from those of community photography, left-wing or women's movement circles," the groups within which Spence positions herself. In fact she clearly understands the "privileging of photography as fine art in the guise of a study of style" (106). Part of Spence's attack is on the conditions of commercial photography and how its handling of its subjects, from wedding pictures to portraits of mother-and-child, encodes circumstances of social power. Yet she is also fully aware of how such questions implicate art photography as well, which has determined much of the structure of commercial photography, and her remarks apply to both. In her

---

15. *Putting Myself in the Picture: A Political, Personal and Photographic Autobiography* (Seattle: Real Comet Press, 1988).

chapter "Remodelling Photo History," she speaks of making strange the routine practices of the trade by seeking "to denaturalize the genres of photography which already consist of fully coded visual signs"; and in taking issue with a classic reading of the function of the frame she argues that "the camera is not a window on the world, nor are meanings of pictures fixed, but . . . visual signs (in this case photographs) are in themselves sites of struggle" (118). Keeping in mind her own experience as a commercial photographer she argues against the credibility of any image of a self in any text. Speaking of photo therapy she argues that this work exists within a framework of debates on media studies, history, feminism, therapy, and memory. The work takes up and questions many of the themes of photography itself, challenging

> the concept of the "decisive" or "perfect" moment, and the "truth" of the photographic image. It exposes the image production process, working against the grain of existing mythologies, for example of family photographs, looking at everyday events and small details, challenging "fixity" and rigid social roles. The work decodes sexuality and gendering and begins to show them as social constructs. (175)

Spence uses herself as an instance of such constructing, wielding autobiography in its capacity as representative life. The images in her autobiography consist largely of three categories of photographs, snapshots from her early history, personal records of herself as cancer patient, and a final series of herself going through photo therapy. All of this variety is put with a sardonic twist that does not seek to disguise Spence's emotional and physical pain but intensifies her consciousness of herself as a wounded woman, fighting cancer as well as the social construction of personality with the sounds (and sights) of a Swiftian indignation. Sometimes the tone turns Rabelaisian: the first image in the book has her sitting on a chamber pot, gazing at her crotch with pursed lips and saying, in large letters, "My God . . . I've got an imaginary lack." She maintains this tone in the caption: "from a photo therapy session on the end of my anal phase." A tongue-in-cheek narcissism makes her the object of her own gaze, but she is also the object of ours at this openly private moment. She is the subject of the image but also, like every photographic subject, at once Other and object, subject, therefore, to photography's puzzles of indexicality. Her lack is the subject of the therapy that, in this anal phase, turns function into allegory, object into possession. And there is more, for example, her complaining about lack while next to her there stands the grossly phallic banister post, certainly the ultimate subject of all this object-deprivation.

Photo therapy of this sort does much of its work by playing out self-images. It is, then, a version of autobiography, though one may well be playing out images of oneself as one's own mother. In fact, it is precisely the narcissistic Othering involved in every sort of self-image that makes possible much of the practice's therapeutic thrust, taking part, as it does, not only in the curative possibilities of self-dramatization but in the self-portrait's way of putting us instantly, irredeemably, into another mode of being. One of the major ironies in Spence's autobiography has to do with how photo therapy counters the immense personal cost of that discourse about others for which conventional portraiture stands as the best-known metonym. At one point in her text she explores in summary form the nature of such portraiture and compares it, in parallel columns, to the conditions of photo therapy (185–86). The portraiture columns on the left emphasize the placement of such images within a discourse that universalizes and therefore dehistoricizes, conferring on its subjects both wholeness and clo-sure as well as the self-esteem of a discourse that silently knows its own power. Steichen's early self-portraits with palette and brush or with camera take in one version of such things; Man Ray's portraits of himself as grimly avant-garde take in still another. Spence's alternative discourse offers oppo-sites and opposition, the columns on the right confirming the struggle of "fully coded visual signs" to which Spence regularly refers, their effects among the subjects of her autobiography.

Yet there are other struggles in Spence's text, struggles of a very different sort, struggles which take it in very different directions from the conflicts between the points of view in those columns in her autobiography, which are based on the play of signs but play in addition with largely subtextual implications that go beyond questions of gender, though never forgetting those questions. Consider, again, the frontispiece. Whatever else happens in this image it puts Spence's body at the center of the scene. Her position and words speak of the body as object and therefore as susceptible to wounding of all sorts, the "imaginary lack" being only one example. Subject to all that the text will explore not only of imaginary lacks but of the very real changes that threaten to eat her body away, her corporeality is, finally, the subject of the subtext that this frontispiece strongly suggests. That text about the body takes in more than the body as text (the subject of the set of contrary columns) but the body as *also* bodily, creaturely, flesh as well as sign. No sense of that reading of body appears in any of the columns (in fact the portraiture columns actively ignore it) but it appears, with varying openness, in every aspect of the book, for example in her early, embarrassed awkwardness at the size of her breasts, most potently in those images of herself as breast cancer patient. All of this is suggested early in the positioning explored in the frontispiece photograph. It puts the body at the center not only literally in the image (her body takes up most of the space within the frame) but on the chamber pot as well. Though the image puts the point in a thoroughly tongue-in-cheek way the centering of the body required to use a chamber pot starts off that subtextual positioning of the body's bodiness that is as much the subject of Spence's work as are questions of power and discourse.

Which means that the body has to be seen as not only a gendered body but as a body as such. Flesh and ideology illuminate each other in more ways than Spence's warring columns can hold. Those ways respond not only to the un-thinging of the body in commercialized art photography but (because those ways put the body back into history) to the thingly depersonalizing that artists like Weston and Strand sought to effect. Versions of this reemphasis on the thingness of the body appear in the photographic self-portraits of John Coplans and Lucas Samaras, each responding in up-front maleness to what Spence responds to in her mocking but no less gutsy femaleness. Yet that functioning of the body as simultaneously flesh and sign takes Spence's best work beyond the (too easily reductive) parochialism of the work of Barbara Kruger and Cindy Sherman. One of the photographs of Spence as postoperative patient—crash helmet on her head, hands over her head and resting on the helmet, scarred breast facing the lens, the nipple staring back at our stare at the scar (161)—parodies her earlier photograph of a model, the pose nearly identical, that earlier image part of Spence's exploration of how to produce "visual myths" (40). And if the earlier image had worried over the Othering that engenders myths, the later responds to the more drastic Othering fostered by the medical establishment (the text quoted next to the later photograph equates the treatment of cancer patients with modes of assault on social problems and especially Vietnam). Her later image responds to the making of visual myths with the full-fleshed density of Spence's own body, Spence's telling of these issues on herself.

Yet the image's response to the Othering engendered by the photographic self-portrait complicates Spence's comments about the photograph as a field of visual signs. Those questions are put into a context that complaints about privileged modes of photography can finally resolve. Images like the portrait

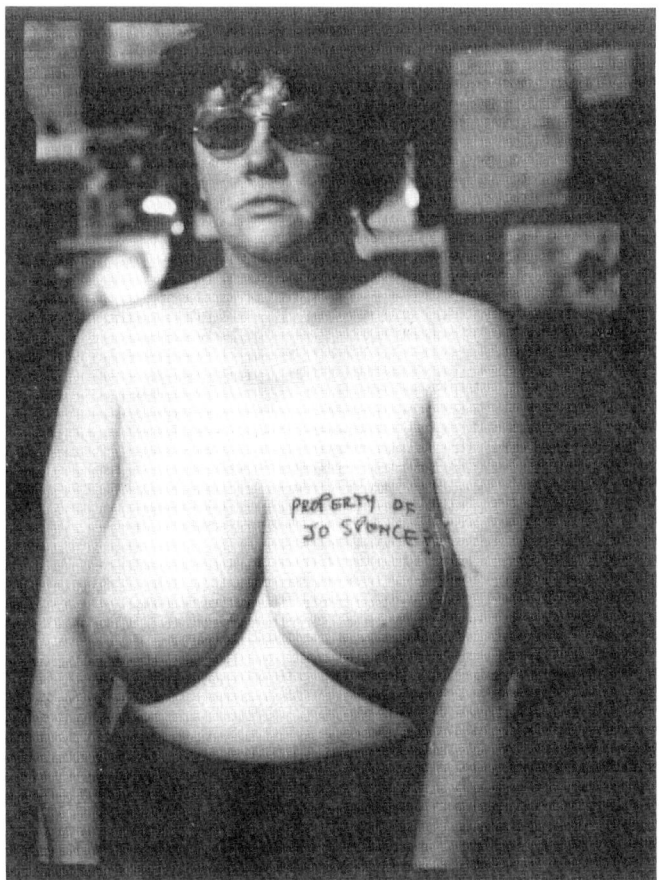

Fig. 7.   Jo Spence, from *Putting Myself in the Picture*

of herself facing the camera just before entering the hospital, "Property of Jo Spence" painted on her partly taped breast (157), can take their intended meaning only when the photograph is taken as a veritable image of the reality that met the emulsion, especially the meaningful personal reality of the breast's proprietor (Fig. 7). That attitude flatly contradicts Spence's comment, quoted above, that "the camera is not a window on the world." If it were not such a window, there would be absolutely no point to "Property of Jo Spence" or any similar image. And if "Jo Spence" were no more than the product of linguistic play, there would be no discernible point to her claims for ownership; indeed, there would be no discernible owner. If

Spence speaks at several points in her text about personalities as processes rather than selves (97, see also 45–46) she speaks at several others in very different ways; and when all are taken together they echo the ambivalence on those issues endemic to every postmodernism, perceptible at just about every point within them. If Spence cannot locate the "real" self of her model or of anyone else (40), she implies by that comment and others like it that self is more likely to be the product of a text than of anything more "essential," which is precisely the conclusion Rejlander saw and did not like. Yet she can argue in the same text for the need, while in the hospital, of representing herself to herself (155), of "providing images in order to have a dialogue with myself" (162). If that dialogue with the image is an encounter with oneself as Other, that which speaks on the other side of the Other, seeking such dialogue, cannot be dismissed simply as the ghost in the machine of discourse, no more than it can in Cindy Sherman or Barbara Kruger, John Coplans or Lucas Samaras or William Wegman, Jerome Rothenberg or David Antin or Ed Dorn or Susan Howe. Why, after all, would a figment of language want a dialogue with a figment of light? Of course there is nothing here like the stubborn Cartesian centering one sees in Gerald Stern or certain aspects of Duane Michals; yet the composer of the blurb on the back of the paperback edition of Spence's autobiography speaks of how "her photography is as much a part of her as her brain, her politics and her subjectivity." What that blurb is responding to in speaking of Spence's subjectivity is suggested in images like "Property of Jo Spence," in comments like those in which Spence speaks of representing herself to herself in order to be able to have a dialogue with self-provided images. It is also suggested in passages like Spence's remark about her sitters generating "such different views" of themselves "as the sitters gave themselves permission to show to me" (27). The unasked question is clear enough: what is it that gives permission? Of course there is a sense in which Spence's remarks about property parody bourgeois notions of property, as though we can lay claim to a part of a body as property; and yet we can and do so claim, and do it meaningfully, do it as though the "Jo Spence" who lays such claim means something that *can* lay claim. The politics of the claim goes even further, asserting as it does a certain personal notion of property against the power structure in the hospital that assumes without argument its "ownership" of the breasts that come into its territory.

Spence's play of text and image is more polyphonic than she claims, more indeterminate than she suggests. Her self-portrait is shot through with a subtextual unsettledness that keeps her field of codes from ever fully settling in, and that deep-seated ambivalence goes far toward fostering the reach of her self-portraits, their complexity of condition, their richness and density.

As for the various languages of power, from fine-art photography to Vietnam, from Rejlander to Richard Nixon, Spence's subtextual unsettledness argues that the field of visual signs encompasses far more than she acknowledges, for it is a site of struggle in which she struggles as much with herself as for herself. Her struggle is a private one as well as a more open encounter with the imperiousness that seeks so fiercely to make her what it wants her to be. Whether those conditions of contention imply a Spencian essence that struggles, in *its* turn, to be what it wants to be—however much that assertion conflicts with her theoretical statements—has to remain a possibility in any reading of her work.

Thus the play of visual/verbal in *Putting Myself in the Picture* makes for a much more writerly text than Spence's ideology would allow. Her autobiography is more of a *text,* more open, more plural, less given to the tunnel vision every ideology demands, than its overt political commitment would seek to have it be. Here too the comparison with the equally ideological Barbara Kruger reveals the latter's relative narrowness of conception. Though Kruger sometimes rises above routine one-liners, she rarely matches the density of "Property of Jo Spence," with all that Spence's self-portrait implies about how we inscribe ourselves in a community or about how a community inscribes itself in us or about the body's bodiness in this context (contest) of textual powers. Spence's image allegorizes the body as the site of the struggle of discourses. That struggle is writerly because the discourses are in no sense ready to reconcile and therefore reduce possibility. Further, if those discourses involve the political they also involve the ideology of that mode of making images in which we are, for once, the object of our *own* gaze. Feeding into Spence's photographs is the specific combination of Othering and narcissism that defines the photographic self-portrait, and her awareness of that combination commands the extraordinary complex that informs "Property of Jo Spence." That complex also includes her awareness of the degree to which *jouissance* seeks to be part of any such picture; her understanding of how questions of the gaze link up with questions of the body-as-object (examine the image of herself with crash helmet that parodies the pose of the model earlier in the book); the relation of her image to the objectifying of the female body in photographers like Weston and Brandt; and the affiliated sense of the body-as-object in the hands of the medical establishment. Finally it takes in the curious status of the body's materiality in the photographic self-portrait, as well as the attendant interplay between what the camera does to bodies and what time does to them. Though the camera always causes instantaneous Otherness, the body's perpetual presence to itself (never, in Spence, a doubtful matter like that of the self's presence to itself) comes stubbornly to the center of Spence's ultimate assertions. The sardonic suggestions of that initial centering on the chamber pot show that, whatever her imaginary lack, there is no lack in her body's immediacy to and in itself, to and in its various times.

It is precisely that question of the body's presence to itself, combined as it is in Spence with an urgent insistence on the specialness of *this* body, that brings to the surface of her work a stubborn subtextual impulse to give to the body what photography always sought to take away from the body as image. Benjamin's "aura" is still the best vehicle for conveying all that the impulse demands.[16] Another way of getting at this is to take into consideration the various meanings of "icon" and "iconicity." Before the Peircian reading of icon as that which carries likeness or resemblance, there is the older reading of icon as an object with special qualities, a representation implying resemblance but with additional, sacral, aspects that make it exceptional in its immediacy, unique and intensely charged, an object of veneration.[17] Those latter qualities tie the fullest meaning of icon directly to the auratic, that which photography, in Benjamin's reading, came into the world to dispel. And yet, *pace* Benjamin, the history of photography, in particular the history of the photographic self-portrait, shows photographers seeking incessantly to restore the lost auratic, to reclaim it for their art even as that art seeks to disclaim it.[18] Rejlander, for example, with all his ironies, suggests the relation of his art to easel painting, the most exalted of the fine arts, its aura part of the academic discourse that surrounds and contains all art; and he sets up an easel to assert exactly that relation. Spence's rejection of photography as fine art disowns that sort of secular auratic; yet her attitude toward her body—its uniqueness, its presentness, its manifold histories—fits in precisely with Benjamin's reading of aura and thus with the body as secular icon. Spence would, of course, deny any such reading of her work, yet this ambivalence is patently one of the defining

16. Walter Benjamin, "The Work of Art in an Age of Mechanical Reproduction," in *Illuminations*, ed. Hannah Arendt, trans. Harry Zohn (New York: Schocken Books, 1969).

17. For the Peircian reading, see *Philosophical Writings of Peirce*, ed. Justus Buchler (New York: Dover, 1955), 102–11.

18. This interplay and combination of the auratic and the iconic defines essential subtextual impulses in early and high modernism, literary and photographic. I keep this history sketchy here in anticipation of my fuller study of this subject.

conditions not only of her work but of any postmodernism, as we have already seen in Barthes and David Antin, among others, and will see again in photographers like Sherman and Kruger. Further, the question of iconicity is another one of those questions which ally Spence's photographs with self-portraits by (for example) John Coplans and Lucas Samaras. These too contemplate the photographer's specular gaze, his recurrent mirror stage.

One of the more significant aspects of the history of the term "iconic" is its use, especially currently, as meaning "having the quality of a thing," that is, immediacy and materiality, substantiality. Further, that meaning tends to blend with the Peircian/semiotic meaning of "iconic" as "representational, having resemblance." For example, Andy Grundberg speaks of the photographs of Thomas Florschuetz as having "a pleasing iconic quality" that "bring[s] to mind the more economical and polished explorations of the human extremities taken by John Coplans."[19] Grundberg's generally accurate description of Coplans's work misses one crucial point: Coplans's photographs are not just of human extremities, they are of *his* human extremities, portraits of his *own* parts. These photographs wander obsessively between generality and specificity, never entirely the one or the other whatever the stress of a particular image. Those points affect, go far toward effecting, the iconic in Coplans, for one cannot separate the meanings of icon as "thing" and "resemblance" from all that the term connotes of the secular auratic.[20]

That play of overt and implied emerges in the first image in Coplans's *Body of Work*, which like Spence's first image, "explains" how one is to read the images that follow. Coplans has so hunched his body that his torso reads as pure rectangle; just above the torso we can see two tautly clenched fists revealing the tension that compels this shape (Fig. 8). The image is monolithic in the way that Stonehenge is, though the stones in the Druid circle take part of their definition from their placement within the group, whereas Coplans's photograph gains much of its own definition from the *monos* in monolithic.[21] Given the punning that plays aggressively in the title of Coplans's book, what this body is working at seems to be its own

19. "Witness to History," *New York Times*, 10 November 1989, C26.

20. Coplans's rhetoric of the body takes in not only his study of the body as a whole, or the torso as a seemingly separate element, but the iconic qualities of individual body parts. He has had fascinating shows, and attendant publications, on his hands and his feet.

21. Similar echoes of the monolithic turn up in Edward Steichen's *Flatiron Building*, a brilliant Photo-Secessionist attempt to recapture the auratic. In a more blatant and pretentious way they also turn up in Stanley Kubrick's *2001*.

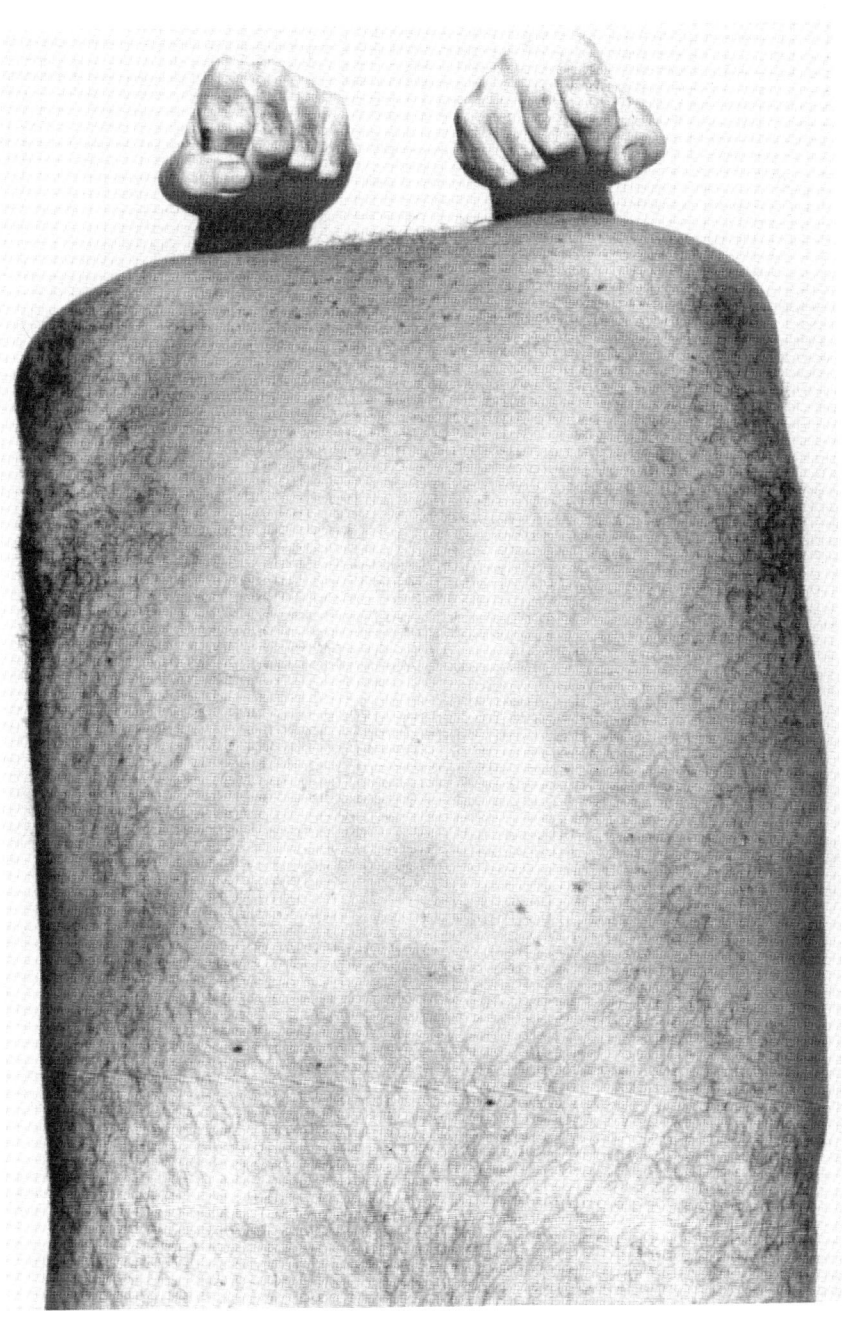

Fig. 8.   John Coplans, "Self Portrait (Back with arms above)"

emergence. It recalls archaic images in which the body and the stone out of which the body is made have not yet quite separated into different modes of being. Such body as there is—the fists that read as antlers, turning the image totemic— seems *just* emergent, the tensed fists the sign of the body's struggle into being. It is a moment of metamorphosis, a point in the history of being, archaic not only because of the art that it recalls but because that which is emerging is so close to origin. It is archaic in one more sense, because it is old but not at the beginning, not at the point of primeval chaos that precedes the archaic. An elemental form holds an elemental condition, an image of emergence appropriate for the beginning of a book (the picture itself continues the punning of the title), though what it is that emerges has yet, it seems, to be fully defined. In that sense the image speaks of Grundberg's *the*, the body as generalized body at a point in aboriginal time and in a context that holds nothing but the body and pure temporality. Around the body is only whiteness, the body itself the up-front subject as is Spence on the chamber pot, yet with none of the contextual emphases that put Spence in a particular place, at the top of the stairs next to a gross banister pole or waiting in the hospital to dispute ownership of her breast. All that the archaic can hold of an impersonal generality seems to enfold this image.

Still, if in one of its aspects this image precedes the fully human, in another it pictures the human at the stage of utmost personal development. The surface and textures of the mass, the heavy body hair, the moles and freckles dotted over the back are defining marks of a particular human body, whatever its generic thrusts and shapes. This body is simultaneously abstract *and* specific, archaic *and* contemporary. It is the locale of a series of related antitheses; no term within any pair is sufficient to define the whole; their open-ended interplay is the only system sufficient to handle the body's varying states. Only after the signs of the developed body come into the viewer's full awareness (of course this happens almost instantaneously) does the image reveal itself as sustaining crisscrossing metamorphoses, from the shape of the mono-lithos to the body of the developed person but also the other way as well, the person transforming himself into the shape of the single stone that will never be fully stone. This comes through as a combination of performance and body art, performance photography at its subtlest. What is performed is a kind of palimpsest that holds within itself all manner of stages of the body's history.

That also includes the body's history in art, a not-quite-subtextual stratum that runs through the work of Coplans in much the same way as it does in the work of Spence. Aside from her echo of her own earlier photograph of a trim, healthy model, several of Spence's nude self-portraits in *Putting Myself in the Picture* parody, for example, traditional nude-in-the-grass images (122–23), genre images (124), and madonnas (131). Coplans, his ideologies less overt, is at once more varied and more insidious, recalling not only ancient art but modern sculpture and his more immediate predecessors in high modernist photography. Yet in Coplans, too, it is history put to service; and where history echoes in Rejlander and his Photo-Secessionist successors in order to place photography within the aura of high art, it echoes in Copland in order for him to comment subversively on that tradition and to stake a place for his own antagonistic making, his own way of handling photography's obsession with the auratic.

Take his relation to Weston. In her excellent comments in the flyer accompanying the exhibit of Coplans's photographic self-portraits, Sandra Phillips remarks on his relation to Weston's "close-ups of legs and torsos" in "an anonymous space."[22] Weston, she argues, seeks to purify flesh of its temporality, but Coplans goes the opposite way, making his art "open to the particularity of its subject." This well-taken point can be refined somewhat more. Phillips asserts that Weston leaves out his subjects' heads in order to stress abstract design, but Coplans' does not ignore or omit the face, he subverts the "natural" sense that the face is a locus of signification, the site where personality emerges, the index of the self's intentionality. Indeed, he sets his work ironically, stonily, against the portraitist's practice of defining the specifics of the face at the expense of other details of the body. And yet in at least one case he acknowledges that tradition in order to sport with its preconceptions. Benjamin makes the point that early photography focused so much on the face because of the "cult value" of the human countenance; that is, its auratic qualities, all that it says about quiddity.[23] In its deliberate flouting of the tradition of the portrait, which means his rejection of that personal element which is most openly auratic, Coplans would therefore seem to be working toward modernist impersonality of the Westonian/Eliotic sort, focusing on the body as object. Yet consider what he does with his reading of Weston's torso of his son Neill, Weston's rereading of classical statuary. The fifth image in *A Body of Work* continues the confrontation with history by parodying Weston's piece, turning Coplans's torso, positioned precisely like Neill's, into a wonderfully

---

22. (San Francisco: San Francisco Museum of Modern Art, unpaged).
23. "Mechanical Reproduction," 225–26.

bizarre face. His torso is as hairy and dumpy as Neill's is smooth and trim, adding to the earlier image a set of shaggy eyebrows, a mouth, even a moustache and beard, the result a Groucho-esque reinscribing of modernist photography's best-known icon of not-quite-nubile male youth. This restoration of the face, its "cult value" intact (no one else ever looked quite like this), bows to Weston but outwits him as well. Weston is at once accomplice and victim, and those are precisely the roles that any body plays in time.

Which is to say that what gives Coplans's body its specificity and uniqueness is also what shows it to be subject to temporality. Put another way, particularity and temporality implicate each other as accomplices do. The pinched-up, drawn-up flesh that inhabits these images of a body in its seventh decade has lost its suppleness and elasticity and has gotten in their place an engraved sense of its immediacy in this temporal occasion. All those metamorphoses played out in the various poses—Coplans as archaic image, as phallic flower, as coy *poseur,* as multiple front line of a (phallic) phalanx— stand as metonyms or allegories of that overall transformation of the body of John Coplans into its current condition. Temporality, that is, is seen as much in the body's acts as in the stained, aged nails, the sagging flesh and belly, the gruff, seasoned maleness. The omission of the particularities that would be supplied by the face is made up for by the particularities of this body in its age. It is precisely that combination of immediacy and uniqueness and the up-frontness of the body at this point in its history, its whatness and whenness inseparable and mutually defining, that give this body its stake in the secular auratic. What Benjamin had suggested about the relations of aura and history comes out in these images fiercely, bluntly. If the photographs of Spence and Coplans put forth body-in-the-world in a way that Rejlander never would, Coplans's purification of context to the body in blank whiteness puts the intensest stress on the body in its time; more precisely, on bodiness-in-time. Whatever Barthes's refusal to accept a narrative for autobiography, the photographs of Spence and Coplans pose a narrative as patent (and potent) as that in Duane Michals; and if Michals and Spence put that narrative out to the surface in their autobiographical self-portraits, Coplans builds up in his image what time has built into his body. Whatever Barthes's refusal of narrative linearity, the upshot of all these contemporary self-portraits is the result of the most rigorous of all linearities (the one that for the most part avoids the surface of Barthes's texts but has within them the most intense subtextual life).

This is in no sense to argue for unbroken continuities in time and in ourselves. Indeed, Coplans's images argue for a multiplicity of selves in the immediate moment, an argument that recalls the suggestions of Rejlander that we are selves for specific moments, shifting as those moments shift; and given what Coplans shows of our relations to long bouts of temporality, the possibilities of self-positioning seem sublimely infinite. Further, if continuities cannot be expected in such a context, they can no more be expected in temporality as such. And yet given all this, we *still* are subject to a narrative, coherent or otherwise, in which we are at once subject and object, the subject of a narrative that shows us subject to temporality, temporality's object. We are that on which it works, that which works along with it, that is, victim and accomplice in more ways than Weston showed.

Which is also to say that the self-portraits of Coplans, like those of Spence in her illness, can only be taken as looking out on reality, the frame of the photograph acting as a window frame. Although the ironies of Coplans's photographs include all manner of specifically male posturings, echoes of classic roles (his work is, *pace* Phillips, in considerable part an examination of such roles), those images are as indexical as the photograph Barthes looks at near the beginning of *La Chambre Claire*, Barthes looking into the eyes that have looked at Napoleon. Further, and precisely as on that occasion in Barthes, that reality is centered on a single, centering figure, the same modernist ghost that haunts every postmodernism. All the varieties of positioning that show Coplans testing out stances for the self are based on the radically up-front positioning of Coplans's body in these portraits. Now we can see how that up-front positioning fuses with the question that turns up in Spence and similar figures, the need to posit a consistently active capacity for self-constituting so that the varieties of positioning can continue to occur—that capacity for self-constituting that not only implies our history but *makes* our history. That is precisely the same situation and capacity seen in the photographs of Cindy Sherman, however different her ideology from those of figures like Coplans and Samaras. She bases her "sittings" on the invariable up-frontness of the same, single body, a centering of the body as the site of the multiple "trials" of self that are acted out in her images just as they are in those of Coplans; acted out, made possible, folded into history by a single, stubborn competence. Coplans differs from Sherman in dispensing with the possibilities of the face, his bodily centering replacing classic facial centering so that he can make his points about bodiness-in-the-world. He shows none of the doubts (and fears) about substantive/substantial meaning that Rejlander shows, whatever convictions they share about the self's occasionality.

What is not occasional, however, is the time within the image, which is no longer the time of Othering but instead, Othered time. Rejlander knew it to be a radically different time from the time *of* the image, the latter being that which the image shares with us and within which it continues to have the sort of being that it has. The up-frontness of Coplans's body in *A Body of Work* is an up-frontness that *was* and that continues to recede from the immediacy of the moment in which we stare at the image of the immediacy of Coplans's body. Whatever Spence's and Coplans's assertions about the actuality of what we see—this breast over which she maintains possession, his torso as temporality's text, the claims of both photographers for the substance of bodiness now and here—we are faced with a play of time and locus that has immensely complex contours. Those contours resist any facile easing into coherence, any easy resolution to the internecine play of image, ideology, and desire that emerges from our specular posturings. What Hippolyte Bayard was one of the earliest to face continues to be faced, though with further twists to the conundrum in a time that has seen performance art move from the up-frontness of late modernist modes to the ironic questions of that condition in postmodern performance artists like Steve McCaffery; the time in which a poet like David Antin, obsessed by the same issues, plays with degrees of up-frontness and their gradual Othering through the various stages of his work.

We have learned a great deal from the encounters of Spence and Coplans with the issues so boldly (for his time) announced by the bourgeois Rejlander. Part of what we have learned, particularly from Coplans, is more than sufficient to put into question some of the assumptions of a classic modernist like Gerald Stern, specifically his centering of his discourse on an unshakable center of self; but other parts of what we have learned continue other assumptions that Stern and figures like Rothenberg and Antin (each in his own way) hold, especially their sense of an immersion in history that entails a dialogue with history. Still, much of that dialogue's content has to do with a condition that neither Stern nor a figure like Carolee Schneemann faces, the shifting nature of the selves that do the immediate speaking. Such shiftiness is another way of confirming the selves' immersion in history, yet that history enfolds the texts that those selves most certainly are, whatever else they are. This blend of history and textuality means that much of the speaking that goes on in the dialogue is profoundly subtextual, the enunciations of a capacity for self-constitution that speaks of its own existence while it also speaks of the shiftiness of the selves it makes. That capacity shows none of the egocentricity of the traditional lyric posture. It is by no means a substitute for the unchanging humanist self. A competence for a kind of action is finally no more or less than a condition of readiness, a positioning for a specific task. That competence and condition and the positioning they entail seem quintessentially postmodern, if not exclusively so.

7

Generating the Subject:
The Images of Cindy Sherman

He wanted to see her naked and vulnerable,
to see her in the refuse, the discarded
plots of old dreams, the costumes and masks
of unattainable states.
It was as if he were drawn
irresistibly to failure.
—Mark Strand, The Story of Our Lives

That one of the earliest events in the history of photography would have some bearing on the work of Cindy Sherman should not, after all, be surprising. Sherman is one of the chief exponents of what it means to be a postmodern visual artist. But so much of what she does bears on generic issues like the nature of the self-portrait, and therefore on the radical nature of photography itself, that her work not only touches on the timbre of the contemporary but has elemental affinities with photography's earliest groupings and earliest questions.

What I have particularly in mind is one of the first open acknowledgments that photography can be a very ironic business. On 14 July 1839, Hippolyte Bayard exhibited a set of thirty photographs made through an early experiment with light-sensitive paper. But the enthusiastic reception of the methods of Louis Daguerre sidelined Bayard's own work, and he responded the following year by making a photograph of himself called *Autoportrait en noyé* (Self-portrait as a drowned man). He noted the following on the back of the print: "The body you see is that of Monsieur Bayard. . . . The Academy, the King, and all who have seen his pictures admired them, just as you do. Admiration brought him prestige, but not a sou. The Government, which gave Daguerre so much, said it could do nothing for Bayard at all, and the wretch drowned himself."[1] Bayard's portrait of the artist as a drowned man is hardly convincing: the body slumps self-consciously against a convenient wall, and the torso shows nothing of the stiff, leaden look of dead flesh. (If anything, he seems to be sleeping off a binge.) But this bit of sardonic dress-up brings into serious question, and very early in the game, all of the awe that photography raises about its relations to the real world, about what it means to be both out there and within the print, about the always-ironic status (note the self-canceling title) of being both Other *and* oneself. Bayard's playacting establishes questions of presence, representation, and selfhood, of fictions and realities that are only partly what they claim, that still haunt the medium. It is not that Hippolyte Bayard is proto-postmodernist, prescient about the shapes of our own acts and theories, but that postmodernism has ways of focusing on central issues that have always been with photography. What Cindy Sherman exemplifies is an especially telling way of making those issues apparent. She took to photography as an art student at the State University of New York at Buffalo and turned out her first important images in 1977, shortly after moving to New York City. That first phase, which lasted into 1980, consisted of a series of images called "Untitled Film Stills." All of the stills focus on a single figure, in every case Sherman herself, decked out in a variety of guises and assuming a range of characters from popular films of the fifties and sixties.[2] Though they are designedly unspecific, which preserves their radical, generic focus, these images take in types that have meaning for more than movie buffs. In one (no. 10) a figure out of any number of Italian films looks up darkly,

1. The image is printed occasionally and was shown at an exhibition of photographic self-portraits at the Museum of Modern Art. It can be found, with the attendant comments, in Beaumont Newhall, The History of Photography (New York: Museum of Modern Art, 1982), 25. It is also reproduced in James Lingwood, ed., Staging the Self: Self-Portrait Photography, 1840s–1980s (London: National Portrait Gallery, 1987), 7.

2. I shall be referring to the images by the Metro Picture numbers as used in the catalogue to her show at the Whitney Museum of American Art in 1987. I want to thank Metro Pictures not only for permission to reprint the images but for their generous help in supplying me with printed commentary on Sherman.

Critics of Sherman's work ought to pay more attention to the photographs of Judith Golden, who was doing a series of parodic self-portraits, herself as Others out of popular culture, in the 1970s. For some comment on Golden's work, see Andy Grundberg and Kathleen McCarthy Gauss, Photography and Art: Interactions since 1946 (New York: Abbeville Press, 1987), 177–78 and 190.

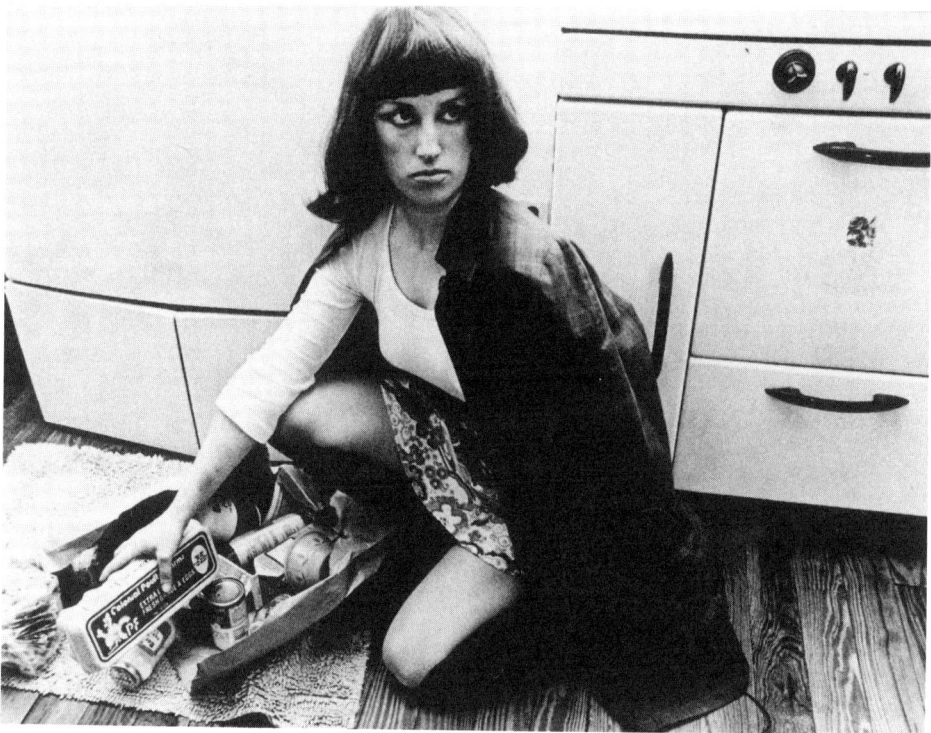

Fig. 9.   Cindy Sherman, Untitled (Metro Picture no. 10). Courtesy of Metro Pictures

poutingly, at an off-camera observer, the high-angle shot and the play of
extreme tonalities defining not only the figure but the passions of the scene.
The place is the kitchen but it might as well be kitchen-cum-bedroom, for
the passion comes to focus on the broken grocery bag pointing to the
darkness of her open crotch, while she picks up (what else?) a carton of
eggs (Fig. 9). In one of the best-known images (no. 21) Sherman takes the
opposite tack, the figure this time a pallid blonde in a business suit, in the
background the blurred images of some very tall buildings. The perspective
is such that they tilt in toward her, which comes partly to account for the
strained anxiety with which she stares out of the image at *something* (closer
definition would thin the fiction) that is, again, in some sort of contact
with her. From domestic sexpot to business waif and everywhere in between,
the spectrum of figures plays out patterns of popular culture, its images of
desire and especially its representations of women. But even this puts too
simply the intricate fields of these photographs, for they also play with how

we seek to constitute ourselves through shared public imagery, modes of self-presentation which, wherever we touch them, give off the feel of semblance, the sense of an artifice which is as much willed as imposed, something of what it means to live in/as fictions.

The black-and-white film stills remain Sherman's best-known work, though what has happened since then takes their implications into broader, more potent patterns. Black and white has given way to an increasingly skilled use of color. The suggestions of narrative inherent in the nature of the film still give way to closer attention to the figure at the center, always "played" by Sherman herself. A series of images with rear-screen projections, in some ways an extension of the stills, were sometimes technically awkward but did bring the subject into higher relief, up at the picture plane and more patently the main point of interest. Whatever their technical weaknesses, these images start an important shift in which the metonymical women in the stills are turned into figures with looser connections to patterns of pop imagery, figures for whom their own inner connections, questions about their connectedness, become the subject of intense brooding.

The next significant move came in 1981, when Sherman was commissioned by *Artforum* to do a series of centerfolds, for these took her established mode, now handled with greater dexterity, toward tenser emotional contexts and further suggestions of strangeness. Though these figures take on the submissive mode built into the vertical thrust of the centerfolds they are always fully clothed (consider what Carolee Schneemann would have done with the same material) and generally pensive and anxious. In no. 96, a ruddy teenager lies prone and open on the floor, clutching a torn piece of newspaper open to a lonely-hearts ad, the studied harmony between her clothes and the tile floor offering an ironic foil for her emergent unease and longing. Moving closer to life size, the images impose, with their brooding occupation of space, a further stress on that radical question of presence which has been in Sherman's work since its inception. It is because of precisely that question that the centerfolds continue to explore those elaborate fashionings of self, the play of text and self, text *as* self, which have obsessed most postmodernisms from their own earliest stages. Then, with that kind of inevitability whose ironies resonate in infinite regress, Sherman was asked, in 1983, by a Madison Avenue boutique to do a series of photographs advertising designer clothes. The images are anything but stylish, the clothes themselves taken more as costumes than daily wear. For the first time a sort of absurd that verges on the grotesque comes into play in the images, as though to confirm the intuition coming down from Thomas

Carlyle that clothes too are texts, and texts cannot be defined apart from what we are (which may well, itself, be text). Our compulsive self-constitutings emerge as bluntly here as anywhere in Sherman's work, whereas the emphasis on high fashion brings out even more openly the subtextual power that impels all such images.[3] But it is the suggestions of the eccentric that link these images most openly to the surprising changes that follow.

In the fall of 1985 Sherman showed a set of thirteen photographs at Metro Pictures, their images life-size though with a life unlike any other she had inspected up to that point. The evanescent cultural surfaces seen in her previous work, with all their attendant codes, give way to substrata that have most of all to do with the permanently unsettling and unbeautiful. Sherman had been approached by *Vanity Fair* to do a series of fairy-tale images, to be run with relevant texts from Grimm and other collections. Like some of her other projects this one did not materialize as originally planned, but it gave her a way of focusing what had already been on her mind.[4] These are no Gretels or Cinderellas but ogres and grotesques from the darkest interstices of the tales, deformed, mutilated, ugly, scary in a way that never goes away. Behind a thin curtain of erect grains a bulky, expressionless figure, with fat face and a prominent eye, stares at us from the top of the image, its head partly cropped but the completeness of its occupation of the scene never in doubt (no. 152). What glints out of those eyes never glinted before this show. Another figure in the series takes over the play of seduction that runs through the canon from the beginning, the play this time reflected in a harem woman with ominously gleaming teeth (no. 146). Sitting behind the entrance of a gauze tent she opens sexuality not only to pop exoticism but to archetypal depths, taking on the shape of a succubus; but the breasts she offers have nothing to do with her, for they are as false as the prosthetic buttocks another figure bares to our eyes. That other image (no. 155) shows only some scattered body parts, giving us, it would seem, all (the little) we want. At one level we are mocked with the tits-and-ass sexuality that runs through the earlier representations, though

---

3. The best study of the fashion photos is Jamey Gambrell's "Marginal Acts," *Art in America* 72 (March 1984): 115–18. See in particular her comments on how male and female stereotypes learn to view each other. Gambrell finds in Sherman's images evidence for the way women transfer the male desire to themselves through "a paradoxically narcissistic game in which the self's assimilation of the other's urge to power results in the self's loss of power" (116). For related comments, see Craig Owens, "The Discourse of Others: Feminists and Postmodernism," in *The Anti-Aesthetic: Essays on Postmodern Culture*, ed. Hal Foster (Port Townsend, Wash.: Bay Press, 1983), 57–82.

4. See Alan Jones, "Friday the 13th," *NY Talk*, October 1985, 44–45.

this time we are told openly that we are getting only a mock-up of what we think we see; yet at another level these images are shown to be grounded in a foundation of elemental myth (several reviewers of the show spoke of the collective unconscious) that takes the implicit anxieties of the earlier images into more permanent territory.[5] Sherman's seeing is oxymoronic, the querying play of inner and outer that informs most postmodernisms taken as a play of contraries that can never quite reconcile and cannot cancel each other out. But it is also, as elsewhere, a play of representations, imagings now not only of women (some of the figures are plainly androgynous) but of ourselves at levels and conditions that are always unshakably active. Sherman's fascination with our imagings of ourselves came by this point to extend into longer-standing modes of figuration.

This is change within continuity, a probing that simultaneously reveals and confirms. In the spring of 1987 Sherman showed a set of images at Metro Pictures that state, restate, and affirm, this time without reference to fairy tales or elemental images, that we are composed of elements, that we make and become offal. A horned mask that could have come from the previous show looks most like a rotting face (no. 174). A pimply pustulated buttock recalls the previous prosthetic version, but this time it images ourselves as filthy and infected (no. 177). The girl in the business suit of the earlier film still has evaporated, the suit, or rather an up-to-date, fashionable version of it, lies empty on a pile of junk. As stagy and melodramatic as the set of mythic images, this group finds its way into other sorts of permanence, repulsed by our physicality (vomit and blood-stained panties and a plateful of worms at a banquet) and the requisite disintegration of all that could be called us, our bodies and our images of self. What we see of Sherman's image is largely fragmentary and indirect—an indistinct background figure, a partial reflection in a mirror or a pair of sunglasses, always several degrees away from anything that can be called immediate or complete. If Sherman can be said to be saying, in this and the previous show, that we never saw her whole, there is more here than a flagrant rejection of all those viewers and reviewers who saw her work as self-exposure. Deeper concerns inform these figments of detritus, for the fragility of the early fictions and the stability of the archetypes come together into scenes of permanent evanescence.

5. See Andy Grundberg, "Cindy Sherman's Dark Fantasies Evoke a Primitive Past," *New York Times*, 20 October 1985, and Gary Indiana, "Enigmatic Makeup," *Village Voice*, 20 October 1985.

In the summer of 1987 the Whitney Museum in New York presented what was called a "survey" of Sherman's work ("retrospective" seemed hardly appropriate for a thirty-three-year-old artist with a career only a decade along), a show which had been touring for more than a year and to which were added some of the latest Sherman images. This show gave what no other could have given up to that point, a rich and detailed sense of the development of her work. It showed not only the rapid series of changes but also the consistency of vision and mode that had been with her from the beginning and appeared with even fuller passion in the most recent productions. What we have seen of the development came out with pristine clarity. More difficult and more disturbing are the stubborn, radical passions that ground this extraordinary work.

What, then, of Hippolyte Bayard and that mixed bag of mockery and poignancy, his "posthumous" self-portrait? Ian Jeffrey has pointed out how Bayard's self-reflexive images like those of Fox Talbot, have as their subject the conditions and possibilities of photography.[6] Bayard's studio pictures, as well as his photographs of architecture around Montmartre, stress the processes of deductive seeing. But the drowned man's self-portrait has even more to do with the phenomenology of photo-making as well as the complex existential status of photo and photo-maker (neither status, Bayard seems to argue, can be taken separately). We pass quickly through the level of fiction (the drowned man cannot take his own picture), though it remains a permanent base from which to work our experience of the image. We know that what we see is life masquerading as death, that we are looking at a (then) quite fleshly Hippolyte Bayard who was, for the moment, holding his breath, that he got up from this leaning position and went to work on the image that we see. To put it another way, we are watching a play of self and persona, though the latter is in fact (even if the extent to which we can speak of "fact" is getting more difficult to define) not all that much of a persona: it is, after all, Bayard *himself* who envisions *himself* in a death that could have happened (we have to think Aristotle at this point) and, most likely in other conditions, will happen.[7] The distinction between the photographer and his self-acted image, not very clear to begin with, becomes even less clear as our witnessing continues, though there is never any doubt that they are not exactly the same, that the moment of coincidence in

6. *Photography: A Concise History* (New York: Oxford University Press, 1981), 25–27.

7. It would be appropriate at this point to recall that the image we are looking at is that of an impersonator who is long since dead. It is perhaps equally pertinent that one of the early functions of photography was to memorialize the dead.

which the image was taken was when they were closest together. (Compare the similar issues in my remarks on Rejlander's self-portraits.) The play of deductive seeing that so fascinated Bayard involves other sorts of deducing than—to use Ian Jeffrey's example—the ambiguous placement of objects in space that occurs in his studio images. And all these forms of deducing obviously involve us as well, for it is we who are called upon to perform the attempts at placement, not only of the objects in space but of the "posthumous" subject in its odd and really quite eerie existential space.

Which may have something to do with the eeriness of Cindy Sherman's later images, for their own ways of being are finally as much concerned with what photography happens to be as with their "personal" qualities. These matters also say much about her initial, intuitive turn toward the genre of the film still as both a source of images and, itself, a way of imaging. Take, again, Bayard's self portrait, as well as Sherman's edgy, reiterated insistence that her images are in no sense autobiographical.[8] Several critics have pointed out that Sherman speaks of her characters in the third person, and her initial fascination with the work of Eleanor Antin gave way to a judgment that Antin believes too much in the characters she makes.[9] We can see why Sherman said that, given her wish to distance herself from the figures in her work; but her comments on Antin are questionable, if we can also ask ourselves how much Bayard believed in the image of himself as drowned. That question, as we have seen, accepts no categorical answers and neither does Sherman's work, whatever her understandable uneasiness about simplistic, diverting, and ultimately gossipy identifications.

Her best-known still shows a blonde in sneakers, bobby sox, checked skirt, and white blouse standing by the edge of a road, behind her a suitcase so sloppily, hurriedly packed that an edge of clothing hangs out (no. 48,

8. In an interview with Lisbet Nilson, Sherman tries, once more, to put the point as plainly as possible: "These are pictures of emotions personified, entirely of themselves with their own presence." See "Cindy Sherman," *American Photographer* (September 1983): 70. To the question whether she considers her pictures self-portraits she answers: "They may be technically, but I don't see these characters as myself. They're like characters from some movie, existing only on film or on the print" (72). With the subsequent question whether, if not self-portraits they are "in some way autobiographical" the exasperation comes through: "They're not at *all* autobiographical" (73).

9. Sherman has spoken often of her early attraction to Antin's work, but in an interview with Paul Taylor she tells of her shift in attitude: see "Cindy Sherman," *Flash Art*, October/November 1985, 78–79. References to Antin turn up frequently in Sherman's work, and appropriately so. Despite her demurrals, despite her status as an icon of postmodernism, Sherman's work is clearly akin to the performance art of Antin and Schneemann, as well as to the performance poetry of David Antin.

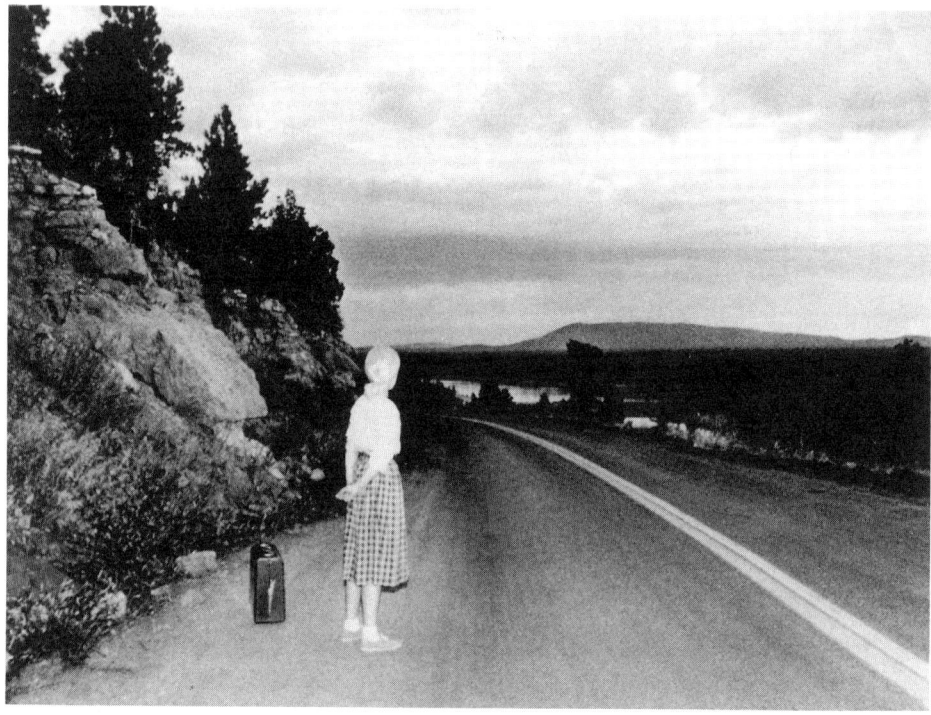

Fig. 10.   Cindy Sherman, Untitled (Metro Picture no. 48). Courtesy of Metro Pictures

Fig. 10). In a layout familiar from classic landscape imagery—memories of Constable will do— the horizon splits the picture across the middle, distant mountain and depth of sky completing their art-historical context with the predictable river but finding also a contemporary highway, its central double stripes confirming the bend of the road to the left and out of the scene. The blonde is hitch-hiking, but to where? To where bobby-soxers went in all sorts of Hollywood films some twenty years before this image (it is dated 1979). And if the image is turned toward our past, the girl is turned toward her own, facing the direction from which cars would be coming, her back to her filmic future in a play of stance and temporality that has as much to do with the nature of the film still as with any inherent story. But elements of such play turn up with regard to any photographic still. Bayard's self-portrait, for example, works with temporality in other, related ways. The time of his drowning is false, the time of his posing is true, just as the time of Sherman's posing is true but the time in the photograph is false to the extent that the image has to be considered a feigning (and also to the extent that one can speak of true and false times, a question implicit in both Bayard and Sherman, and in no sense answered by either). These issues point to some of the ways in which temporality is involved with photographic images. But there are other ways of such involvement: for example, we watch Hippolyte Bayard foreseeing his own death, long after that death has occurred; and no amount of juggling of theories can put aside the fact that it is an image of Bayard himself that we are watching performing that business, a point he wants so badly for us to note that he calls the image the dead man's self-portrait. Temporality and art and self—the play of time, text, and subject—work his photograph into a series of extraordinary complexities, few images in the history of photography surpassing what it does. To the frame Bayard developed, Sherman adds a sense of sociocultural systems and an attendant extension of the play of text and subject that was not possible to Bayard but which he would have taken in stride and perfectly understood.

Take, for example, what happens with the hitch-hiking bobby-soxer. The sox and skirt and blouse imply and implicate a set of definable values, taking in shared modes of understanding and being that begin with Frankie Vallee and specifics of diction and diet, moving from that level of pop sociology to all manner of more complex business. As one instance of the latter, the impress of communal values offers not only the sort of sustaining pressure that animals look for when they huddle, but also the sort of impress achieved when paper is stamped with preexistent images. Thus the play of pressure and impress, the kind of pressure known by lemmings but also the various kinds known by those more sardonic sorts who cannot resist the movies that make them—even though they know full well how they (themselves *and* the movies) are made. The film still, then, comes to stand not only for communal passions but for that play of self and semiosis, modes of temporality and degrees of fictionality, at which Sherman's work begins.

In his essay in the Whitney catalogue of her work Peter Schjeldhal says of the stills that "these pictures are at least tentatively about the film frame as a sign for a fictional world," a useful way of putting one of the frame's semiotic aspects.[10] Any film still is a snippet from a much larger fictive framework. It is literally an enclosed frame in which, in the case of Sher-

10. "The Oracle of Images," in *Cindy Sherman* (New York: Whitney Museum of American Art, 1987), 8.

man's work, a central figure is caught at one point in an action.[11] In every film still that Sherman recalls, the figure is impersonated by an actress, perhaps the representative of a type. Sherman's early reviewers spoke often of Monica Vitti, and it is part of the artist's point to render characters of that sort, characters with a curious existential status because we can speak of them as typical and generic (a Monica Vitti *type*) and yet as particular and specific (a *Monica Vitti* type). (Sherman's sensitivity to such apparent anomalies is one of the defining characteristics of her work, and it lifts her far above similar attempts by others to engage with public semiosis.) All of this leads to what some consider to be an infinite regress of fictions. In playing out the self-*makings* that film stills impress, we play with intricate levels of *feigning*, for what we are looking at in the still is an actress playing a role and playing it in a genre that is itself hardly "true" because it is only a single piece of a much longer strip of film, a fragment of a full-length, self-enclosed fiction. Thus the still is an image of an image, a metonymical snippet of an hour or two of feigning. In terms of Sherman's work one can complicate this further by noting how Gina Lollobrigida plays a Gina Lollobrigida type (see no. 35); but that is only part of the context that involves Cindy Sherman because with image no. 35 we have to speak of a photograph of Cindy Sherman playing Gina Lollobrigida playing a Gina Lollobrigida type. To this string of quasi-mirroring and existential states one has to add that her images of stills are designedly generic, speaking not of a single film but of a mode of making images. They are role-playings about role-playing, figments of fictionality, leaving both open and claustrophobic the question of egress from this complex.

One has to consider equally closely the related business of how we generate self through—under the impress of—such public packagings of the unreal.[12] That business fosters another sort of open-endedness, the result being further elements that never quite jibe, that are more than Sherman's varied connections with codes and images and fictions can handle by themselves.

11. I go along with the convention of speaking of Sherman's images as film stills rather than production stills. In fact, though, many of her images read more like production stills, and production stills have a relation to the film as narrative that may well be tangential at best. The distinction does not seem significant in working with Sherman's images, but in other contexts it may well have considerable importance.

12. This is, of course, a version of what I spoke of in my comments on John Coplans, what some theorists have argued is not a classical humanist self but a capacity for self-constituting. If Sherman shows a version of such capacity, she is not defined or controlled by it, since we shall see in her work a curiously consistent *absent* figure for whom the question of self-constituting seems never to come up.

Sherman is well aware that our participation in systems is an ironically creative act, maybe the only kind of creativity known to most of us; yet it is, obviously, a creativity within limits that leave the areas of choice potentially narrow and perhaps hardly existent. Hers is a more-than-usually ironic reading of the dream to "be" the images one sees on the screen. And it is an irony that reaches further than most such readings of codes, for it reaches toward conclusions that would involve codes and more but seem never to succeed in finally coming about. Who or what is the agent of that ironic creativity that public role-playing permits? Where, in terms of the photographic image, is that "who" or "what" to be found? Do our viewings of these images involve other kinds of nostalgia than memories of Lollobrigida? However we eventually resolve what is turning out to be a potent oxymoron, there is clearly more at play here than matters of semiosis and the exposing of codes. We seem to be working our way back to Bayard once again. He has, in fact, been continually muttering in the background.

Bayard begins and ends with himself in a way that, whatever his ironic demurrals, is very much of his time and place. He is present in every phase, a proto-*auteur* who sets up the scene of the image, setting himself down within it as a prefigurative figment of himself and getting the image taken as well, eventually bringing it to light. Part of his point is a parody of romantic visions of the artist as almighty creator: he has, after all, been so unsuccessful that he was compelled to drown himself (a point we might be able to guess at without the comment on the back, but find confirmed through that comment. Among his multitude of prefigurations one can include Bayard's guess at the ambiguous matter of captions). Of course this is Wertherian, Hugoesque nonsense; and yet Bayard's own work exemplifies a far less tacky version of the point because no place in the complex of events and results that centers upon this image is without his active participation, untouched by his many-faceted capacities. This means that the question of how to take him cannot easily be resolved because his ways and his arguments, that which he does and that which he mocks, are at ironic loggerheads. No genre he could have worked in would have left such matters so open. With Bayard one sees quite clearly why photography upset, and continues to upset, so many of the principles that created the canons of the arts. No one could come out of such events entirely satisfied, not even Bayard himself.

Cindy Sherman contributes her own upsettings, not least to photography itself, its own revered canons. What she adds raises problems and possibilities that are not *quite* in Bayard. His image is a self-portrait, a playing of oneself in a hypothesis. Sherman's images are of figures that come to her out of public fictions and are never of herself in the special way that Bayard's is of himself. That source is the same not only for the film stills but for the fashion photographs as well, and even for the fabulous characters of the 1985 show. However much a Jungian reading would put the latter into a collective unconscious, we know those figures largely through their traditional representations. Thus, even with the crones and the succubi there are essential, crucial differences between the figures in Sherman's work and the one that appears in Bayard's sardonic self-portrait. To play oneself, even in a hypothetical condition, is not the same as playing figures that are always-already-fictive. (The case of the *Monica Vitti* type, based on the typecasting of an Antonioni actress, is several steps closer to what Bayard actually does but is by no means precisely the same.) Sherman, unlike Bayard, appears to be enwrapped in a tightly enclosed, self-generating complex from which there is no perceptible egress, a complex whose rigid self-enclosing finds its most ironic commentary in the inherent incompleteness of the stills from which it was made, which goes far toward explaining several accepted readings of Sherman's work, typical of which is that in Douglas Crimp's significant essay "The Photographic Activity of Postmodernism."[13] Crimp worries about questions of presence (in various meanings), performance, and representation, arguing for a special kind of presence "effected through absence, through its unbridgeable distance from the original, from even the possibility of an original" (94). That, he argues, is the quality of postmodern photographic presence. Noting the importance of Benjaminian "aura" in this context, Crimp sees not only the depletion of aura in the art of the sixties and seventies (referring, surely, to Pop and Minimalism) but also more recent attempts to "recuperate the auratic" in "the resurgence of expressionist painting and the triumph of photography-as-art" (96).[14] But postmodern photography subverts this tendency, Crimp argues in his essay, by stressing the purloining of images, the unlocatability of the original, the fact that "even the self which might have generated an original is shown to be itself a copy" (98).[15] Crimp refers, inevitably, to Sherrie Levine's

13. In *October* 15 (1980): 91–101.
14. Walter Benjamin, "The Work of Art in the Age of Mechanical Reproduction," in *Illuminations*, ed. Hannah Arendt, trans. Harry Zohn (New York: Schocken Books, 1969), 217–51.
15. Of course this subversion would have to include, among its victims, the neo-expressionism to which Crimp refers. Yet it is precisely along such lines that the ambiguities of the situation, and especially of Sherman's work, make their appearance, for Sherman turns up as a significant figure in an essay by Michael Brenson in the *New York Times*, 5 January 1986, "Is Neo-Expressionism an Idea Whose Time Has Passed?" But the ambiguities extend into Brenson's essay itself: at the

appropriations of Edward Weston (one could add Barbara Kruger to the package). His remarks on Cindy Sherman follow logically from his premises. As Crimp puts it, she attacks the idea of "the supposed autonomous and unitary self," showing it to be "nothing other than a discontinuous series of representations, copies, fakes . . . an imaginary construct" (99). Two sentences of his paragraph on Sherman are particularly useful:

> Sherman's photographs are self-portraits in which she appears in disguise enacting a drama whose particulars are withheld. . . . The pose of authorship is dispensed with not only through the mechanical means of making the image, but through the effacement of any continuous, essential persona or even recognizable visage in the scenes depicted.

There is no question that Crimp is correct in much of what he says about Sherman, that her images reveal a great deal about the generating of the subject through public fictions, that her work shows how the possibilities within such generation may well be so restricted that any idea of an authorial-directorial figure (and therefore of the pure *auteur*) is called seriously into question. Yet that is not by any means the entire story about Sherman, even of her work up to 1980, the time of Crimp's essay, for as Crimp puts the issues, they are as unitary and totalizing, as rigid and categorical, as any of the limiting conditions Sherman ponders in her work. The result is an unconscious, mirroring complicity with authoritarian social structures, one that would lead an Hippolyte Bayard to suspect that the culture has colonized even the criticism that seeks to subvert it. At least this version is so colonized. Crimp shows persuasively how Sherman functions within the "directorial" mode she shares with photographers like Duane Michals and Les Krims, but that she craftily, cannily seeks to subvert the mode from within. Something very similar happens with Sherman's relation to work like that of Crimp, and the result of that partial subversion is a deeply felt ambivalence, a rejection of the categorical, and an insistence on open-endedness that get close to some radical qualities of postmodern experience.

This is not the place to make a detailed response to Crimp's essay. How does one deal with his remark about the negation of authorship "through

beginning he lists Sherman among artists linked to the movement but later he wonders whether she "may or may not be identified with Neo-Expressionism." Brenson's hesitations seem more the mechanical means of making the image"? His point is the same as what some critics have called the "automatism" of the photographic image, a point we touched on in our reading of Rejlander's self-portraits, the actual making of the image accomplished by the camera's combination of technology and chemistry. Joel Snyder and Neil Walsh Allen have sketched out some basics of the issue in "Photography, Vision, and Representation," quoting from critics like Stanley Cavell and Rudolph Arnheim, who make a case for automatism.[16] Snyder and Allen make a strong, plausible case for the rejection of so sweeping an assertion, arguing for choice, for the manipulation and selectivity possible to the photographer both before and after the taking of the image. Though one turns that taking over to machines and nature, one designs the taking and its aftermath to derive full advantage from what is there to be taken. Sherman herself often refers to the extensive preparation, sometimes taking several days, that goes into the making of her images. To speak exclusively, as Crimp does, of the mechanical aspects of photography is to promote a totalization that is patently specious. And to say that Sherman "simply chooses [these guises] in the way that any of us do," as though that were all that happens (and as though the choice were "simple"), is only to enforce an unacceptable narrowness and rigidity, an attempt to reduce a complex body of art to a preexistent scheme.

Crimp's comments eventually lead us, as most such comments do, to one of the prime perennial issues in the very difficult question of photography and representation. Snyder and Allen quote Arnheim as saying that "the physical objects themselves print their image by means of the optical and chemical action of light" and therefore that photographs have "an authenticity from which painting is barred by birth" (64). Arnheim is especially useful in showing the relation of automatism and what he calls "authenticity." It has often been pointed out that the imaged object in the photograph, whatever its nature, its sobriety or fantasy, its claims for documentation or its denials of such, *has to be there* to be photographed, and that point remains valid whatever happens to the image during the process of bringing it to light. No other art form can (or indeed is willing to) make such a claim, and in making that claim photography has troubled theorists

appropriate to what happens in Sherman's work than the formulaic categorizations to which she is so often subjected.

16. Joel Snyder and Neil Walsh Allen, "Photography, Vision, and Representation," in *Reading into Photography: Selected Essays, 1959–80*, ed. Thomas F. Barrow, Shelley Armitage, and William E. Tydeman (Albuquerque: University of New Mexico Press, 1982), 61–91.

from Baudelaire to Arnheim and beyond. Snyder and Allen correctly point out, however, that Arnheim is wrong in saying that the objects print their images, because it is the light reflected from the image and refracted through the lens that is the agent in the process (70). Arnheim is, in effect, turning the making of photographic images into a form of pathetic fallacy, animistic, ultimately sentimental. To put the matter in a different way that leads deeper into central issues, all that is required of the object is its presence to the light and the lens, a presence *which remains where it was* as the light goes about its business. It is only by stressing that leaving-behind that we can avoid the suggestion—the superstition—of a continuation of the object's presence within the photographic image; yet the matter does not end there because that point about light calls in another factor in the matter of photography and representation. There is not only the question of the object's requisite *being-there* but the further, related fact that the image we are viewing was made by light bouncing off an object and striking an emulsion in a way that "fixes" the image. Subsequent work with that light brings the image directly to us, where the sequence ends. Roland Barthes was so intrigued by these points about light that he argued for a special kind of continuum between the viewer and the imaged object, and therefore for all manner of paradoxes in the nature of the photographic image.[17] Rosalind Krauss and others argue that the Peircian idea of the index is essential to an understanding of how photographs mean.[18] It should be clear by this point that Crimp's comments pick out only one of several threads in an extraordinarily complex weave, and that no single thread in the text/texture of photography can handle all the contours of these issues.

That Sherman acknowledges such insufficiency is patent from her work, some of which is involved not only in exploring public fictions but in countering what she considers to be fictions of herself, generated by all sorts of viewers, including some of her astutest critics. In so doing she also counters, toys with, all sorts of public attitudes toward photography itself, especially the tendency of viewers from the earliest stages of the art to trust in the actuality of what the photograph shows. To "exist" in a photograph, so it has always been felt, is to be true, to be real. One gives the image

17. His most extended comments on the suggestion of a continuum appear in *Camera Lucida*, trans. Richard Howard (New York: Hill & Wang, 1981), but they can be found throughout his work.

18. Rosalind Krauss, "Notes on the Index: Part 1" and "Notes on the Index: Part 2," in *The Originality of the Avant-Garde and Other Modernist Myths* (Cambridge: MIT Press, 1986). Working the concept of the index in terms of photography seems to me difficult and probably dubious, as I made clear in some of my comments on the photographic self-portrait.

credence because of the mode in which it is proffered. Every photograph, in this view, is a documentary. Experiments in "Photorealism" play mockingly with this point, the term drawing on assumptions about the nature of photography but also generating a subtext that counters, at every step, what the term seems to imply.

One of the results of Sherman's play with public fictions is a commentary on that veristic reading of photography. Allied to that reading and derived from its preconceptions is the view that all her images are autobiographical, performances of aspects of Sherman herself, a series of self-explorations in the manner of Carolee Schneemann but much less openly. Impelled by the driving assumptions of photographic verity viewers probe beyond the dress-ups, compulsively insisting on their autobiographic import because photography, after all, is ultimately true, and the truth one sees in these, beyond all the role-playing, *must* be the truth of Cindy Sherman. At this point we see more of the difficult balancing act in Sherman's handling of the viewer. She is especially adept at taking the viewer on as accomplice, for her images, early and late, depend heavily on memory, not only of old films but of images from old tales and even what it looks like to dress for success—a series of given selves, the import of which we fill in. But at the same time Sherman seeks to undo other assumptions with which we approach her images, not only our radically documentary view of the photographic image but, what follows from that, what we think it (*and want it*) to document of the photographer herself.[19] There is a sense in which the 1987 show at Metro Pictures, with its pervasive disintegration/fragmentation of personal being, can be seen as a rebuff to such readings of her work, and the various prosthetic devices in the 1985 show surely can be taken the same way. Yet from the beginning of her work Sherman has been undoing the most general version of such readings, undermining what seems like a permanent longing for veracity.

Still, the point I made earlier about the text/texture of photography holds true in several ways for Sherman's work as well, and not only because they are photographs but because of how she handles them. No single mode of approach can take in all that she sees at once, all that she senses to be *simultaneously* existent, which generally comes to mean that we can expect

---

19. Such comments, as I have noted, have been made by some of the astutest critics around. See, for example, Craig Owens's classic essay "The Allegorical Impulse: Toward a Theory of Postmodernism." In it he argues that "Sherman's works are all self-portraits, but in them the artist invariably appears masked, disguised." In *Art after Modernism: Rethinking Representation*, ed. Brian Wallis (New York: New Museum of Contemporary Art, 1984), 233.

an encounter of elements that do not sit comfortably together. Take Douglas Crimp's remark that "the pose of authorship is dispensed with . . . through the effacement of any continuous, essential persona or even recognizable visage in the scenes depicted." The comment about the lack of a recognizable visage is arguable, but we can put it aside for a much more difficult and ambiguous one, some of whose implications appear in Crimp's phrases. Isn't the phrase "essential persona" inherently self-contradictory? What can the idea of the persona—a figment, facade, fiction, a mask, role, device— have to do with anything essential, with questions of essence? "Essential" can hardly mean "necessary" in this context, since the "necessary" object is lacking. It can only mean "basic" or "radical," having to do with "essentials"; and it is there the problems begin. It seems likely that Crimp, a fine and subtle reader of photographic images, is responding with particular sensitivity to an oxymoronic play in Sherman's handling of her work, an encounter of incompatibles that is one of its radical features and perhaps the commanding one. Take, further, the other sentence by Crimp that I quoted earlier: it says in part that Sherman's photographs are "self-portraits in which she appears in disguise" (precisely the point made, almost verbatim, by Owens). Given that Crimp is on record as having called the subject in Sherman "a discontinuous series of representations, copies, fakes," how can these *also* be portraits of "self," and who is the "she" involved who is behind all these varied appearances? Who is it that is in disguise? To put it in Crimp's own words: if Sherman "simply chooses [these guises] in the way that any of us do," who is the Sherman who does the choosing? If Crimp wants to argue that there is *only* disguise, his language is actually, doggedly, saying something quite different. Indeed, one could argue that Crimp's language reveals a stubborn residual nostalgia that he cannot quite pack away, and that this nostalgia may be the cause of such patent contradictions. We have seen such nostalgia elsewhere, and could see much more of it in readings of other artists and critics. One also could argue that such nostalgia is built into the language and cannot be avoided, since we have to use language to talk about these images. Both arguments, I think, are correct. In either case the ambivalence of these responses is triggered by, responds to, an ambivalence built into the shape of Sherman's art and essential to its nature. One can hear its voice outright in some remarks Sherman made in the interview with Alan Jones. Responding to a question about photography and other arts, she said "a photograph is less of an *icon*. And because it's a photograph you remain aware of an event in *real time*" ("Friday the 13th," 45). This points directly back to what Barthes spoke of as the sense of having-been-there that every photograph has, and it ties eventually to what Arnheim spoke of as "authenticity." Later in the interview, responding to a question about "the Vito Acconcini self, the Bruce Nauman self," in terms of "the Cindy Sherman self" she said:

> Maybe there *is* no difference. I like the way those people used their bodies. *They* didn't think of themselves as being up there on the wall. They were too concerned with the conceptual aspect of the *any body*. That's what their photographs document. They just happened to use themselves. That's the way I feel about it myself, even though I am under make-up or a wig or a costume. I wouldn't want to have done what they did, though. If I didn't have things to hide behind I'd be more aware of being up there on the wall. (45)

The relation of the last sentence to the rest of Sherman's comment is puzzling only if we refuse to acknowledge her own ambivalence about these issues. It is precisely this tonality to which Crimp and his language are responding, and it is surely a related matter that the structure of selfhood explicit in Sherman's last sentence is precisely the one implicit in some of the comments of Crimp and other critics.

And there is more. Crimp remarks, quite properly, about the lack of continuity in the persona, that status which leads him, again quite properly, to speak of fragmentation. But if there is no continuity in the look of the images, there is an absolute continuity elsewhere within the circumstances of Sherman's art. Though one may reject the idea that the images we see are variations of Cindy Sherman, *it is always Cindy Sherman who performs the variations.* It is she who is doing the posing, and whatever else we have, we have an unbroken set of images of her doing exactly that. This is not, however, to argue for any sort of "essentialism" in the photographic image, but indeed for quite the opposite. Whatever presence she had in those acts remains back there with the acts and cannot be carried over in that history of the work of light which so fascinated Barthes. Sherman's comments that in photography, as compared to the other arts, we are more aware of "real time," shows how her sense of the workings of the medium has the profoundest sort of relation to the images she makes out of it. More precisely, it relates to how she works those images, the stance she takes toward them, the persistence of that posing figure which, whenever we get to it, is always-already-other, always-already the subject of transience. We have seen a version of these issues in the self-portraits of O. G. Rejlander, and in fact see it everywhere in this art obsessed with absence. Photographers learned early that figures who move through the field of a long-exposure shot turn out to be barely visible, ghosts in the machine, and perhaps not visible at all, however firm their original stride. It is matters of just that sort that Sherman's work recalls.

For though Crimp insists that absence is the *defining* property of postmodern photography, it is surely the property of every photograph ever made, and this is as true for Talbot and Stieglitz as for any of our contemporaries. We have seen what Hippolyte Bayard did with the intricacies of this issue. We are, in fact, just catching up to him. In every photographic image there is an explicit, emphatic absence, one that is necessarily as intense (the ratio is exact) as the "lost" presence of the object struck by the light. In responding to a photographic image we are responding to a lacuna, its spaces filled with figments. If Sherman is obsessed by the fact of the fragmented figment, she is equally obsessed by the irrevocable lacuna, that lack so intense that we cannot put away for a moment our awareness of its emptiness; but her stress on the persistence of herself as performer shows that she sees the vacancy as part of a system whose discourse inevitably speaks, if only in negative terms, of that lost and unattainable Other whose losing has caused the lacuna. It is to an awareness of such ambiguities in the nature of photography that we must attribute what is still the most striking fact about Sherman's images, their consistent, insistent foregrounding of Sherman-as-model. Whatever the shifting faces, there is always the same made-up face. Whatever the shiftiness of the issue of photographic reality and of Sherman's particular bent toward role-playing about role-playing, there is a stubborn repetition (theorists of repetition could have a field day with Sherman's work) of the figure that speaks of shiftiness, that undoes fellow *auteurs*. That was one of the major impressions left by the Whitney survey of her work, which began with the publicity-size, black-and-white film stills and went through her various stages to the massive grotesques and dismemberments. The effect is quite extraordinary and maybe a bit spooky, for that sameness pursues the viewer through all the places where it is not.

What we have, then, is a play of absence and continuity, an odd, anomalous pairing that does not reach its fullest capacity until we add the fragmentation that many viewers have noted, an addition that puts into place a complex oxymoron. Despite the unshakable up-frontness of the figure of Cindy Sherman, there is, confronting the viewer, a series of scattered images that owe the coherence they have to membership in that series. But despite all the fragmentation there is an obsessive continuity that thrusts itself at the viewer in even the space of a single show and intensifies its pitch as the immersion continues. Though it is clearly the continuity of an absent figure, it is, all the same, an absolute continuity, fragmentation's requisite Other. That it is the stubborn continuity of a necessarily *transient* figure only increases the intricacy, the paradoxes, of Sherman's basic mode.[20] This encounter of contraries is most likely the basis of that intense underlying emotion that several critics have noticed, a deep, searching anxiety that moves very close to terror.[21] The eeriness in Bayard carries over to this body of work, which is clearly so very different, yet so very much the same. What we see in this encounter is the acting-out of such feelings, a postmodern morality play, for wherever one touches that lineup of photographed images one touches an absence intensified by that insistent, obstinate figure who always stays just out of reach. To say that Sherman can be scary has very little to do with fairy-tale ogres and much to do with the interplay of the elements that make up her world.

And it is precisely that interplay which has the most to say about the status of Sherman's work, its place in the histories of photography and contemporary art. Sherman's appearance in two significant collections of photographer's self-portraits shows not only the continuing refusal of some students of photography to accept her insistence that her work is in no way self-referential but what is ultimately more important, that what she does has more than occasional forebears (see the anthologies by Billeter and Lingwood). After Bayard there is a continuing history of photographers dressing-up, in everything from chains to Near Eastern exotica, as every-

20. In her January 1990 show, which parodied the ongoing codes of art history and the related codes by which we make images of each other, the continuity of the same face from image to image was particularly striking. That Sherman made no attempt to disguise it shows at least a subliminal acknowledgment of such continuity, though it can equally well be seen as an ironic riposte to her critics in this show which speaks of public figment-makings.

21. Gary Indiana puts it as follows in his review of the 1985 show "Enigmatic Makeup," *Village Voice*, 20 October 1985: "Sherman's work has always seemed suffused with latent horror of *reduction* (to roles, to appearances); one of its tensions (and conceits) is the artist's/subject's difference from herself, played against the viewer's awareness that 'they' . . . are all really 'her'—the artist, a larger ironical personality hidden under the makeup, even when there is no makeup." The implicit structure of selfhood seen in the comments of Sherman and Crimp is the same as the one seen here. It can be found in much of the criticism of Sherman's work, which clearly becomes a test case for the ambivalence resident in so many contemporary discussions of these issues. Take, for example, these comments from the fine essay by Lisa Phillips in the Whitney catalogue: "Her hall of mirrors, her masquerade conceals her real identity: Cindy Sherman is hidden in her self-exposure" (16).

thing from volunteers to Christ. Some of the issues that were to appear in Sherman's work persist all through this history—the play of self and/as text, the business of the *auteur*—but there is no one before Sherman who carried out the play with dress-up to the degree that she does, that is, everywhere and always. This means that nowhere before her postmodern photography has there been precisely this kind of interplay between absence and continuity, with all that it entails. By taking these recurrent practices into postmodern experience, Sherman does with the photographic self-portrait what has never been done before but was always potentially possible, needing only the appropriate milieu to bring itself forth.

More immediately, there is the question of her relation to modernist and late modernist figures as well as the more general attacks upon Greenbergian modernism/formalism with its criteria of wholeness, coherence, identity, and closure. Sherman takes part in those attacks, as all postmodernists do, and one could set her work up against that of a holistic modernist portraitist, Avedon for example, with foreseeable results. More interesting is Sherman's position vis-à-vis portraitists like Sanders and Arbus, both of whom, she says, influenced her ways of working.[22] One can see the relations of Arbus's grotesques and her images of suburbia to a range of Sherman's work, whereas the matter of the masterly Sanders is probably a good deal more subtle, having to do with, among other things, the semiotics of role-playing. But Sherman differs from both on at least one point that makes an immense difference: the images of Sanders and Arbus are always of the figures named in the title of the image—the German industrialist, the suburban couple— but Sherman's images are not only unnamed but have an odd, anomalous status that is not clearly fact or fiction. Whatever the gaps in the nature of selfhood, the images of Sanders and Arbus may show they have none of that special sort of lacuna endemic to Sherman's work, the sort that has made that work some of the most searching in our time. These images which draw so much on oxymoronic states not only continue history but subvert it.

22. See Andy Grundberg, "The 80s Seen Through a Postmodern Lens," *New York Times*, 5 July 1987.

8

The Syntaxes of Barbara Kruger

Barbara Kruger's images vary in size according to the mode in which she produces them, and each of those modes has ironies peculiar to its dimensions and style. At their smallest they show up as matchbooks, consumer society's epitome of the expendable, and the ironies begin whether we use them as we would other matchbooks or whether we put them on display in some safe place as examples of postmodernism's play with generic boundaries. At the other extreme are billboards that use advertising's classic synecdoche to subvert the social constructions that advertising builds. Between these extremes come postcards, T-shirts, posters, and, best known, the large, red-framed images that have been absorbed by the very museum culture that is one of the objects of her ironies. Still, it is not only the modes of production that give Kruger's images their aspect of complicity (the figment of full participation that is one of her cannier strategies); that aspect also includes the media images she appropriates from sources like old magazines to form the primary stuff from which her work begins. Such appropriation makes possible one of the more elaborate examples of that ironic positioning through which Kruger manages to be, simultaneously, in and out of the discourses she spends her art examining. Kruger and Sherrie Levine have built much of their postmodern art out of the business of appropriation; but where Levine reproduces old photographs precisely as they appear, challenging the modernist reading of authorship, Kruger complicates the issue by confronting the appropriate image with a text of her own devising that skewers the image with a pitiless irony that comes partly from the encounter between visual and verbal figures, partly from the positionings that encounter creates, partly from her appropriation of the appropriator of the female subject's imagining. Whatever the size of Kruger's images, they take on much of their meaning from the milieu in which they are found, the statements shifting in import from matchbook to museum wall. Kruger's play with generic boundaries is central to the undoing that activates her work. Language, size, and locale are all part of that undoing, potent and playful participants in these site-specific scenes.

The images, then, come out of the *déja-lu*, the realm of the preexistent and pre-interpreted, and seem about to be drawn into a terrorist interrogation. Hers is a kind of re-photography, different from Cindy Sherman's practice because Sherman makes mock-ups of the sort of figments that Kruger maneuvers. Through cropping and enlargement, Kruger aims to displace a conventional reading of the image to expose its covert rhetoric, not only its persuasions about products but those deeper, more sinister persuasions that seek to make products out of the voices that speak in her images (the "I" or "we" of Kruger's images is always female). To these images she adds her text; but the text is neither caption nor title, placements that would suggest separate but related orders of signification, giving the photograph primacy and privilege. Instead, the text comes in as an overlay, usually superimposed on the photograph, occupying the same space. It shares the world within the frame yet makes its own claim for privilege because of its role within the frame. Since these are the common conditions of many advertising graphics, part of the function of the superimposing placement is to generate ironic recall. Still, there is more to the question of placement, for the text in Kruger's work is always distinctly unfriendly, the superimposition giving it the status of an invading power that imposes itself on an antagonistic discourse. One could call this, then, the rhetoric of positioning or, more precisely, the rhetoric of rhetoric's positioning, that placement of verbal figures which causes them to speak before they are spoken. To put it still another way, that positioning suggests a mode of speaking that our speaking of the words confirms beyond any mistake.

Which is not to say that the relations of text and image come clear all that quickly. In fact, Kruger designs those relations to forestall what Craig Owens has called "the instant legibility of graphic design techniques."[1] She does that because, as Owens and others have pointed out, she wants to pry apart that easy folding-in of image and attendant text that advertising solicits.[2] Such carefully crafted collusion creates the mutual reinforcement that orders commercial persuasion and gives it unitary speech. Kruger's purpose is to subvert that speech by exposing what it will not utter, to speak the implicit and unspoken within the image's codes, to depose habitual (unitary) modes of reading by disjoining image and text and thereby compelling us to attend to *all* the voices within the image. The *déja-lu*, it seems, has not been sufficiently read. The modes of unitary reading are structured to suppress any meanings that counter the glossy. Kruger subverts the selectivity of such readings by prying text from image to open up a field in which the fullest play can take place.[3]

In "Untitled (We won't play nature to your culture)," one of Kruger's best-known works, the close-up of the woman's head forces us to attend to the leaves covering her eyes (Fig. 11). We have seen versions of such images before, in old movies or *National Geographic* or courses on archaeology, with coins on the eyes of the dead designed to buy a passage to Paradise. The leaves in Kruger's image take the place of such coins, showing how the woman is seen by the image's male viewers (Kruger's "you" is always male) as all that is natural, instinctive, organic, life-giving, supportive.[4] That is

1. "The Medusa Effect or, The Spectacular Ruse," in *We won't play nature to your culture: Barbara Kruger* (London: Institute of Contemporary Arts, 1983), 7. For other comments by Owens on Kruger, see "The Discourse of Others: Feminists and Postmodernism," in *The Anti-Aesthetic: Essays on Postmodern Culture*, ed. Hal Foster (Port Townsend, Wash.: Bay Press, 1983), 57–82.

2. Aside from Owens, see also Lita Barrie, "Beyond the Looking Glass: Your Truths Are Illusions," in *Barbara Kruger* (New Zealand: National Art Gallery, 1988), 27, and especially Kate Linker, "Representation and Sexuality," in *Art after Modernism: Rethinking Representation*, ed. Brian Wallis (Boston: Godine, 1984), 414.

3. Compare the following, from Barthes's "Rhetoric of the Image": "The text *directs* the reader through the signifieds of the image, causing him to avoid some and receive others. . . . With respect to the liberty of the signifieds of the image, the text has thus a *repressive* value and we can see that it is at this level that the morality and ideology of a society are above all invested." *Image-Music-Text*, trans. Stephen Heath (New York: Hill & Wang, 1977), 40.

4. Much contemporary play with pronouns establishes "you" as male. See, for example, Jenny Holzer's *Electric Sign* (from the *Under a Rock* series), the text of which utters a long, accusatory speech, most of it addressed to a "you" as phallic as any in Kruger. In an interview in *Eau de Cologne* 2 (1987): 65, Kruger acknowledges her alignment with Holzer in addressing how power is

all the phallic/paternal order offers her as role in the binary play of nature
and culture, where culture is clearly the more advanced and superior element. Thus does "you" honor woman, even (especially?) when dead. Our
codes define our status (true for both viewer and object) and our images
grow from those codes—images so obtuse that they cannot see the irony in
putting into the same context a scene from an old cult of the dead and an
equally old ordering that makes woman the source of life-giving nurture.
And what are we to do with the coins that, however invisible, however in
a shadow-text that functions like lenticular images, the coins appearing to
our awareness as we shift our speculations and probe the ancient codes?
The coins' potent implicitness turns this old binary play into a play of
subject and commodity, releasing the unsaid words on which this media
image rests.

Some of the words likely to be unsaid are the pronouns that characterize
most of Kruger's texts, the pairing of "me" and "you" in "Untitled (We
won't play nature to your culture)," the implicit, speaking "I" in "Untitled
(Your fictions become history)," the more deeply implicit "you" in "Untitled
(I shop therefore I am)." Part of what Kruger releases is the unspoken
pronominal play in most public images, their rhetoric based on the wooing
of an implied addressee who has to be coaxed and persuaded for the image
to earn its keep. Much of what she argues for has to do not only with the
persuading on which such images thrive but with far more sinister assertions,
endemic to contemporary culture and extending far beyond commerce,
about the addressee as subject—taking "subject" to include not only that
subject which is created within systems of grammar but all that appears
about power and positioning in the phrasing "subject to."

In fact, much of Kruger's work plays with the relations of positioning and
multiple signification. Steeped in contemporary theory, she draws on material that has much of its source in Benveniste's work on pronouns as well
as his attendant comments on history and discourse.[5] Though Benveniste
says nothing directly about the relations of pronouns and power, Kruger
builds on what he implies to release what these images contain of an unspoken ratio that never calls attention to itself but has to be recognized for the

---

used. For a useful linking of Holzer and Kruger in terms of their handling of institutions, see Hal
Foster's "Subversive Signs," in *Recodings, Art, Spectacle, Cultural Politics* (Port Townsend, Wash.:
Bay Press, 1985), 99–118.

5. The essays collected in *Problèmes de linguistique générale* (Paris: Gallimard, 1966), have been
translated by Mary Elizabeth Meek as *Problems in General Linguistics* (Coral Gables: University of
Miami Press, 1971). I shall be referring, in the text, to the pages in the translated edition.

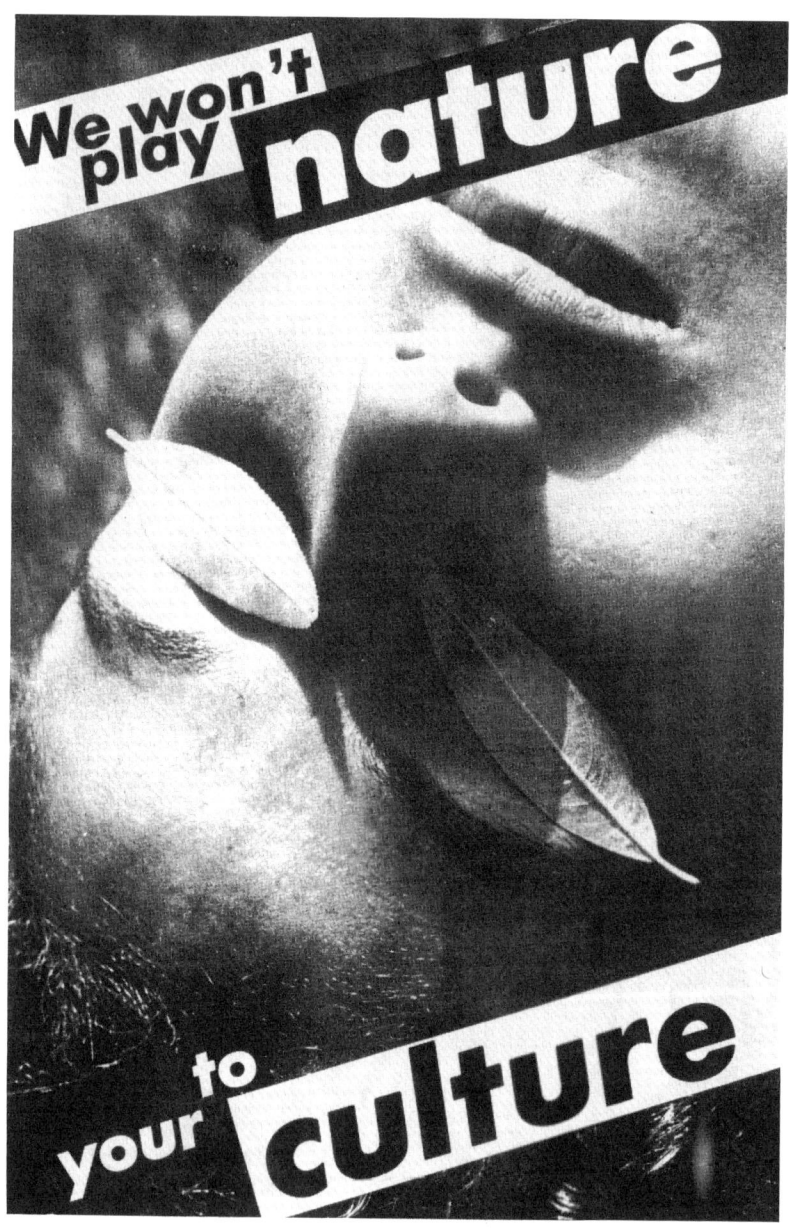

Fig. 11. Barbara Kruger, "Untitled (We won't play nature to your culture)."
Courtesy of Mary Boone Gallery, New York

image to function at all. Even when she uses only one pronoun, that pronoun implies the other. We have to take two steps in order to clarify the relations of Kruger and Benveniste, beginning with his assertion that we constitute ourselves as subjects only through the radical nature of language. Every instance of discourse that utters or implies an "I" posits us as subjects, establishing our subjectivity within that specific instance of discourse; yet it is a mistake to argue that this "I" has anything like objective reality. Though we can speak of a concept "tree," we cannot speak of a concept "I" that would take in every "I" spoken every time discourse occurs (218, 226). To claim reality for each or any would be to court Babel, for each "I" would be speaking in a language peculiar to itself, each language would be unique and therefore no use to communication. The second step follows from the first, specifying other radical tensions in Kruger's pronominal play. Every occurrence of an "I" implies a contrasting "you," spoken or unspoken. Every utterance of the subject is therefore dialogical, the "I" not only necessarily constituting an addressed "you" but giving "you" the potential to designate itself as "I" when it takes over the role of speaker (224). Neither "I" nor "you" can exist outside these verbal relations, but within them each exists in all its potential fullness, which includes all the fullness of their relations to each other. This means, further, that we can speak of subjectivity only in terms of those persons who exist within the instance of discourse, that is, "I" and "you." Utterances that deal with "he" are "objective" or "historical," "he" being a nonperson because "he" lacks subjective status (221).[6]

Kruger's best-known work, which concentrates almost exclusively on first- and second-person pronouns, creates a running critique that takes in not only modes of self-constituting through language but the relations those modes create; the result is a running allegory of the relations of language and power. Part of that allegory involves the ironic creativity of the male who wields and gazes, his capacity for the making of fictive selves. Consider, for example, "Untitled (I am your almost nothing)." Reductiveness takes in not only the tiny banner of text but all that "I" is permitted to be; the woman is reduced not simply to her fetishistic hair (her radical sensuality, as in Hawthorne's Hester Prynne) but to the hair as diaphanous web, there but barely so, a series of undefining strands without substantial coherence. "Almost nothing" comes through as an ironic term of endearment, some-

6. Also see, in *Problems in General Linguistics*, the chapter "The Correlations of Tense in the French Verb."

thing like "little woman;" but the play of text and image turns out far more ominous tones, the scanty web of threads edging the female toward nonexistence.

It is "you" in its role as an "I" which constitutes her as "almost nothing," existent only insofar as she *is* her sensual hair. Though Kruger's text never speaks directly in the voice of a male "I," that voice has had to utter itself as subject in order to make this nearly nonexistent object, which now takes its turn as "I." Thus Beneveniste's argument that any "I" and "you" will inevitably become the other takes an ironic turn in most of Kruger's work because though it is always the woman's voice speaking in her images, that voice speaks out of a situation determined largely by the male as subject, who turns the woman into an object most comfortable to himself; in this case something that is almost nothing, a cutesy figure that has only as much substance as the man wants it to have. This also comes to mean that the constituted (female) subject is not only the victim of power but also, at the same time, an instrument of power as well, for this figure is a cliché or stereotype that the phallic order retains, partly for its own gratification, partly to keep itself dominant. In images such as Kruger's the stereotype "replaces physical violence with semiotic coercion."[7] Clichés have power because they are clichés, widespread and unquestioningly accepted just like any stock response. In "Untitled (I am your almost nothing)," the image reifies the cliché, that minimalist term of endearment echoed in the bare existence of the diaphanous web. Kruger's reifications are finally best seen as allegorical acts, lessons in how to turn radical pronominal gestures into figurings of how subjectivity becomes subjection.

Some of the import of that allegory can be understood by querying the lack of pronominal gestures in certain modes of late modernism. For Clement Greenberg there can be no dialectic of "I" and "you" of the sort we have been inspecting, and therefore no dialogic structure of address. In "Avant-Garde and Kitsch" Greenberg argues that the nonobjective art of the avant-garde is valid in the way that nature is valid, that is, autonomously so, beholden to no meaning outside of what it is in itself.[8] That paring down of business results in an exclusive stress on the "processes or disciplines by which art and literature have imitated" the world of experience (6). "What we have here," Greenberg argues, "is the imitation of imitating." (The phrase inevitably recalls Friedrich Schlegel's discussion of "Poesie der

---

7. Owens, "Medusa Effect," 7.
8. Clement Greenberg, *Art and Culture: Critical Essays* (Boston: Beacon Press, 1961), 5–6.

Poesie.") A structure that embraces itself so tightly leaves no space in its world for anything other than itself, certainly not for its viewer/reader or, when its work is accomplished, for its maker (a point made by the New Critics through their doctrines of the intentional and affective fallacies). To speak of autonomy in such circumstances, as Greenberg has to do, is therefore to speak also of a peculiar isolation, that object which is all medium sharing the world with nothing else, taking part in no other space than the space it needs to occupy in order to fulfill itself. When it speaks, it speaks only to itself, which means that the only kind of dialogue in which it can take part is a species of infinite mirroring, a *mise en abyme* that can open up only to more of itself. This is another way of saying that it can only occupy spaces that are coterminous with itself, a fusing of self with mirrored image that is radical to Greenberg's work despite the occasional references to social order. (Modernism's rejection of classic [Brunelleschian] perspective, itself a claim for radical autonomy, ends in the fierce autonomy of Greenbergian modes.)

The species of postmodernism identified with Barbara Kruger takes a very different position toward the extent and content of space, an attitude that her pronominal gestures characterize and strengthen. In Benvenistian terms the relations of "I" and "you" (relations that cannot fail, for where there is one there is always the other) are necessarily dialogical. Such pronominal statements, always addressed, always involve an "object" over against the speaker. Thus the spaces in which Kruger's images do their work are never coterminous with those images but always contain an object of address necessarily outside the image's boundary.[9] Part of the purpose of Kruger's handling of address is therefore to create a space in which "you" can be addressed, in which "you" can be confronted and accused. Kruger makes that space in the act of confronting and accusing (much of her work's effect comes from its simultaneous gestures). Yet that does not exhaust her need for the making of spaces: since so much of the impetus for Kruger's images comes out of the import and acts of the gaze, she has to create a space in which both seer and seen can perform their defining roles, a space not

9. Of course the "you" is within the individual work in the sense that the work enacts the dialogue, but the "you" is also, simultaneously, outside in the sense that the work addresses readers/ viewers as they strike Kruger's matchbooks or walk through the galleries. This form of multiple positioning relates significantly to what I shall be speaking of as Kruger's copulative structures.

One can gain some significant readings of the differences between a late, transitional modernism of the sort David Antin evinces in much of his work, and an *echt* postmodernism of the sort Kruger evinces, by comparing what they mean and what they do with "address."

necessarily identical with the space of accusation. That all these spaces can ultimately be seen as performance spaces goes far toward explaining the radical significance of performance for those species of the postmodern for which gesture is something more than the act of a centering "I." She enacts pervasive issues of recent performance art, from the transitional late modernism of Eleanor Antin and Carolee Schneemann to the pure postmodernism of Steve McCaffery; and by enacting them in and through photographs she brings together the two genres that focus most closely the problems of every postmodernism. In so concentrating on the question of the subject and its spaces she shows that there is no place for autonomy (defined in this context as being coterminous with oneself) in any aspect of her work, or indeed most modes of postmodernism.[10]

Another way of understanding this question is to put it as Michael Fried does in "Art and Objecthood," one of the key documents in late modernism's formalist phase. Fried distinguishes "literalist" (read "Minimalist") art from modernist painting and sculpture through the latter's efforts to suspend its objecthood by emphasizing pictorial (not literal) shape.[11] Where the modernist work offers only itself, literalism is concerned with "the actual circumstances in which the beholder encounters" its kind of work (125). It therefore can be called theatrical, a stance which, Fried repeatedly argues, threatens the death of all art, at the least its degeneration, and must be fought if the arts are to survive. Two points relate directly to what we have observed in Kruger. First, though the literalist object stands as the focus of the situation, "the situation itself *belongs* to the beholder" and in it the object confronts, obstructs, and extorts the complicity of the beholder (127). In so doing literalism creates a situation in which the beholder is distanced and turned into a subject and the work of art into an object. Literalism, as some would put it (Fried would not be among them), creates the viewer's role as subject, creating, specifically, the syntactical relations in which that role can be enacted. But the Greenbergian modernist work, interested only in what it can offer out of itself, sets up no such relation, seeking to represent only its modes of representation. Second (extending,

10. The opening out of a space that includes the viewer is not only antiformalist but leaves room for the application of reader-response criticism, which takes much of its impetus from its antiformalist bias. Though I shall not take up the issue here, the reading of Kruger *and* Fried in terms developed by, say, Iser and Fish, would open a number of relevant issues. This is still another way in which Kruger's modes touch on the relations of subjectivity and genre.

11. Michael Fried, "Art and Objecthood," in *Minimal Art: A Critical Anthology*, ed. Gregory Battcock (New York: E. P. Dutton, 1968), 120.

it seems, the idea of theatricality), Fried argues that literalism emphasizes an endless or indefinite duration, whereas in modernism "the work itself is wholly manifest" in a "continuous and entire presentness" that ultimately defeats theater (144–46). Fried seeks to distinguish carefully between presentness and presence, the latter obviously what objects qua objects have, the former, presumably, that fullness of being in a continuous present that "true" (modernist, Greenbergian avant-garde) art indubitably has.[12] Fried's final words come straight out of the modernist understanding of Benjaminian aura, at the same time suggesting a code that art has taken part in since its inception: "Presentness," he concludes, "is grace."

Despite Fried's rather narrow basis and his melodramatic remarks about literalism/Minimalism threatening the death of art, he was on to something important in his distinctions (the validity of which Kruger supports and clarifies in her work). In a later piece Fried argues that what he once called literalism has now become postmodernism.[13] In fact his comments about the theatrical make good sense not only out of Kruger but Cindy Sherman as well. What Fried speaks of as theatricality can also be described, as I have done above, in terms of the making of spaces, spaces that Kruger's art shares with all modes of performance. In "Untitled (You are getting what you paid for)," shown at the Mary Boone Gallery in May 1987, the dripping nipple of a baby bottle pushes up to the picture plane, confronting the viewer immediately and intimately. Placed at the center of the image the nipple is tilted down slightly and aimed directly at the viewer's mouth. The text itself is so placed as to imitate the dripping of the milk. Thirsting for what we read, we are the (loving?) object of the maternal voice's attention. (Six feet by four feet, the image centers a nipple that is larger than the viewer's head, mocking one's giant thirst with this monstrous shape of satisfaction). The recipients of this proffered object and therefore sharing the performance space, we are obviously complicitous (Fried, we recall, speaks

12. For a postmodernist reading of the play between presentness and presence, see the discussion on Steve McCaffery in Chapter 5.

13. A special issue of Critical Inquiry, "The Politics of Interpretation" (9 [September 1982]), has an essay by T. J. Clark, "Clement Greenberg's Theory of Art," with a response by Fried, "How Modernism Works," and a counterresponse by Clark, "Arguments about Modernism." Clark's and Fried's essays have been reprinted, with additional comments, in Pollock and After: The Critical Debate, ed. Francis Frascina (New York: Harper & Row, 1985). Though Fried's arguments are somewhat weaker than in "Art and Objecthood," they reflect a refinement of his formalism if no essential change within it. In "How Modernism Works," Fried says: "In the years since 'Art and Objecthood' was written, the theatrical has assumed a host of new guises and has acquired a new name: post-modernism." Pollock and After, 78 n. 17.

of the viewer's "complicity") but in a broader and grimmer way than the Fried of "Art and Objecthood" would have it. Kruger's command of the viewer's involvement implicates not only the male spectator, asking for maternal solace from that which he seeks to control, but also the codes and (multiple, contradictory) roles endemic to his society and the power structures within it. The scene of enactment, then, turns out to be more than the gallery that holds this grotesquely large image. That scene spreads out to take in an entire social order and the variegated desires perpetually at play within it.

Autonomy does not address an other; it does not indulge in dialogue; it—necessarily—goes without relation. A valid autonomy would defeat the Benvenistian claim (that "I" always calls to "you") made by Kruger and most other postmodern artists; however, in postmodernism's terms, modernist claims for autonomy are not valid. Autonomy of the modernist sort can only be the desire of those who can imagine themselves or their art as utterly self-sufficient. Autonomy is inextricable from the intellectual/social institutions that make it possible to conceive of autonomy at all, a point that emerges as part of the tradition in which the autonomists partake. Behind their assertions stands a long and varied history that belies such claims for independence from the social order, including the claims of those romantics (the immediate source of similar modernist claims) who argued themselves to be independent of systems other than the ones they create for themselves.[14] That there is something of Byron in the claims for autonomy made, explicitly or otherwise, by Greenberg and Fried and, for example, Roger Fry is not, after all, surprising; and that Byron, a master of romantic irony's mode of direct address, was therefore a master of the theatricality Fried abhors, is only one more among the ironies this situation holds.[15] Still, in terms of Kruger's art it may not hold enough. The Benvenistian positioning of subject and object within Kruger's performance spaces has to do with more than dialogue, for it comments with potent cogency on contemporary modes of conceiving the nature of art. That is, the play of genre and subjectivity that impels Kruger's work drafts an implicit history that necessarily includes her own work as well, a point which that work does not acknowledge. If that participation suggests the potential for the species of ironic self-distancing that gives art extraordinary resonance

14. For an elaboration of this point, and a reading of part of its history, see my *Autonomy of the Self from Richardson to Huysmans* (Princeton: Princeton University Press, 1982).

15. See my *Self, Text, and Romantic Irony: The Example of Byron* (Princeton: Princeton University Press, 1988).

(Jasper Johns mastered it early), Kruger has not developed anything more than the suggestion. It is a kind of ultimate positioning to which her work, with all its Conceptual complexity, has not yet arrived.

II

Whatever their dense effect there are more than Benvenistian ironies that inform Kruger's play with subjectivity and syntax. Consider, in addition to "I am your almost nothing," the following texts from her untitled works: "I am your slice of life," "We are your circumstantial evidence," "I am your reservoir of poses," and "I am your immaculate conception." Kruger's texts are studded with copulative verbs and their attendant predicate nominatives, the activities of noun and verb at least as insidious as they are in the Benvenistian mode, since they make even firmer assertions about matters of identity. The point of coupling the copulative verb and predicate nominative is to give that noun the same referent as the subject of the sentence; in effect, to rename the subject. Such constructions can therefore be argued to assert identity, the nouns that straddle the verb looking at each other as one looks into a mirror. (Copulative structures are clearly related to the Imaginary.) In fact, the copulative system works like pronominal play in establishing the subjectivity that language brings into being, since that system advises each side of the structure that it is a reconstituting of what stands on the other side. To utter a copulative sentence is, therefore, to build a being; or to put it more specifically within Kruger's concerns, to utter such a sentence is to compel identification (the term "compel" stretching out to include coercion and indoctrination).

Take, once again, the text "I am your almost nothing." The act of equation here confirms the reduction of the woman to the near nonexistence of the diaphanous web of hair because each side of the equation can only hold as much as the other does, or so, at least, the language would lead us to believe. As Kruger shows copulative language working, it seems to be asserting that the predicate renaming exhausts the potential of the subject that is renamed. An assertion is put forth as an objective, radical fact, and we tend to accept it as such because the syntax says it is so, our language in complicity with the powers that wield copulative verbs. More accurately, less melodramatically, one could say that the language, never innocent in itself, becomes far less than innocent when it becomes an instrument of power.[16]

The speaker of such language is no more innocent than the language that is spoken. In Kruger's case that points to an anomaly that runs throughout her work, because her speakers are always the *victims* of the power commanding the play. Wielding her habitual duplicities Kruger manages to undo that appearance of complicity even as she shows it working. Speaking the copulative "is" in a way that creates the contours and limits of identity can be done, in Kruger's terms, only by the speaker of the phallic order (the phallic order in its paternal mode, since the Father is the Wielder of the Word that creates). Yet there is no Kruger work in which that order speaks directly, for the voice that comes out of the text, whatever the nature of the image, is always the female voice. Thus when that voice utters a text like "I am your almost nothing," the voice is speaking *as if,* speaking the sounds of the phallic assertion, what that assertion wants the speaker to think she fully is. The voice we hear in this image speaks the sounds of the phallic order even though it is that order's victim. The result of this masquerade is a bitter, ironic ventriloquism, part of whose function is to question *any* assertion of identity since it seems difficult to locate the precise source of the voice. That indecision sets the tone for the undoing of any suggestion of unwitting complicity (to be carefully distinguished from the witting kind that Kruger performs), and it works in perfect collusion with Kruger's handling of the relations of text and image to put the suggestion of such complicity permanently aside. The voice that emerges from a Kruger work never can sound like innocent complicity if we attend the guerrilla grilling the text executes on the image. The sounds the ventriloquist mouths are the sounds of unwitting complicity but not the substance. If Benveniste is correct that subjectivity is credible only within the acts of language (and as Kruger's ventriloquism suggests, perhaps not even there), then what we hear as unwitting complicity has not even that much.

Take, as still another example, "Untitled (Your comfort is my silence)," which pushes the copulative structure to the point of breakdown. Similar images appeared on any number of cautionary posters during the second World War, urging silence about, for example, troop movements or other dangerous data. The implied danger comports oddly with the pleasurable

16. One of the subtler ways in which that thinking about essence seeks to get confirmed has to do with the widespread readings of photographs as veritable images of reality. The codes through which we encounter the medium claim that the photograph says "is" in a way that no other medium does.

symmetries of the order within the frame, which includes, in part, the diagonal shape of the head and hat, in part the balanced parallelism, visual and verbal, of the two banners of text.[17] This binary balance echoes the copulative assertion of equation (copulative structures are most often binary), so that the order of Kruger's text and the formal order within the image provide still another instance of equating at work. "Untitled (Your comfort is my silence)," is beginning to look like an endless hall of mirrors, its actions leading toward a *mise en abyme* of equations, but the *abyme* gets quickly closed off when we fill in the unspoken in the language of the text, when we get it finally to say, "Your comfort is *purchased at the price of* my silence." Only then does the cost of equating come fully into the open, showing, further, that the equating of roles is a sham. Only then do we perceive that all the acts of equating are designed to support the phallic claim for the pervasiveness of equating, especially between the elements that straddle the copulative verb. Kruger handles those claims as though they were true, showing how they seek to achieve and assert their credibility; and yet, at the same time, she destroys that credibility through her reworking of the image and what she gets her text to say. The text so positions itself that it is, at once, involved and metatextual, within and above the world that the copulative seeks to make true. This context puts all sorts of ironies into the term "copulative," not least because Kruger's work (and all photography) profoundly embraces questions of desire. Those ironies find considerable room for play in Kruger's art, especially in terms of the interplay of power and "positioning" (the latter, of course, has its own ironies hovering about). She suggests related ironies in "Untitled (You reenact the dance of insertion and wounding)," an image that is largely text, the photograph showing a man bending down to kiss a woman's hand. Putting this text together with scopophilic clichés such as "the penetrating gaze" (the fuller meaning of which comes out in the putting-together) shows how gaze and copulation come to be metaphors for each other. The play of power and sexuality in Kruger's work is pervasive, potent, intricate, and devious.

The question of complicity (complicated here in terms of the copulative) gets far more intricate when we consider that Kruger's dialogue of "I" and "you" is always, simultaneously, a dialogue of text and image. (Kruger's texts are always antagonistic to the photographs with which they share the im-

17. The diagonal shape rests on the hand as a bust does on a stand, giving this media piece the aura of the museum, extending Kruger's ironies into still another dimension.

age's space.) This relation parallels the enforced mutual support of "I" and "you" that Benveniste points out, taking the question of complicity into still another set of dimensions. It also highlights that peculiar balance of the fixed and the fluctuating seen in both Benveniste and Kruger. If there is a sense in which our roles are forever necessarily shifting, there is another, related sense in which the framework of roles is fixed, just as the framework of shifters is fixed, just as the framework of text and image remains always the same no matter what appears in each.

That web of complicitous positioning suggests some encompassing statements about the possibilities of positioning envisioned in Kruger's work. If there is any single factor that specifies the nature of Kruger's postmodern art, it is her obsession with the potential varieties of positioning and (what follows from her awareness of the plethora of its modes) the radically shifting nature of positionality as such. In a very important sense she is Gerald Stern's polar opposite. Part of the reason for Kruger's play with pronouns is their status as shifters, the point that their content is open to circumstance. This means that since subjectivity is constituted only within language, there is no fixed locale where subjectivity can always sit, certain of its site. Those usages of language that constitute subjectivity guarantee that no stability will ever lock it in. Much the same kind of shifting positionality occurs in copulative structures, for not only can subject and predicate nominative readily change places, but there is an important sense in which each side of the copulative equation is, simultaneously, on the other side as well. Thus when the text asserts "I am your reservoir of poses," the interchangeability of "I" and "reservoir" makes it possible to see both in the mirror at once. To be everywhere at once is to be nowhere in particular. The opposite circumstance, where one is capable of being everywhere at different times (the result of pronominal play), is the requisite mirror image of copulative simultaneity. The effects of both are precisely the same, substantiating the pervasiveness of shifting positionality.

And yet these linguistic musical chairs are only one kind of cause for the repositioning that is always at play in Kruger's work. Insofar as the woman is the object of the gaze she is necessarily immobile, set up as spectacle, acting out all manner of passive verbal constructions such as Kruger's deliberately clumsy locution "We are being made spectacles of." Prone, head down, her mouth open in a curiously ecstatic grin as her lover strokes her neck, the woman images all that is acted upon, all that she is when she is object/spectacle. The segmenting of the image through the strips of blankness and text cuts into the fullness of the spectacle in a series of antagonistic

thrusts, threatening (as Kruger often does) the breakup of the image, undoing the control of the gaze over the image as a whole. Yet that is clearly
not quite enough to undo the effects of the passive pose, the construction
of the sentence dangling awkwardly, helplessly, in its concluding "of."
Thrusting themselves between the viewer and the object of his gaze the
banners of blankness and text seek to undo the effects of the gaze's assigned
positions; yet though they succeed in unsettling the order, they never quite
overcome its power. The flaccidity of the passive sentence is the ultimate,
irrefutable sign of an incomplete assault. There are other signs as well. To
be made a spectacle of means to be made a public fool. (Consider the more
active phrasing: "You're making a spectacle of yourself.") Whatever the
assault upon the dominance of the passive image, the woman is not even
given the option of making a fool of herself, for that option is taken over
by the power that knows itself as power. Even the luxury of self-induced
foolishness is taken away from her, apparently irrevocably.

Still, the power relations implicit in the positionings through which the
gaze is ordered come apart often enough for Kruger's viewer to be uncertain
that he will always be where he is. Take, for example, "Untitled (You are
a captive audience)"; its obvious grotesqueness is only its most immediate
effect. Insofar as the "you" is the viewer as addressee, he is outside the
context of the image, observer of the frame's content but not part of the
content itself. Yet the copulative text (this time turned on the wielder of
the gaze in a sardonic act of revenge) pulls the viewer into the image at
the same time as he stands outside, putting him on both sides of the system
of the gaze. As that system works in this image, it identifies viewer and
object in precisely the same way that the copulative system identifies subject
and predicate nominative. Each system echoes and reinforces the other,
becomes a metaphor for the other's ways of working. Just as the referent
that is both subject and predicate nominative can be everywhere at once,
so can the viewer and viewed in this image: the viewer not only, through
close cropping, takes the position of the dentist but also that of the dentist's
patient who has just yielded up a tooth. The dental mirror within the
patient's mouth locates the meaning of the image with sardonic precision,
sign of an allegory of the activities of this gaze, which forces a fusion of
viewer and viewed. It is the word "captive" that gets the final ironies going.
The wielder of the gaze has locked himself into a system as much as he has
locked in the object of his gaze, so that he is, this time, his own victim as
well. That there is masochism in such a context comes clear through the
kind of laugh such a grotesquerie arouses (that mockery being still another

function of Kruger's magnificently gross close-up). Putting these points another way: insofar as what he looks at is a fiction he has constructed to
make the world more pleasing to himself, the viewer is looking into a
mirror. What he thinks he sees of the object is finally no more than himself,
the mirror reflecting not only *what* he sees but also *as* he sees. The copulative
system and the system of the gaze work together to put him on both sides
of that mirror. They make him, finally, the subject of his own text, wielder
and object of a dominating power, both dentist and patient, an operator
on himself.

The status in which one becomes subject to oneself (in every sense of
that phrase) appears also in "Untitled (Your life is a perpetual insomnia),"
where "you" is, once again, the star of his own seeing. Kruger crops the
image to balance lines and figures in exaggerated symmetries (triangles
openly meet and echo, broad diagonals fix and ground the image), a gesture
that turns up occasionally in her work and always recalls that academicism
that her work has to abhor. Here, though, the ironies have to do with more
than the politics of art history. The tonality of the image's order matches
and echoes the formal tonality of the man's clothing. The only easing of
that formality appears in the unbuttoning of a single wrist button, that
easing emphasizing, by contrast, the up-tightness of the tie, the obviously
expensive pin-striped shirt, the multiple rings. (What looks like a wedding
ring—signifier of another formality—is not on the third finger of the left
hand, suggesting the possible undoing of still another signifier of the social
order.) Part of what we are being told by precisely this type of dress is that
this is an image of wealth, class, and power, the hints of gray hair in the
eyebrows suggesting (as our codes urge us to believe—consider the air of the
actor John Forsythe) that such status has now been achieved, the hierarchy
ascended. Classically formal modes of ordering art couple, gently but firmly,
with images of accomplished power, their echoing a confirmation of their
ultimate intimate linkage.

Yet what they get together to render is a suffering that won't quit, so
that image and theme cohere into a system that refuses to stay stable.
Affirmation and denial assert themselves to no conclusion; their dialectic
is as perpetual as the insomnia they figure. What, then, of that dentist who
operates on himself? Here the allegory is less open but the result is the
same. It is our public visual discourse that urges us to identify people who
look like this with wealth, status, and power. In fact, this image is as much
a stereotype as any of those clichés Kruger uses to describe the positioning
of women. Here, though, the action turns sourly self-reflexive because the

figures who create such clichés, whether of men or women, are precisely those power figures whom this stereotype recalls. "You" has made the original image, and Kruger turns it into his sardonic autobiography, revising it into a mirror in which he sees both himself and his stereotype at once; sees himself, that is, inside and outside his stereotype, sees what he has made and decides that it is not very good. Narcissitic masochism can get very canny; so can those acts (never without some masochism) in which we operate on ourselves.[18]

Kruger's questionings of the relations of scopophilia and power seem to be shifting in focus, seen particularly in her uneven show at the Mary Boone Gallery in January 1989. A long lenticular image holds photographs of five babies, the lenticulation showing, from one viewing position, "feed me," "hug me," and the like, from the other, "psychotic," "neurotic," "schizophrenic," "hysterical," and "paranoid." The latter, coupled with the images, recall nineteenth-century catalogues of photographs of insane or criminal types, one of the purest flexings of power to which photography has been put. A less successful piece in the show has a nineteenth-century engraving of a scientist or physician, standing over the nude corpse of a young and beautiful woman, holding a heart in his hand. It is titled, flatly, *No Radio*.

III

The "you" who suffers and creates (creating not only his image of woman but his suffering as well) gets the finger pointed at him (points the finger at himself) only after another kind of shift in position. As Kruger put it in an interview with Carol Squiers: "With the question of You I say that there is no You; that it shifts according to the viewer; that I'm interested in making an active spectator who can decline that You or accept it or say, It's not me but I know who it is."[19] Implicated in the making of address, Kruger's spectator contributes to the paranoid tone of the society that informs such images. (To say that he becomes an informant is only to add to

18. For other comments on the relations between scopophilia and narcissism, specifically in relation to film, see Laura Mulvey, "Visual Pleasure and Narrative Cinema," in *Film Theory and Readings*, 3d ed., ed. Gerald Mast and Marshall Cohen (New York: Oxford University Press, 1985), 807–8.

19. Carol Squier, "Diversionary (syn)tactics: Barbara Kruger has her way with words," *Art News* 86 (February 1987): 80.

the meanings of that act.) Yet her point that "there is no You" can be understood in several other ways; so taken, in fact, that it takes part in a radical ambiguity, tinged deeply with ambivalence, that pervades postmodernism and gives it much of its special character.

Some of that ambiguity emerges in Kruger's dispute with Baudrillard over his reading of her work. In an essay printed in the catalogue of her 1987 show at the Mary Boone Gallery, Baudrillard argues that Kruger's use of personal pronouns is "violently ironic," exposing "a society with a weak identity," addressing authorities that are now disappearing.[20] In fact, "you" and its repetition "actually emphasize the absence of the other, of the interlocutor—or at least his problematical presence." To put it plainly, "there is no one at the other end of the sign." The masculine can respond to challenges to its power "only by vanishing, which it has already done." Kruger's images, says Baudrillard, denote a condition where there is no "virtual antagonist" or even any masses, "thereby underlining the unreality of our state of things." In a sense Baudrillard is arguing that Kruger's images are Baudrillardian simulacra, images that represent, precisely, nothing, though their status is actually more broadly postmodern.

Kruger's reaction was swift and sharp. In an interview with the artist, published in *Flash Art* later that year, Anders Stephanson argues that Baudrillard has to be wrong because he ignores Kruger's stated desire to effect changes in power/social relations.[21] (That Stephanson is asking Baudrillard to react to Kruger's pronouncements on her images rather than the images themselves complicates the issue in a way familiar to questioners of intention.) Kruger responds by, first, refusing to accept this reading of her work as essentially incorrect, a position about readings she often holds; then arguing that "some kind of incremental communication" seems always to exist, "closer than we might suspect"; then flatly rejecting what Baudrillard saw to be the necessary implications of her practice:

> Of course I disagree with Baudrillard in his pronouncement that power and the masculine no longer exist, which strikes me merely as a hilarious idea for a 90's screwball comedy. Nothing crawls as profoundly between laughter and tragedy as power's cutely disingenuous attempts at self-effacement.

20. Jean Baudrillard, "Untitled," in *Barbara Kruger* (New York, N.Y.: Mary Boone Gallery, 1987), 3.
21. *Flash Art*, October 1987, 56.

Whether or not Baudrillard is being that disingenuous, there is no question that Kruger is correct in rejecting his comments about male power. Taken by themselves or in relation to the realities of such power, Baudrillard's comments are patently absurd. Still, it is possible to see how he gets where he does, how his thinking gets him to the center of a puzzle that informs not only Kruger's work but a great deal of postmodern thinking on the issues he raises. What Baudrillard arrives at is based on the persistent postmodern position (it is one of postmodernism's defining principles) that the subject does not exist outside the realm of discourse, that any suggestions of its actuality are only the residues of a humanism (Western-white-male oriented) that has long since collapsed. (These are, by now, the clichés of a period well into its decadence.) Baudrillard comes to his position directly from a discussion of Kruger's use of pronouns; and pronouns, in that pervasive postmodern reading we looked at in its Benvenistian form, grant no actuality to the ghost in the machine of discourse. In fact such readings routinely point out how easily we are duped into assigning actuality on the basis of the function of pronouns. Baudrillard is not forcing connections but following out the course of a position so well established and so familiar to his readers that most will inevitably make precisely the same connections. In fact, Jane Weinstock, an excellent reader of Kruger's work, has made just those connections, though she would never accept the idea that male power has vanished. Arguing for the variety of constructions of "you" in Kruger's work, Weinstock says that "you" is not "a biological entity, an unalterable identity; rather, it is a series of positions legislated by language."[22] Still, Weinstock continues, "you" has a sexual identity, marking "a series of power positions which historically have been occupied by white men. Kruger's works, then, cannot be considered as attacks, for if the 'you' has no referent, there is no-one to attack" (13). Weinstock's "then" argues for the inescapable logic of the point about nonreference, precisely the same conclusion Baudrillard came to, and for precisely the same reasons. Her point that "there is no-one to attack" comes from precisely the same thinking as Baudrillard's "there is no one at the other end of the sign." That she would never pursue this line of thought to Baudrillard's conclusion only increases the anomalies in this dispute.

The puzzle, then, remains; each element within this self-contradictory dispute presents a case that is irrefutable within its own terms. Each, taken separately, is convincing in different ways, on different sorts of evidence.

22. Jane Weinstock, "What she means, to you," in We won't play nature to your culture, 12.

The result is aporia, the species of irreconcilability that some Yale School postmodernists find in every manner of argument, including, sometimes, their own.[23] The stepping-back referred to by figures like de Man creates metacritical irony, precisely the species lacking in this aporetic discourse. That lack is equally patent elsewhere in postmodernism, especially on many issues that touch on the nature and status of the subject. Critics like Mary Kelly and Constance Penley argue that feminist theory is frequently bedeviled by suggestions of essentialism, but the same surely holds for postmodernism as a whole, which rarely escapes the touch, however subtle, of that which it seeks everywhere to refute.[24] Kruger's refusal to acknowledge the reasons why Baudrillard's argument got where it did, reasons built into the pronominal discourse that structures so much of her work, leaves the quarrel hanging, a condition typical of many similar situations in postmodern discourse. (See my comments in the previous chapter on Cindy Sherman and her critics, as well as my related comments on Jo Spence.) One could argue that, though "you" and "we" exist only as positionings within discourse, they still take active part in damaging power plays, still may be cause or recipient of harm, sometimes both together. Yet what, precisely, is harmed? A ghost in the machine of discourse? That is another version of the conclusion that Baudrillard had to come to.

What is surely not harmed is what we arrived at in my comments on John Coplans, the *capacity* for positioning, that which structures all discourse, establishing the shifting conditions that characterize the acts of the subjects residing, for the moment, within the pronouns. That capacity has to be ever present, continuing, and dependable, for discourse to take place at all. That such capacity has, therefore, some basic trappings of the "essential," that it can be said to reinstate, surreptitiously, a "self" (reinstated in the status of the positioner), may well be one of the reasons for the pervasive

23. Any argument for the nonreliability of argument necessarily implicates itself in the claims it is making, a metacritical irony that is as requisite as it is rare. Paul de Man makes a version of that point about self-implication in *Allegories of Reading* (New Haven: Yale University Press, 1979), 125. There he comments on a complication "characteristic for all deconstructive discourse: the deconstruction states the fallacy of reference in a necessarily referential mode." See also 208, where de Man is speaking of Rousseau but making the same point: "The loss of faith in the reliability of referential meaning does not free the language from referential and tropological coercion, since the assertion of loss is itself governed by considerations of truth and falsehood that, as such, are necessarily referential."

24. See Kelly's "Re-viewing Modernist Criticism," 97–98, and Penley, "'A Certain Refusal of Difference,'" 378, in *Art After Modernism: Rethinking Representation*, ed. Brian Wallis (New York: New Museum of Contemporary Art, 1984).

postmodern inability to escape the sounds of essentialist speech, however *sotto voce,* however deeply muttered. In *Allegories of Reading* (174) de Man argues that Ricoeur's reading of Freud comes to similar conclusions: "The subject is reborn in the guise of the interpreter." He argues for more of such rebirth in Starobinski (on 171) and Heidegger (on 175). This maneuver, which transforms "the nothingness of the self into a new center of meaning," is, de Man states, "a very familiar gesture in contemporary thought, the ground of what is abusively called modernism" (174). That it is also perceptible throughout postmodernism, and in much the same terms, offers still another instance of radical continuity where there are supposed to be only breaks. Similar positionings in terms of the essentially human appear, perhaps less surprisingly, in the work of Stanley Fish. See, for example, his comment in "Interpreting the Variorum" on the capacity to interpret: "The ability to interpret is not acquired; it is constitutive of being human."[25]

If there are more ironies here than Kruger has so far controlled, that means that she is bound within the spaces she describes. She is implicated in a way that Steve McCaffery, aware of the need to question even (especially) his own preconceptions, most emphatically is not.

And that, in penultimate irony, sets up patterns and echoes in her work that resonate in areas where we did not expect them: if Kruger is involved in an aporitic context where some of postmodernism's radical theoretical positions cannot seem to affix themselves, that instability echoes the shifting positionality that is, itself, one of those radical positions. Her work becomes, in several ways, a representative body of art, defining its context in defining itself. Consider, for example, the question of "border" in late modernist meditations on the making of art. Such speculations affirm a single creative centrality, fixed in a position that looks out benignly toward the horizon of its own boundaries; and that is a condition that Kruger, committed neither to benignity nor fixity, could never seriously assume. Her way of undoing images of power by showing them helplessly stuck in webs of their own devising are most closely akin to a different kind of border relations: for example, her undoing of accepted generic boundaries by giving her images much of the flavor of the media presentations they seek to undermine. If Kruger's texts invade her antagonist's turf through guerrilla modes of disguise, they do so in a parody of the way words work in media, faking complicity (assuming duplicity) in order to undo from within. The odd

25. See Rick Rylance, ed., *Debating Texts: Readings in Twentieth-Century Literary Theory and Method* (Toronto: University of Toronto Press, 1987), 170.

territorial quirk in which her viewers get to be put on both sides of their own boundaries appears once again in one of the ways her art functions.

Still, the quirk appears so often, in so many aspects of her work, that it comes out to be the radically stable force that controls and defines that work. It appears in that language which is, at once, participatory and bellicose, complicitous and metatextual. It appears in the way that titles can stay the same from one work to another though the images are different ("You make history when you do business"); in the way that images stay the same and titles change (a hand, a vegetable, and a vegetable brush are seen as "The Power of Art. The Art of Power" and, rearranged, as "You make history when you do business"); in the way Kruger has been making more frequent use of lenticular images, the viewing of which requires us physically to shift viewing positions, to perform the allegory. Yet those quirks appear in much more than these examples. The refusal of fixity that we saw in her use of syntactic and scopic systems turns up not only in her images but in their relation to their modes of production, from matchbooks to billboards and including (in a continuation of the irony for which Warhol set the model) the absorption of her art into the forms of museum culture. Positioned in that distancing which posits the antagonist as Other in order to see where to get at it, Kruger works from within as well, working the modes that emblem what she seeks to undo. Thus the shifting positionings of subjectivity and genre not only determine modes of production but get modes of production that ironically echo themselves. This demonstrates not only the determinative force of both subjectivity and genre but their own intensive mirroring, each implicated directly in what the other does.

That mirroring may be, however, more than implication. Kruger's work exemplifies the postmodern version of the point that subjectivity and genre are not only essentially related but may turn out to be exactly the same elements viewed from differing perspectives. If that sounds very much like the shape of a copulative system, it only confirms our growing sense that we are dealing with a set of metonyms, any one of which can take its place up front as a synecdoche for the whole.

Yet the one that seems most fully to represent them all is that pervasive territorial quirk which they all seek to instance. That is because the radical shiftingness for which these instances are metonyms echoes its own acts and problems in the very way it works. This means that it can function as a synecdoche for itself, not only standing for that complex which *is* itself but standing in the fullest possible way *because* it is itself. Consider the overall pattern. The quirk which is so pervasive that it appears at every point is an act that promotes instability; yet its unfailing reiteration exhibits and exemplifies precisely that stability it seeks everywhere to undermine. This makes it exactly analogous to what we have already seen about the capacity for positioning, that which engenders the quirk: it, too, takes as its business the need to reveal instability; yet, given the order of the world Kruger describes, it has to be regular and unfailing or that world cannot work. The way of being of Kruger's unstable world contains invariable, essential elements, taking "essential" in the sense of "requisite" but taking awareness of the fact that other senses of "essential" (themselves allied to "requisite") can never be entirely absent from a world that functions this way. That anomalous bag of contraries turns up all over postmodernism and in some of its finest artists, Sherman and many others. In Kruger's case there is a characteristic reflexivity, characteristic in the sense that not everyone has it, though figures like Sherman and Lucas Samaras have their own versions. Kruger's territorial quirk echoes itself in its acts, for it cannot make up its mind whether it is stable or unstable (of course it is both at once). Rejecting any binarism, any claims for either/or, it regularly, dependably, images instability as it goes about the process of defining itself. At the deepest reaches of Kruger's art there is an ultimate aporia, where the model of stability finds itself promoting its opposite, arguing fiercely and dependably for the potency of its contrary. In an art that everywhere comments on the corruption of desire this is about as far as its ironies can go.

Index

ABC—We Print Anything—In the Cards (Schneemann), 95–96
Acconci, Vito, 7, 146–52 passim, 154; Following Piece, 146–48, 151, 157–59
Activities (Kaprow), 141
Allegories of Reading (de Man), 232–33
Allen, Neil Walsh, 204
American Photographer, 197n.8
Anderson, Laurie, 113n, 135–36
Antin, David, 4–5, 9, 16, 42, 61–85 passim, 120, and Coplans, 188; "dialogue," 71, 74; "how long is the present," 73–74, 84; immediacy, 119, 120; "is this the right place?" 61; and Kaprow, 128; and Kruger, 219n; late modernism, 116; and McCaffery, 110, 121, 124; "a more private place," 61, 62, 80–81; "a private occasion in a public place," 61, 63, 65; and Rejlander, 174; and Schneemann, 93, 95; "sociology of art," 83; and Spence, 179, 188; and Stern, 35–36, 84, 188; talking at the boundaries, 65, 78, 80, 120; "talking at the boundaries," 73; "Talking to Discover," 71, 75n, 81n; tuning, 63, 65–66, 71, 73, 120; "tuning," 74; "what am i doing here?" 61; "what it means to be avant-garde," 66, 67

Antin, Eleanor, 220
Anxiety of Influence (Bloom), 67
Arbus, Diane, 211
Armstrong, Louis, 141
Arnheim, Rudolph, 204
Artaud, Antonin, 91, 92
Artforum, 193
Ashbery, John, 29
Assemblage (Kaprow), 122
"At Bickford's" (Stern), 20
Atget, Eugène, 1–2
Autoportrait en noyé (Bayard), 190–91
"Avant-Garde and Kitsch" (Greenberg), 218–20
Avedon, 211

Bakhtin, M. M., 111
Ball, Hugo, 3, 52–53, 130–31
Barthes, Roland, 13, 15–16, 86, 87, 92–93; and Benamou, 112; Camera Lucida, 168–69; La Chambre Claire, 109, 187; and Coplans, 186–87; and light, 205–8; and McCaffery, 109, 113; Roland Barthes by Roland Barthes, 17–20; and Schneemann, 94, 97; and Spence, 186
Battaille, Georges, 87, 92
Baudelaire, Charles, 143
Baudrillard, Jean, 155–56, 230–32
Baum, L. Frank, 3

Bayard, Hippolyte, 8, 14, 188, 197, 203, 209; and dressing-up, 211; early experiments of, 190–91; and Rejlander, 165; self-images, 142–43, 196, 198–99; and Sherman, 201–2
"Bee Balm" (Stern), 34
Before the Law (Kafka), 117
Benamou, Michel, 57, 111–12, 116
Benjamin, Walter, 1, 2, 12, 15, 60, 110, 112–13, 185, 202; and Coplans, 186; and Spence, 181
Benveniste, Emille, 8, 215–17, 226
Blake, William, 3, 10, 47, 54, 103, 126
Blanchard, Marc Eli, 167
Bloom, Harold, 16, 67–70; *Anxiety of Influence*, 67
"Blue Skies, White Breasts, Green Trees" (Stern), 22
Bly, Robert, 32
Body of Work (Coplans), 182, 185, 188
Byron, Lord (George Gordon), 222

Cabaret Voltaire, 58
Cage, John, 56, 66, 79
Calle, Sophie, 6, 7, 15, 88, 91, 129, 148–59 passim; "The Detective," 149–50; "Les Dormeurs," 149–50; *L'Hôtel*, 148, 150, 156; "Sortie," 157; *Suite vénitienne*, 150–59 passim
Camera Lucida (Barthes), 168–69
Cantos (Pound), 2
Caramello, Charles, 112, 116
Carlyle, Thomas, 193–94
Cassirer, Ernst, *Language and Myth*, 98
Castle, The (Kafka), 117, 147
Catscan (Schneemann), 96
Cavell, Stanley, 204
Cervantes, 111
La Chambre Claire (Barthes), 109, 187
Chatterton, Thomas, 10, 20
Chin, Daryl, 92
Christensen, Paul, 45, 55
Christo, 62
Clarissa (Richardson), 95
"Climbing This Hill Again" (Stern), 29
"Cokboy" (Rothenberg), 46

Coleridge, Samuel Taylor, 8, 11
Coplans, John, 7, 13, 180–89 passim; *Body of Work*, 182, 185, 188; and Kaprow, 129; and Rejlander, 174; "Self Portrait (Back with arms above)," 182; and Sherman, 200; and the thingness of body, 177
Crimp, Douglas, 13, 203–9 passim; "Photographic Activity of Postmodernism," 202

Daguerre, Louis, 190–91
"The Dark Bar Scenario" (McCaffery), 118–20
Day, F. Holland, 161
de Man, Paul, 108, 232, 233n.23, 233; *Allegories of Reading*, 232–33
Derrida, Jacques, 108, 111, 167
Descartes, René, 3, 8, 10, 54
"The Detective" (Calle), 149–50
"dialogue" (Antin), 71, 74
"The Dogs" (Stern), 33
"Les Dormeurs" (Calle), 149–50
Dorn, Ed, 179
Duane Duck (Michals), 130–33
Duchamp, Marcel, 4, 114

Echo-logy (Kaprow), 125
Eliot, T. S., 4, 5, 55–56, 185
Emerson, Ralph Waldo, 3–4, 8, 57
Erickson, John, 52
"Esther K. comes to America" (Rothenberg), 46

Finley, Carol, 6
Fish, Stanley, "Interpreting the Variorum," 233
Following Piece (Acconci), 146–48, 157–59
"For Black Tarrantula" (Schneemann), 99–100
The Four Horsemen, 90
Fried, Michael, "Art and Objecthood," 220–222
Frost, Robert, 72
Fuses (Schneemann), 91–92, 94, 98

"Galicia Nights, or a Novel in Progress"
     (Rothenberg), 46
"gambling" (Antin), 73
Gambrell, Jamey, "Marginalized Acts,"
     194n.3
Ghost Rev (Schneemann), 94
Ginx's Baby (Rejlander), 162, 171–72
Ginx's Baby and Co. (Rejlander), 163,
     172–73
Golden, Judith, 191n
"Grapefruit" (Stern), 41
Gray, Spalding, 126
Greenberg, Clement, 14, 69, 126, 151,
     211, 222; "Avant-Garde and Kitsch,"
     218–19
Grundberg, Andy, 182, 184

Happenings (Kirby), 125
Hard Times (Rejlander), 160, 165
"Here I am Walking" (Stern), 33
"Hidden Justice" (Stern), 30–31
Hockney, David, 34
Hölderlin, Friedrich, 47
L'Hôtel (Calle), 148, 150, 156
Howe, Susan, 4, 10, 179
"how long is the present" (Antin), 73–74,
     84
Hoy, Ann, 15–16
Hugo, Richard, 35
"Human Universe" (Olsen), 50

"I am your almost nothing" (Kruger),
     223, 224
"I am your immaculate conception"
     (Kruger), 223
"I am your reservoir of poses" (Kruger),
     223
"I am your slice of life" (Kruger), 223
I Build a Pyramid (Michals), 136–39
"I Do a Piece from Greece" (Stern),
     36–38
Indiana, Gary, on Sherman, 210n.21
"I Need Help from the Philosophers"
     (Stern), 26
Interior Scroll (Schneemann), 98–100
"Interpreting the Variorum" (Fish), 233

Iser, Wolfgang, 120n.2
"is this the right place?" (Antin), 61

Jeffrey, Ian, 196–97
Jespersen, Otto, 107
Jewish Book (Rothenberg), 45
Johns, Jasper, 223
Jones, Alan, interview with Sherman,
     207–8
Journal (Thoreau), 9, 10
Jung, C. G., 56

Kafka, Franz, 117, 150, 154; Before the
     Law, 117; The Castle, 117, 147; The
     Trial, 147
Kaprow, Allan, 6, 15, 121–30 passim,
     144; Activities, 141; and Antin, 72;
     Assemblage, 122; Echo-logy, 125; Pose,
     141; Poses, 126–28, 129; Routine,
     122–24, 127; and Schneemann, 91;
     Testimonials, 125
Keats, John, 20, 40–41, 138
"Keeping Things Whole" (Strand), 10, 12
Kelly, Mary, 232
Khurbn and other Poems (Rothenberg), 48
"The Kingfishers" (Olsen), 50
Kirby, Michael, Happenings, 125
Kitsch's Last Meal (Schneemann), 98–99
Klein, Yves, 143–48 passim
"Knowledge Forwards and Backwards"
     (Stern), 35
Kostelanetz, Richard, 126
Krauss, Rosalind, 13; Peircian index, 205
Krims, Les, 203
Kruger, Barbara, 8, 11, 14, 212–35
     passim; "I am your almost nothing,"
     223, 224; "I am your immaculate
     conception," 223; "I am your reservoir
     of poses," 223; "I am your slice of life,"
     223; and McCaffery, 107; No Radio,
     229; "The Power of Art. The Art of
     Power," 234; and Rejlander, 174; and
     Rothenberg, 58; and Spence, 177, 179,
     180; "Untitled (I am your almost
     nothing)," 217–18; "Untitled (I shop
     therefore I am), 215; "Untitled (We

won't play nature to your culture),"
214–17; "Untitled (You are a captive
audience)," 227; "Untitled (You are
getting what you paid for)," 221;
"Untitled (You reenact the dance of
insertion and wounding)," 225;
"Untitled (Your comfort is my
silence)," 224–25; "Untitled (Your
fictions become history)," 215;
"Untitled (Your life is a perpetual
insomnia)," 228; "We are your
circumstantial evidence," 223; "You
make history when you do business,"
234

Lacan, Jacques, 110n
Language and Myth (Cassirer), 98
"Language-Writing: From Productive to
Libidinal Economy" (McCaffery),
108–9
"The Last Self-Portrait" (Stern), 20
Lawson, Thomas, 15
Levine, Sherrie, 8–16 passim, 203, 213;
Torso of Neill, 12
Library of Cruelty, The (McCaffery), 112
Lovesick (Stern), 34, 38
Lucky Life (Stern), 20, 22, 25–26, 31, 33

Mac Low, Jackson, 56, 58
Magritte, René, Le Viol, 132
Malte Laurids Brigge (Rilke), 2
Manifesto on Feeble Love & Bitter Love
(Tzara), 56
"Marginal Acts" (Gambrell), 194n.3
Mask (Schor), 100–104
The Maximus Poems (Olsen), 2, 108
McCaffery, Steve, 5, 8, 16, 88, 91,
100–117 passim; and Antin, 72, 85;
and Coplans, 188; "The Dark Bar
Scenario," 118–19, 120; and Kaprow,
129; and Klein, 146; and Kruger, 220,
233; "Language-Writing: From
Productive to Libidinal Economy,"
108–9; The Library of Cruelty, 112; and
mediation, 42; and Michals, 135; North
of Intention, 100–116 passim; Of

Grammatology, 115n; Scenarios,
118–19, 120, 124, 141; and
Schneemann, 93, 95; and Spence, 188
McEvilley, Thomas, 144
Meat Joy (Schneemann), 93–94
Mental Distress (Rejlander), 161–62
Merveilles d'Egypts, 133–34, 139
Metro Picture images (Sherman): no. 35,
200; no. 48, 197; no. 174, 195; no.
177, 195
Michals, Duane, 6–7, 129–39 passim,
143, 179, 203; and Coplans, 186;
Duane Duck, 130–33; I Build a Pyramid,
136–39; Myself with a Feminine Beard,
131, 133, 135; Ritual Fire at Luxor, 134;
and Rothenberg, 48; and Spence, 186
Mill, John Stuart, 63, 72
Miller, J. Hillis, 9
"a more private place" (Antin), 61–62,
80–81
More than Meat Joy, Schneemann's cover
design, 88, 89
Mottram, Eric, interviews with
Rothenberg, 53, 55–56
Myself with a Feminine Beard (Michals),
131, 133, 135

Nature (Emerson), 57
Neue Gedichte (Rilke), 2
"New Models, New Visions; Some Notes
toward a Poetics of Performance"
(Rothenberg), 43, 51, 53
New Selected Poems (Rothenberg), 45–46;
the Pre-Face, 50
Newspaper Event (Schneemann), 90–91
Nichol, bp, in Open Letter, 105n, 108
Nilson, Lisbet, 197n.8
"Nobody else Living" (Stern), 39–40
"No Longer Terror" (Stern), 41–42
No Radio (Kruger), 229
of Intention (McCaffery), 100–116 passim
"No Wind" (Stern), 23–24

Of Grammatology (McCaffery), 115n
Olson, Charles, 2, 109; The Cantos, 108;
"Human Universe," 50; "The

Kingfishers," 50; *The Maximus Poems*, 108; and McCaffery, 108; "Projective 2, Verse," 50; and Rothenberg, 50–56 passim
"One Bird to Love Forever" (Stern), 26, 32
"One Food in the River" (Stern), 20–21
Open Letter. See Nichol, bp
Owens, Craig, 214
Owens, Rochelle, 89

Palmer, Michael, 10, 72, 106
Paradise Poems (Stern), 31, 33–34
Payne, Andrew, interview with McCaffery, 107, 108, 110
Penelope, 48, 49, 50
Penley, Constance, 232
Performance in Postmodern Culture (Benamou), 111
Perloff, Marjorie, 66
Phillips, Lisa, 210n
Phillips, Sandra, 185–87
"The Photographic Activity of Postmodernism" (Crimp), 202
"Photography, Vision, and Representation" (Snyder), 204–5
Picasso, Pablo, 3
"Picking the Roses" (Stern), 31, 32
Plato, 127
PO&SIE, 71
Poe, Edgar Allan, 3, 11
"Poesie der Poesie" (Schlegel), 219
Poland, 1931 (Rothenberg), 45, 48
Poor Jo (Rejlander), 165
Portrait of Dorian Gray (Wilde), 168, 170
Pose (Kaprow), 126–28, 129, 141
Pound, Ezra, 2, 108
"The Power of Art. The Art of Power" (Kruger), 234
"The Power of Maples" (Stern), 30
"a private occasion in a public place" (Antin), 61, 63, 65
"Projective Verse" (Olsen), 50; and Rothenberg, 53–54
"Property of Jo Spence" (Spence), 178–80

Proust, Marcel, 26, 153
"Psalm" (Stern), 22
Putting Myself in the Picture (Spence), 180, 185

Rabelais, François, 111, 175
Ray, Man, 3, 176
"Red Bird" (Stern), 26
"The Red Coal" (Stern), 23–24, 33
Rejlander, Oscar Gustave, 7, 14, 15, 160–74 passim, 181; and Bayard, 187; and Coplans, 186–88; *Ginx's Baby*, 162; *Ginx's Baby and Co.*, 163, 172–73; *Hard Times*, 160, 165; *Mental Distress*, 161–62; "O.G.R. introduces himself as a volunteer to H.P.R.," 161–67 passim; *Poor Jo*, 165; and Sherman, 208; *The Two Ways of Life*, 160
Rejoicings (Stern), 21–22, 31, 33
"Remodelling Photo History" (Spence), 175
"Revolution and Independence" (Wordsworth), 41
Ricoeur, Paul, 233
"Riding Around on a Cooking Spoon, 1969" (Hockney), 35
Rilke, Rainer Maria, 2, 5, 6, 7, 11, 16, 20, 143; *Malte Laurids Brigge*, 2; *Neue Gedichte*, 2; and Rothenberg, 54; and Stern, 35
Rimbaud, Arthur, 54
Ritual Fire at Luxor (Michals), 134
Robinson, Henry Peach, 161
Rosenthal, Nan, 144
Rothenberg, Jerome, 5, 16, 20, 42–60 passim, 64–66, 84; and Antin, 72; "Cokboy," 46; and Dada, 3–7 passim, 44, 47, 49, 58; "Esther K. comes to America," 46; "Galicia Nights, or a Novel in Progress," 46; and immediacy, 119, 140; *Khurbrn and other Poems*, 48; and late modernism, 116; and McCaffery, 109–10; and Michals, 138; Mottram interviews, 53, 55–56; "New Models, New Visions; Some Notes toward a Poetics of Performance," 43,

51, 53; *New Selected Poems*, 45–46, 50; *Poland, 1931*, 45, 48; Riverside interviews, 54–55; "Salamanca A Prophecy," 60; and Schneemann, 95, 104; *A Seneca Journal*, 45, 60; and Spence, 179; and Stern, 188; "The Suicide of Dada," 46; *Symposium of the Whole*, 53; *Technicians of the Sacred: A Range of Poetries from Africa, Asia, Europe and Oceania*, 45, 56; *That Dada Strain*, 46–47
Routine (Kaprow), 122–24, 127

Sade, Marquis de, 87
"Salamanca A Prophecy" (Rothenberg), 60
Samaras, Lucas, 14, 48, 129, 177, 179, 182, 235
Satisfaction (Kaprow), 125
Sayre, Henry, 44
Scenarios (McCaffery), 118–20, 124, 141
Schjeldhal, Peter, 199
Schlegel, Friedrich, "Poesie der Poesie," 219
Schneemann, Carolee, 5, 6, 9, 15, 88–128 passim, 188, 193; *ABC—We Print Anything—In the Cards*, 95–96; and Antin, 72; and Calle, 148; *Catscan*, 96; "For Black Tarantula," 99–100; *Fuses*, 91–92, 94, 98; *Ghost Rev*, 94; immediacy, 119, 126, 140; *Interior Scroll*, 98–100; *Kitsch's Last Meal*, 98, 99; and Klein, 146; and Kruger, 220; and late modernism, 116; and McCaffery, 85, 103–4, 107, 109–10; *Meat Joy*, 93–94; and Michals, 135; *Newspaper Event*, 90–91; and Rejlander, 174; and Sherman, 206; *Water Light/Water Needle*, 88–89, 96; *Up to and Including Her Limits*, 96
Scholem, Gershom, 51
Schor, Mia, 100–101; *Mask*, 100–104 passim
Self-Portrait Asleep in the Tomb of Merekura at Sakkara (Michals), 133–34

"Self Portrait (Back with arms above)" (Coplans), 182–84
Seneca Journal, A (Rothenberg), 45, 60
Shakespeare, 111
Shelley, Percy Bysshe, and Stern, 35
Sherman, Cindy, 8, 9, 14, 190–211 passim; *Artforum*, centerfold no. 96 in, 193; and Coplans, 187; enacting, 153; "Enigmatic Makeup," 210n.21; and Klein, 146; and Kruger, 221, 235; Metro Pictures images, 195, 197, 200; and Samaras, 187; and Spence, 177, 179; *Vanity Fair* images, 191, 192, 194
Shifters (McCaffery), 108
"The Shirt Poem" (Stern), 24–25
Smithson, Robert, 62
"Snow Man" (Stevens), 103
Snyder, Joel, "Photography, Vision, and Representation," 204–5
"sociology of art" (Antin), 83
"Some Secrets" (Stern), 21
"Something New" (Stern), 33
"A Song for the Romeos" (Stern), 35
"Sortie" (Calle), 157
Spanos, William, interview with Rothenberg, 44, 51, 55
Spence, Jo, 7, 15, 100, 129, 140, 174–89 passim; "property of Jo Spence," 178–80; "Remodelling Photo History," 175
Spurlock, William, 62
Squires, Carol, interview with Kruger, 229
Stations (Wilson), 136
Steichen, Edward, 8, 54, 176
Stephanson, Andres, 230
Stern, Gerald, 4, 11, 12, 20, 17–42 passim, 179; and Antin, 84; "At Bickford's," 20; "Bee Balm," 34; "Climbing This Hill Again," 29; and Coplans, 188; "The Dogs," 33; "Grapefruit," 41; "Here I am Walking," 33; Hidden Justice," 30–31; "I Do a Piece from Greece," 36–38; "I Need Help from the Philosophers," 26; immediacy, 140; and Klein, 146;

"Knowledge Forwards and Backwards,"
35; and Kruger, 8, 226; "The Last Self-
Portrait," 20; *Lonesick*, 34, 38; *Lucky
Life*, 20, 22, 25–26, 31, 33; "No
Longer Terror," 41–42; "No Wind,"
23–24; "Nobody Else Living," 39–40;
"One Bird to Love Forever," 26, 32;
"One Foot in the River," 20–21;
Paradise Poems, 31, 33, 34; "Picking the
Roses," 31–32; "The Power of Maples,"
20; "Psalm," 22; *The Red Coal*, 33;
"The Red Coal," 23–24; *Rejoicings*,
21–22, 31, 33; and Rothenberg, 58;
"Some Secrets," 21; "Something New,"
33; "A Song for the Romeos," 35;
"Steve Dunn's Spider," 32; "Stopping
Schubert," 38–39, 40; "There I Was
One Day," 37, 40; "Turning Into a
Pond," 33; "Two Trees," 26;
"Washington Square," 40; and
Whitman, 29
"Steve Dunn's Spider" (Stern), 32
Stevens, Wallace, 103
"Stopping Schubert" (Stern), 38–39, 40
"The Story of Our Lives" (Strand), 190
Strand, Mark, 4, 8–16 passim, 31;
"Keeping Things Whole," 9, 11; and
Spence, 177; "The Story of Our Lives,"
190
"The Suicide of Dada" (Rothenberg), 46
Suite vénitienne (Calle), 150–59 passim
Symposium (Plato), 169
Symposium of the Whole (Rothenberg), 53

Talbot, William Henry Fox, 196
talking at the boundaries (Antin), 61, 63,
73, 78, 80, 120
"Talking to Discover" (Antin), 71, 75n,
81n
*Technicians of the Sacred: A Range of
Poetries from Africa, Europe and Oceania*
(ed. Rothenberg), 45, 56
Testimonials (Kaprow), 125
That Dada Strain (Rothenberg), 46–47
"There I Was One Day" (Stern), 37–40
Thoreau, Henry David, *Journal*, 9, 10

Torso of Neill (Levine), 12
Trial, The (Kafka), 147
tuning (Antin), 63, 65–66, 71, 73, 74,
120
Turner, Victor, 57
"Turning Into a Pond" (Stern), 33
"Two Trees" (Stern), 26
Two Ways of Life, The (Rejlander), 160
Tzara, Tristan, 43, 52, 56; *Manifesto on
Feeble Love & Bitter Love*, 56

"Untitled Film Stills" (Sherman), 191
"Untitled (I am your almost nothing)"
(Kruger), 217–18
"Untitled (I shop therefore I am)"
(Kruger), 215
"Untitled (We won't play nature to your
culture)" (Kruger), 214–17
"Untitled (You are a captive audience)"
(Kruger), 227
"Untitled (You are getting what you paid
for)" (Kruger), 221
"Untitled (You reenact the dance of
insertion and wounding)" (Kruger), 225
"Untitled (Your comfort is my silence)"
(Kruger), 224–25
"Untitled (Your fictions become history)"
(Kruger), 215
"Untitled (Your life is a perpetual
insomnia)" (Kruger), 228
Up to and Including Her Limits
(Schneemann), 96, 104

Vanity Fair images (Sherman): no. 10,
191; no. 21, 192; no. 145, 194; no.
146, 194; no. 152, 194
Vitti, Monica, 200
Le Viol (Magritte), 132

Wakoski, Diane, 55
Warhol, Andy, 234
"Washington Square" (Stern), 40
Water Light/Water Needle (Schneemann),
88–89, 96
Wegman, William, 126, 179
Weinstock, Jane, 231

Weston, Edward, 1–3, 12, 13, 15, 35,
    177, 180, 185–86
"what am i doing here?" (Antin), 61
"what it means to be avant-garde"
    (Antin), 66, 67
Whitman, Walt, 35, 54
"who's listening out there?" (Antin), 75
Wilde, Oscar, The Portrait of Dorian Gray,
    168, 170
Wilson, Robert, Stations, 136

Wordsworth, William, 19, 41, 87;
    "Resolution and Independence," 41
Wright, James, 35

Yeats, W. B., 20, 107
"You make history when you do business"
    (Kruger), 234
Young, Edward, 13; Conjectures on
    Original Composition, 2

Zukofsky, Louis, 54, 108